THEY MUST BE MONSTERS

A Modern-Day Witch Hunt

*The untold story behind the McMartin phenomenon:
the longest, most expensive criminal case in U.S. history*

Matthew LeRoy & Deric Haddad

Copyright © 2018 by Deric Haddad & Matthew LeRoy

All rights reserved. No part of this book may be reproduced or transmitted in any form or by any means, electronic or mechanical, including photocopying, recording, or by any information storage and retrieval system, without permission in writing from the publisher.

The Manor Publishing House
San Diego, California

July 1, 2018

ISBN: 978-1-7324489-0-2
ISBN-10: 1732448906

Library of Congress Control Number: 2018907325

Website: www.theymustbemonsters.com

Cover by Hector Munro Colosio

Printed in the United States of America

Dedication

To Heather, my beloved, for your unselfish contribution, for your patience and compassion, for your willingness to lie alone in bed so many nights wondering if my work would ever be done. For you, for your generous spirit, for your dedication in helping me to fulfill my dream, I dedicate this to you—and only you.

—Deric Haddad

This incredible and arduous project is a living testament to the strength and unconditional love that comes from family.

To my remarkable mother, Deneen – Thank you for believing in me
To my best friend and beautiful wife, Brenda – Thank you for marrying me
To my amazing daughters, Gabby & Jackie – Thank you for inspiring me

—Matthew LeRoy

In Loving Memory of
Jill Patricia Loustalot and Carl Richard LeRoy

Author's Note

"History, with all her volumes vast, hath but one page."
—Lord Byron

In the summer of 1990, as we packed our things, ready to go our separate ways, I said to Matthew, "Twenty years from now, our discoveries are really going to mean something." And I was right. I knew it then just as I know it now. The information we'd obtained would forever be bound to history's need to understand its significance.

Over the next thirty years, as we both experienced love and life, raising children of our own, America dramatically changed—and I suspect that McMartin had something to do with it; that an event which touched so many people for so many years must have had an irreparable impact on such an impressionable society.

Today, understandably, teachers are far more reluctant to hug their students, or to make any type of physical contact with a child. Openly discussing sex—and perverted acts in particular—is now part of our nightly conversation, as if what once seemed unbecoming has been brushed with a tint of glamour.

Ironically, I'm afraid, with all of our progress and advancement, we've devolved in the most subtle ways. A simple accusation, true or contrived, enters the news cycle and moves across the airwaves before facts are verified, destroying reputations before due process takes form. False narratives incite angry mobs into the streets, where they loot and burn down businesses in some misguided act of retribution. Across the globe, our fellow countrymen are beheaded by zealots, and yet our interest wanes as the next newsflash hits our smart phones.

Sadly, after so many volumes of history as our reference, common sense and decency continue to take a backseat to a salacious story. People hear what they choose to hear. They believe what they choose to believe. There is no defense against a wave of passion. There is no reasonable defense.

—Deric Haddad

"We are what we always were in Salem, but now the little crazy children are jangling the keys of the kingdom, and common vengeance writes the law!"

—Arthur Miller, author of *The Crucible*,
in a 1996 interview with *The New Yorker*

Contents

Part I   Manhattan Beach 1
Part II   Changing Society 47
Part III   Only the Beginning 89
Part IV   Forsaken 159
Part V   Crucible 197
Part VI   God Help Us All 267
Part VII   Blood of the Lamb 307
Part VIII   The Proverbial Snowball 351
     Epilogue 371
     Author's Postscript 375
     Acknowledgements 377
     Timeline 379

This book brings an end to a thirty-year journey. The story is true, tragically so, a compilation of personal interviews, authentic memoirs, transcripts from various court proceedings, news reports (thousands of articles from dozens of journals), video footage, and—most paramount—our personal interactions with the people touched by the event. All dates, locations, episodes, and other general occurrences are real—factual documentation—and yet, for the effect of recapturing certain moments, creative dialogues have been provided based on collective testimonies. The names of characters considered public figures are real, whereas tangential characters—those who were relevant but whose name identification is nonessential; mainly children—have been given pseudonyms.

Prologue

We never imagined it would take thirty years—that our "college paper" would become so much more—but here we are.

Like the general public, we were captivated by the story: Allegations of an insidious crime, a small town overcome with fear, home to the longest, most expensive criminal case in U.S. history.

But those headlines, that narrative, only scratched the surface. A closer look revealed something else: A tale of human interests within the upscale city of Manhattan Beach, a lovely place that gave rise to frenzy, to a devastating crucible.

And so, as naïve as we were in 1987, we chased it, leaving college on a three-year investigation, our best efforts to record a moment in time that would have otherwise been lost.

Cautiously, we reached out to those on both sides, and to their credit, they welcomed us into their homes. Some wept as they relived those forsaken days, while others, their accusers, shifted nervously in their seats, finally grasping that they had falsely implicated those they'd once considered friends.

From a historical perspective, it's difficult to compare this occurrence to other episodes in our nation's past. Many have called it the "modern-day Salem Witch Trials," but even that doesn't reflect the unique wickedness of what took place in Manhattan Beach, for the tragedies of 1692 were, if anything, profoundly contemporary.

In this event—the heart of the 1980s—with its advanced learning and social correctness, good people, proud intellectuals, fell prey to their deepest fears. They went mad.

Today, three decades after the passion subsided, most have moved on. Still, their anger, their wrath, changed American society forever. It changed how we interact with our children: the careful use of our words and the cold distance of our touch.

Yes, the rage has dissipated, but the hysteria lives on, patiently surveying the landscape.

PART I
Manhattan Beach

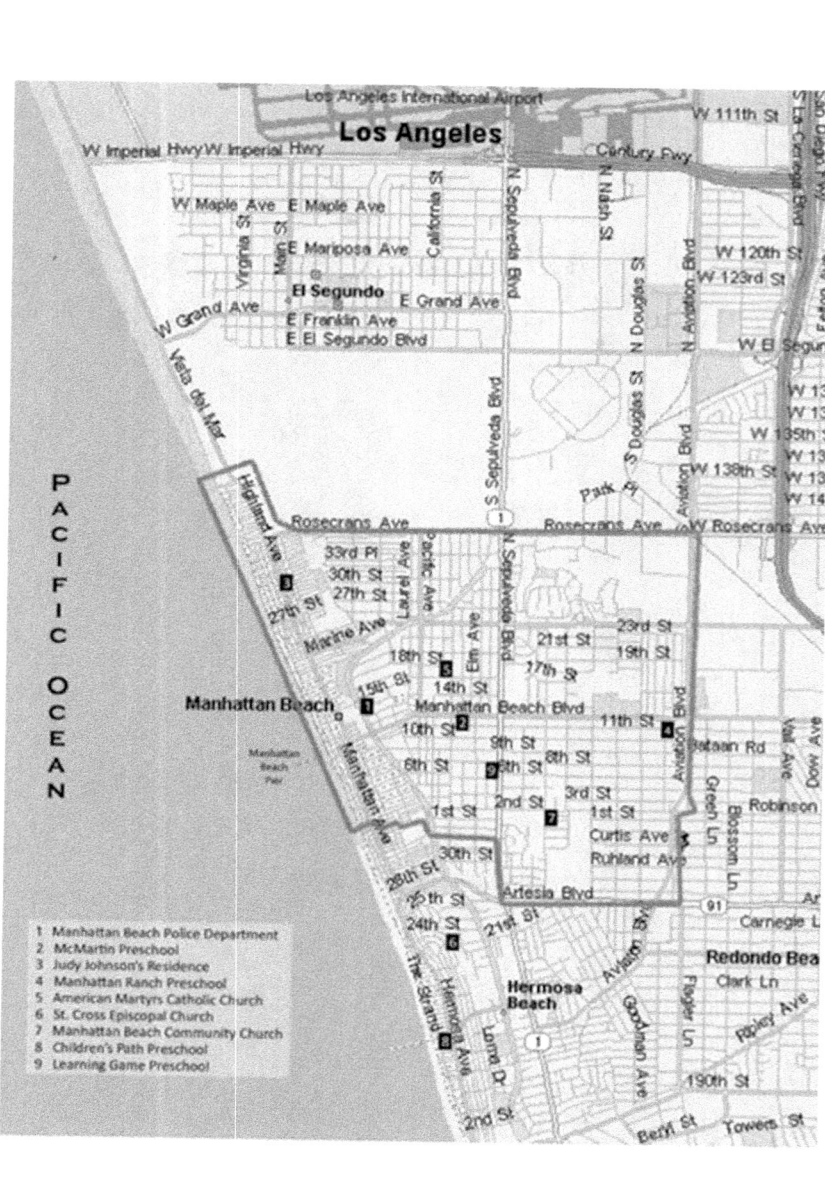

CHAPTER 1

December 1982
Manhattan Beach, California

The morning, like so many winter daybreaks in Southern California, felt cool but trended comfortable. Virginia McMartin, seated on her balcony, finished her crossword puzzle and enjoyed the ocean view. Just before 10:00 a.m., she reached for the phone and dialed.

Peggy Buckey, Virginia's daughter, answered. "Good morning, McMartin Preschool."

"Mornin', Peg," Virginia said in her slow, Southern drawl. "Tell Ray I'm waitin'."

"All right, Mom, I'll send him down."

Virginia's grandson, Ray Buckey, a twenty-five-year-old instructor at the preschool, left his class and drove to her beachfront home, a three-minute drive. He would pick her up and bring her back to the school, where she would sit and watch the children play.

Two months shy of her seventy-sixth birthday, and unable to chase after toddlers, Virginia had become a figurehead at the preschool, handing the reins over to Peggy, who, treating it like the family business it was, hired Ray, her son, a two-time college dropout in need of a break.

Ray pulled up in his Volkswagen Van and waved to Virginia who stood on her porch, leaning on her walking stick.

"You ready, Gram?" Ray called out to her, stepping out as she ambled toward him. He lifted her hand, guiding her into the passenger seat. He went back around and jumped in, turning the ignition.

That short drive back was a tender scene for the young man and his grandmother, a moment they cherished with time running its course. Virginia, an icon of Manhattan Beach, had entered her twilight years, and Ray, her awkward legacy, was always eager to assist her. Ray's love for his family ran deep—somewhat of a mama's boy whose older sister had been his best friend—but it was his "Gram," the matriarch, whom he most adored.

Virginia, careful not to shower Ray with undue praise, had a hushed admiration for him. He wasn't an achiever by any means; in fact, to some, Ray was the classic loser. While most of his high school classmates thrived in their careers, Ray lounged around the beach, living rent-free in an apartment his parents owned, taking advantage of his mother's unwillingness to force him into manhood.

Despite his laziness, though, Virginia knew Ray to be honest, kind, and thoughtful—traits that escaped most men his age. It pleased her more than he knew. Ray had a keen love of nature and animals, an emotional connection to the vulnerable and meek. A peculiar fellow, some surmised, Ray shied away from the new wave of yuppies that had taken hold of Manhattan Beach. A private guy with a quiet demeanor, Ray seemed to relate better to children than he did adults. Once he settled in as a full-time teacher, some parents took notice.

"It's *so* nice to have a male influence around these kids," one mother had told Peggy in front of Ray, as he grinned and dropped his head. "My husband's away on business half the time, and Jimmy just doesn't get enough of that at home."

"Well," Peggy had said, looking proudly upon Ray, "he *really* has a way with the kids. They all flock to him."

Ray and Virginia reached the school, and he helped her out of the van. Holding her arm, he escorted her along the sidewalk toward the entrance. Above them, facing the street, hung a wooden plank with "Mc-Martin Pre-School" in pale yellow letters carved neatly across its face, the fine craftsmanship of Chuck Buckey, Ray's father.

The building, a stick-built structure with stucco exterior, had four rooms shaped in an "L" and large bay windows. The grounds, a narrow concrete slab, had a sandbox with a jungle gym surrounded by handmade wooden play fixtures, also courtesy of Chuck.

Trees shaded the property. Virginia went to her favorite spot near the entrance where her wheelchair waited. She sat, resting her walking stick against the fence, looking on as the children ran about.

A three-year-old blond girl approached her. "Miss Virginia! Miss Virginia!"

The girl leaned in to hug her, and Virginia reciprocated, caressing her back and gracing her with a smile.

Sharon Nash, the mother of a former McMartin student, turned left from the corner of Walnut Avenue onto Manhattan Beach Boulevard and, seeing Peggy and Virginia conversing in the yard, slowed up, honked, and rolled down her window.

"Good morning, ladies!" Sharon said cheerfully, a gesture repeated by other women throughout the morning—the customary niceties of friends in a small town.

A typical day at McMartin began at 9:00 a.m., when mothers escorted their children to the entrance and jotted their names onto the sign-in sheet. Most days, before heading off, a handful of mothers conversed with Peggy at the gate. Peggy, a genial woman, was always open to conversation, and so they lingered, chatting about the flavor of the week.

Amongst this group, a certain clique stood apart—the women of the nearby American Martyrs Catholic Church, the exquisite structure within Manhattan Beach's "Tree" section, the woodsy neighborhood that bordered the preschool. These non-working wives certainly lived the good life—expensive homes, new cars, fashionable clothing—and enrolling their children at McMartin was, in a way, an added touch, a few precious hours each morning to slip away, to jog the strand, play tennis, or to simply return home for some peace and quiet.

As fellow parishioners and close friends, they had a penchant for community activism. Some were members of a women's philanthropic club, The Sandpipers, and volunteered their time to help the needy and abused, a sense of social consciousness the church had long fostered.

Unlike the other mothers, the women of American Martyrs considered themselves "close friends" of Virginia and Peggy. Each year, as a gesture of appreciation, they pitched in for a teacher's gift. The previous Christmas, they gave Peggy a hand-woven blanket with "Thank You" embroidered on it. Other times they sent cards, letters, and small trinkets to show how essential the preschool had been to their children's upbringing—their way of saying that the McMartin-Buckey family was an extension of their own.

Once their children graduated from McMartin, they went on to American Martyrs Parochial, just a few blocks away, where their kids remained classmates and companions.

* * * * *

Half a mile due west of the McMartin Preschool, a quiet drive through the Tree section, the dome of the American Martyrs Catholic Church comes into view. Its bell-tower—a contemporary architecture of earth-tone brick—reaches higher than any other point in Manhattan Beach.

Just before 5:00 p.m. on the Monday before Christmas break, Daniel and Patricia Tilden, loyal parishioners, stormed into the rectory, demanding to speak with Monsignor Robert Deegan. The receptionist led them to his office.

Seeing them enter, sensing their anger, Deegan came to his feet. "Dan...Patty...what's wrong?" he asked. "What's happened?"

Patty shook her head slowly. Tears welled in her eyes. Dan put his arm around her.

"We just had a talk with Melissa," Dan said. "She said she was touched...*touched inappropriately*...by that janitor. She said he took her into his workshop."

Monsignor Deegan assured the Tildens he would take whatever measures they wished, even if that meant "contacting the police." But he forewarned them of the damage this could do to Melissa, emotionally and psychologically. "Making a case out of this," Deegan said, "might do more harm than good."

Deegan promised to privately council the janitor, ensuring them that these unspeakable acts would not recur. The Tildens accepted the clergyman's resolution.

A quarter mile east of the rectory—down 15th Street then left onto Laurel Avenue—was the campus of American Martyrs Parochial School, a modest facility with a large playground and ballfield. At the far corner of the grounds stood a shack, a wooden structure with a metal roof—the "workshop" Melissa Tilden had spoken of.

Inside, Clement Renaud, the fifty-four-year-old senior maintenance man, organized his tools. Tucked away on the shelves, high in the corner, was a short stack of adult magazines. A glass jar sat on the counter next to the door filled with a ready supply of chocolate and lollipops.

"Mr. Renaud." The distant voice broke his concentration. "Mr. Renaud!" The voice drew near. It was Sally Koller, an administrator. Renaud moved to the door, sticking his head out.

"Monsignor Deegan wants to see you," Sally yelled. "He wants you to go up to the rectory. He said it's important."

Renaud waved, acknowledging her request. He locked up the workshop and went to his van, an older model Chevy with tinted windows in the back. He drove to the rectory, a sixty-second trip. He parked, stepped out, and noticed Deegan standing on the rectory steps, arms folded, more stoic than usual.

Seeing Deegan waiting there, his eyes burning, Renaud had a good idea of why he'd been summoned. He knew he had gone too far. He knew that Melissa had been a risky choice, a Martyrs student and parishioner, a "good girl" by every measure. Renaud had told her "not to tell," that she would "get in trouble" for going into the workshop in the first place.

Renaud walked past Deegan, head down, his eyes too ashamed to admit what he was about to confess.

Deegan, a large man at sixty-one years old, had the pale skin and sharp blue eyes of a second-generation Irish-American. His deep baritone voice added to his forceful presence at the pulpit, while his natural warmth and marvelous sense of humor made him personable and approachable to all. He had a way of persuasion, a keen understanding of human motivation—and it did not take him long to break down Clement Renaud.

Deegan told Renaud that his only option was to begin counseling sessions. They would meet once a week to discuss Renaud's sickness.

Clement Renaud agreed to Deegan's offer. Their counseling began after the Christmas break and continued through Easter.

From Deegan's perspective, after four months with no further complaints, the controversy faded.

But then, in the third week of April 1983, Deegan got word that the story had been exhumed, that a salacious rumor had afflicted the parish community.

That word came from Bob Currie, one of Deegan's most outspoken parishioners. Currie, the parent of three American Martyrs students, knew the Tilden family well. Currie arrived at the rectory highly upset.

"What's going on with this janitor?" Currie asked Deegan. "I know what this guy did."

"I'm really not at liberty to discuss this, Mr. Currie. It's a private matter. If the family wishes to speak with you about it, that's their choice."

"I know what you're doin'," Currie said. "You wanna make this go away. You wanna sweep this under the rug, right?"

Deegan said nothing. His resigned glare told Currie that he'd heard enough. Currie shook his head and left.

If Bob Currie knew about the janitor, Deegan suspected, others knew as well. The lurid details were circulating from home to home—the idea of what had happened to Melissa Tilden—and it was sure to leave an unholy stain on the Church.

Deegan's internal struggle, however, soon came to an end—and not by his own doing. Shortly after his confrontation with Bob Currie, Deegan suffered a massive heart seizure. His sudden death sent shock waves through the faithful, as their beloved figurehead, their noble leader, had fallen.

Coincidentally, shortly after Monsignor Deegan's passing, Clement Renaud was let go from his position at American Martyrs. He relocated to Texas.

* * * * *

Three weeks later

The morning of Thursday, May 12, 1983, seemed to go as planned for Peggy Buckey. For three hours, her students did arts and crafts, sang songs, and played in the yard. At eleven-thirty, they returned to their classrooms and settled down for some quiet time before their mothers began arriving at noon.

One by one, the mothers came to the fence, signed the sheet, and stepped away with their children. "Bye, Miss Peggy!" a four-year-old girl yelled as she and her mother stepped along the boulevard toward the vacant lot adjacent to the school. Peggy smiled and waved back.

As Peggy turned, facing the entrance, she was taken aback to find a small blond boy, no more than two years old, standing near the entrance with a paper bag at his side. Peggy stepped toward the boy, unable to recognize him. He definitely wasn't a McMartin student. She looked around, trying to spot the adult who had accompanied him, but there was no one.

"Hello," Peggy said as she approached. "What's your name?"

The boy stared at her but did not speak.

"Can you tell me your name?" Peggy asked. "Who brought you here?"

Still, the boy said nothing. Peggy held out her hand and said, "Come with me," as she led him to the office.

Peggy sifted through the paper bag, looking for clues. There, crammed between some snacks and a change of clothes, was an enrollment application. It was from a different preschool, half-filled out, but it had his name, Mitchell Johnson, as well as the contact information for his mother, Judy Johnson.

Grabbing the phone, Peggy called nearby preschools to see if someone, maybe a babysitter, had left him at McMartin by mistake. Obviously, no responsible adult would knowingly leave a child at the wrong preschool and step away. *This has to be a mistake.*

Peggy called the Magic Rainbow preschool. No one there had ever heard of Mitchell Johnson. She called the Learning Game and Wee Tot preschools, both within walking distance of McMartin. Same result.

Babette Spitler, a thirty-four-year-old McMartin teacher walked into the office. "Well, who do we have here?" Babette said upon seeing the unfamiliar child.

"I wish I knew," Peggy said. "I found him standing near the gate with this bag at his side." Peggy handed Babette the generic application. "Have you ever heard of Judy Johnson?"

Babette looked it over, shaking her head. "No...never."

Peggy called the phone number on the application but got an answering machine.

"I'm calling for Judy Johnson," Peggy said to the recorder. "Mrs. Johnson, this is Peggy Buckey at the McMartin Preschool. I believe we have your son, Mitchell. I'm thinking there must be some mistake...like maybe someone dropped him off at the wrong school. I'm not really sure what happened. But we'll keep him here for a while. Please get back to me right away."

Two hours passed, and they hadn't heard from Judy Johnson.

At 2:15 p.m., Peggy asked Babette to wait with Mitchell. Peggy rarely stayed that late. The McMartin Preschool was primarily a morning school, with only a handful of kids staying until 4:00p.m. Peggy normally left around one-thirty to take Virginia home.

"If no one comes for him by three-thirty, call me," Peggy said. "We'll have to contact the police. We'll have no choice."

Peggy handed Babette a note to give to Judy Johnson in case she came before Peggy returned.

Once Peggy left, Babette waited with Mitchell, making sure he was comfortable. She gave him a snack and a toy, and he played quietly, unaffected by the situation. With each passing minute, though, Babette grew anxious. None of this was right. Peggy should've already contacted the police.

At 2:45p.m., Babette saw a blond woman approaching the entrance, a woman she'd never seen before. The woman had an awkward, almost shameful look on her face. She appeared to be in her late-thirties, attractive, trim, and healthy-looking.

"Hello," the woman said as she neared. "I'm Judy Johnson…Mitchell's mother. I'm so sorry about this."

Judy told Babette that she had an unexpected crisis and needed somewhere for Mitchell to stay during the afternoon.

"My oldest son…he has brain cancer, and he needed immediate care. I had to get him to the emergency room, and I just didn't have time to come in and speak with someone in charge."

Babette said nothing, puzzled by it all.

"I felt safe leaving him here," Judy said. "So many people have told me what a wonderful school this is."

"This *is* a great preschool," Babette replied, "but there's no excuse for what you did. We were minutes away from calling the police," Babette said. "We *should've* called the police. Do you know what would've happened if we did?"

Judy nodded, dropping her eyes, acknowledging how irresponsible she had been. "I'm truly sorry."

Babette handed Judy the note. "You need to call Peggy Buckey right away. She wants to discuss this."

"I understand," Judy said. "I'll talk to Peggy. Thanks."

Judy held Mitchell by the hand and they stepped away. They walked to Judy's Volkswagen Bus, climbed in, then drove west down Manhattan Beach Boulevard.

Babette called Peggy and filled her in.

Around five o'clock, having not received a call from Judy, Peggy phoned the Johnson home. No one answered. She left another message. She repeated that process twice more before 8:00p.m. Judy did not reply.

The next day, Peggy tried again, leaving her fourth message on Judy's answering machine.

Finally, on her fifth attempt, just before 8:00p.m., Judy answered.

"You know, Mrs. Johnson," Peggy said, "you could've at least called us or left a note or done something, anything to give us an idea what was going on. I should've called the police."

"I know. I understand," Judy replied. "It's just that I was desperate, and I knew if I would've come inside and asked if I could leave Mitchell for just a few hours, the answer might've been no. And yesterday, I couldn't take no for an answer."

Judy explained that her first-born son, Mark, a thirteen-year-old, had been suffering from an inoperable brain tumor for the past five years. He'd recently come out of remission, and he was not expected to live much longer. Mark required constant treatment, but Judy, unfortunately, had to find a job because her husband had just left her. "He's barely giving me enough money to feed the boys," Judy said.

The day before, Mark had awakened nauseated, vomiting, a reaction to his medication.

"I had to get him to the doctor," Judy stressed, "and I had nowhere to turn. The only thing I could think of was to take him to the McMartin Preschool. Everyone says your family is so wonderful."

Peggy remained silent, listening carefully, flattered but unmoved.

"Mrs. Buckey," Judy asked, "is there any chance I could enroll Mitchell into your school?"

"Oh, I'm sorry, Mrs. Johnson, but that's just not possible," Peggy said. "Our weekly classes are full. They always are. Besides, there are only three weeks left in the school year. I would never enroll a new child this late."

Peggy waited for a response, but Judy did not speak. After an uncomfortable silence, Peggy unguardedly said, "We might be able to fit him into our summer sessions, if we get a cancellation, but I can't guarantee you anything. And, so you know, our summer classes don't start until the last week of June, so what would you do in the meantime?"

"Don't worry," Judy assured her. "I can work something out."

Peggy told Judy she would have to consult with her mother, Virginia McMartin, before a final decision could be made, even though Peggy knew precisely how Virginia felt—and it was not in Judy's favor.

The prior evening, while Peggy had called Judy's home repeatedly, Virginia sat next to her daughter, appalled by Judy's actions. "After twenty-seven years, I've never known anyone to pull a stunt like this," Virginia had said. "This is crazy."

Virginia couldn't reconcile Judy's actions: how she'd gambled with her son's safety in the midst of a crisis. Mitchell was only a toddler; he had no concept of his proximity to danger. Judy had dropped him off at noon, when the streets filled with lunch-hour traffic, when the majority of mothers arrived to pick up their children, when dozens of people crowded the school's entrance. Mitchell could have easily followed another child out of the gate, stepped into the middle of the street and been hit by a car—and nobody would have known who he was or where he'd come from. This was not bad judgment, Virginia argued, this was a reckless act.

Still, the decision was not Virginia's to make.

"I don't like what she did," Virginia said, "but you're the director, Peg. You'll be the one dealing with her in the future. This is *your* call."

Peggy, determined to help, phoned Judy to tell her she could enroll Mitchell into the summer sessions. His first day would be Tuesday, June 21, five weeks later.

"Oh, thank you so much, Mrs. Buckey," Judy said. "I can't tell you how much this means to me."

"No problem," Peggy replied. "I'm just glad we can help. We'll see you in June."

Peggy hung up, feeling good about her decision—but later that afternoon she received a call from the owner of the Wee Tot Preschool referring to the "mystery boy" Peggy had called about.

"Didn't you say his name was Mitchell Johnson?" the woman inquired.

"Yes, that's right," Peggy said. "His mother came back a few hours later, and we figured it all out. We're enrolling him into our summer classes."

"Oh, really?" the woman replied, somewhat confused. "Why do you ask?"

"Well, his mother, Judy Johnson," the woman said, reading from the application, "just enrolled him here at Wee Tot. After she left, I remembered the name, so I thought I would let you know."

"Thanks for the call," Peggy replied as she hung up, contemplating how strange it all seemed.

CHAPTER 2

The summer of 1983 brought extreme heat to the entire nation, and Los Angeles was no exception. Temperatures spiked to 84 degrees in mid-May, well above the historical average, as the heavy rains of winter—the cry of a devastating El Niño—was long gone. The air had turned markedly dry, a strange climate, and the people of Manhattan Beach felt it.

Judy Johnson stepped onto her back patio and found her plants thirsty. She filled her watering can, showering the bed back and forth to soften the soil. The sporadic rainfall usually kept them vibrant, but the stretch of sunny days with zero precipitation had left a bunch wilted.

Judy picked a handful of the liveliest daisies, clipped the stems, and set a fresh bouquet atop her small kitchen table. She stepped to the window, pulled back the curtains, and opened the panes, allowing the cool breeze of the Pacific to rush in. Judy plopped onto her sofa, legs stretched out, enjoying a peaceful moment while Mitchell napped in his bedroom.

The Johnson home, located at 3112 Vista Drive, a 672-square-foot adobe cottage, had been built within the narrow streets above Highland Avenue. From her doorstep, Judy could walk five minutes to Grandview Avenue, with its panoramic vantage point of Manhattan Beach's backlands, or in that same time she could trot to the strand and relax near the shore, something she did quite often. The home was quaint: a two-bed, one bath with a modest kitchen-living room blend. Judy kept it clean and organized, her meticulous tradition—the classic American homemaker.

Judy heard footsteps on the porch, then the clanking sound of the mailbox. She went to the door and opened it, seeing her mail carrier, Joanne, walking away.

"Thank you," Judy yelled, lifting the stack of mail from the box.

Joanne stopped and turned back. "You're welcome," she replied. Joanne's smile dampened into a look of concern. She knew of Mark's condition.

"How's he doing?"

"Not bad, but not great," Judy said. "Touch and go."

Joanne had worked this neighborhood for years. She'd watched Mark grow from a healthy little boy into a cancer-stricken teenager. It broke her heart each day she filled their box with another stack of envelopes from Kaiser Hospital.

"Well, I'm always thinking about him," Joanne sympathized.

"I know you are," Judy said. "God bless you."

Joanne carried on with her route.

Sifting through the mail, Judy came across an envelope—a letter from her estranged husband, Brad. It had no postage or return address, but she recognized his handwriting. He must've dropped it off on his way to work.

Judy opened it and laid the letter flat upon the kitchen table. She read it carefully, skeptically, knowing that, once again, Brad was giving her the calm after the storm. He'd come by the day before to discuss their "financial arrangement," and he didn't particularly agree with her demands. He'd left in a huff, yelling something profane as he slammed the door.

In the letter, dated May 23, 1983, just three weeks since he'd moved out, Brad apologized for his "performance" the day before. "I make myself mad when I talk to you," he wrote. "I have complicated feelings for you and the boys that cause me to get very upset." But he promised, "From this day forward, I will treat you as a very good friend—no more swearing."

Brad wanted to resolve their settlement quickly, to be formally separated by Christmas, which put them on pace to file for divorce by the following June.

Brad's contrition, sincere or not, did little to change Judy's perspective. Brad had an endgame, and it did not include her. He'd abandoned her while she cared for their dying son, and he didn't have the decency to provide her with the resources to get by.

Days later, on the evening of Sunday, May 29, Judy sat alone in her kitchen, writing down her thoughts:

> *Brad comes over two hours late to pick up Mitchell who was just going to sleep for a nap.*
> *Says he wants to file immediately. If we are married 14 years he has to pay alimony for life to wife.*
> *He also developed a new thing called "discounting." Claims repairs will be 250 dollars a month which is split. Even though half the property is his and landlord takes care of his property.*
> *Who ever said this world was fair!*

Despite her desolation, Judy stayed focused on keeping the boys active in the community. Her May and June calendars tell her story—where she took them to a "picnic at Live Oak Park" and to a "concert at Polliwog Park," how she took Mark to "scouts" and "baked a cake" for a birthday party, and how she "painted the lattice" and did other home improvements—the normal facets of her daily life prior to the separation.

Still, the fact that her marriage had failed continued to occupy Judy, and she searched for answers. On the evening of June 1, Judy watched a documentary titled, *Divorce: Kids in the Middle*, where divorced parents, through amicable joint custody, made the transition less traumatic on their children.

So far, Judy and Brad were not doing so well. Every encounter turned bitter; every fruitful discussion ended in a volatile hissing match. It wasn't healthy for the boys to see, and they'd witnessed every last word of it.

The following week, to break away from that setting, Judy packed the boys into the VW Van and drove to Phoenix to visit her younger brother Steve and his wife, Debbie. The six-hour drive—the peacefulness of the highway that Judy treasured—gave her time to reflect.

When they pulled up to Steve and Debbie's home, the van door slid open and the boys rushed out, tackling Steve. They all fell to the ground in laughter.

Steve and Debbie Knutson had been married for two years, both employed at Sears. Steve, thirty-four, was in management, while Debbie, thirty-two, was a buyer. Working full-time and saving their money, preparing to raise a family of their own, the Knutsons could not make it to

Manhattan Beach very often, at least not for recreation. They'd planned to spend a week with Judy and the boys at the end of July, but they just couldn't get there any sooner.

The situation had really weighed on Steve, being so far away from the Johnsons as Mark's condition worsened. Steve knew that Judy needed help, but he also knew she would never ask for it. Judy was too proud—his older sister who'd always carried the load. She kept acting as if nothing was wrong.

Once the boys finally let him up, Steve gave Judy a hug.

"How ya doin', sis?" Steve said, kissing her cheek.

"I'm good," she said, leaning in for another hug.

After their embrace, they went inside and chatted before dinner. Mitchell, twice the size from their last visit, ran around the living room entertaining them all.

"He's getting so big. My god," Debbie said. "He looks like a little man."

"He's growing like a weed," Judy said. "You should hear the things he says."

Over that three-day visit, from Steve's perspective, Judy seemed to be holding up well. Her only concern was Mark's treatment. Judy was convinced Mark could beat it. They just had to keep battling.

* * * * *

Tuesday, June 21, 1983

Just before 9:00 a.m., Judy and Mitchell arrived at the McMartin Preschool for his first official day.

"Hello, Mitchell," Peggy said with a smile.

Mitchell remembered Peggy. He was excited to see her.

"Thanks again," Judy said, signing him in. "He's been looking forward to this."

"Well, I'm glad," Peggy said. "We're happy to have him."

Peggy checked the sign-in sheet. She noticed Judy had written "4:00 p.m." as the pick-up time.

"So he's staying for the afternoon session?" Peggy verified.

"Yes," Judy said. "He'll normally be a noon pick-up, but today I need a few more hours."

"No problem," Peggy said. "I won't be here then, but just come to the gate and someone will bring him out."

Judy waved goodbye to Mitchell and stepped to the vacant lot. She jumped into her VW Bus and pulled away. She felt relieved. She could look for work while she tended to Mark, just as she had told Peggy.

However, on that first day of preschool, Judy had other plans. From the vacant lot, Judy turned left on Manhattan Beach Boulevard—away from the coast—and right onto PCH. She headed to San Pedro for a 9:30 a.m. appointment with Dr. Frank M. Kline, a psychiatrist. Working in affiliation with UCLA-Harbor Medical Center, Dr. Kline specialized in adult ADHD, alcohol abuse, anxiety, bipolar disorder, depression, stress, and schizophrenia.

Seven hours later, just before 4:00 p.m., Judy returned to the McMartin Preschool. Babette Spitler saw Judy standing outside the fence, and she retrieved Mitchell. Babette escorted him out, and the Johnsons headed home. As far as Judy could tell, Mitchell's first day at McMartin had been a success.

But sometime that evening, Judy noticed Mitchell sitting uncomfortably, moving from side to side in his chair. He complained that his bottom hurt. Judy checked it out, and she noticed redness on his anus.

In the days that followed, as Mitchell attended McMartin on Tuesdays and Thursdays, usually from 9:00 a.m. to noon, Judy documented his illnesses and irregularities on her calendar.

On Thursday, June 23, his second day at McMartin, Judy wrote, "Mitchell Fever"; on July 6, 7, 8, and 9, she wrote "Sick" and that he suffered from diarrhea.

Week after week, the redness on Mitchell's bottom persisted.

Then, on July 18, Judy went to an appointment at Kaiser Hospital to see Dr. Mark Segal. Judy had contracted vaginitis. She took Mitchell with her.

During the exam, Judy made a bizarre statement to the doctor.

"Mitchell's anus has been itchy," Judy told Dr. Segal. "I think I might've given him my vaginitis."

Dr. Segal smiled dismissively, shaking his head.

"No, that's not possible," he said. "He can't have vaginitis. He probably has some form of eczema."

* * * * *

Eleven days later, Friday, July 29, Steve and Debbie Knutson arrived in Manhattan Beach for their much awaited vacation. Since the Johnsons' last trip to Phoenix, Steve couldn't take his mind off Judy and the boys.

Mark's recent decline had Steve more worried than ever. While in Phoenix, Mark had had moments of excruciating pain, and with his father having moved out, Mark seemed further depressed. Steve could see Mark's emptiness, a deepening void that needed filled.

Steve, the fun-loving uncle, had always been Mark's pal. Despite the miles between them, they'd developed an understanding, an unspoken acceptance of Mark's imminent death. Mark knew what was happening to him—that his time was fading—and Steve helped him to live in the moment, turning ordinary situations into colorful memories.

That Friday, once the Knutsons settled in, Steve hid on the rooftop above the garage, armed with a water gun. Mark and Mitchell were across the street at the home of Gayle and Jeep Schaeffer. The Schaeffer's son, Jason, was Mark's age—the two boys were lifelong friends, like brothers—and Judy and Gayle were also close, neighbors who'd raised their boys together for thirteen years.

As Mark and Mitchell came back across the street, Steve prepared his attack. Once they stepped within range, Steve called out, "Hey! Who goes there?" They stopped, looked up, and were met with a stream of water to their faces. Mitchell giggled uncontrollably, while Mark hurried around the side of the house and turned the spigot. Mark came back with the hose and fired upon Steve from the back side. A major water fight broke out.

Steve, out of ammunition, threw his arms in the air, surrendering to Mark, but his nephew showed no mercy, drenching Steve until he laid flat, shot dead. Mark continued spraying as Steve carefully climbed down from the roof. Once on the ground, Steve chased Mark around the house and out of sight. Moments later they walked back—Steve's arm around Mark's shoulder—and they dried off, ready for a sunset barbecue.

For the Knutsons, as precious as those moments were, they were just as heart-wrenching, watching Judy bear witness to the gradual demise of her first-born son. The water-fight was a lively event, but it was gone in an instant. The next minutes were uncertain. Mark's illness, his relentless pain, could dampen any joyous occasion.

Later that evening, however, to Steve and Debbie's surprise, it was Mitchell who seemed most disturbed. He was distant and withdrawn.

"Come sit on my lap, Mitch," Steve said, inviting the boy to jump up. But Mitchell shook his head and stepped back. Later, when Steve tried to hug him, Mitchell pulled away. Knowing that Brad had recently left, Steve figured the boy was going through a phase of mistrust.

The next morning, as Steve emerged from the shower in the Johnsons' tiny bathroom, Mitchell came running through the doorway and socked his uncle in the genitals, yelling angrily and aggressively before darting away.

To Steve it did not seem that Mitchell was simply horsing around. It appeared instead to be "reactionary," a defensive hostility.

A day later, again in the small bathroom, Steve needed to use the blow dryer, but there was no electrical outlet. He stepped around the corner into the kitchen where Mitchell sat on the floor playing with his toys. Steve plugged in the dryer, flipping the switch—and Mitchell jumped back, screaming. He ran into his bedroom and hid under the bed. Mitchell would not come out until Judy went in to settle him down.

Later that night, with the boys sound asleep, Judy discussed it with Steve and Debbie.

"I don't know what it is," Judy told them. "He's been acting so strange lately."

"Do you think it's because Brad moved out?" Steve asked.

"Maybe. I'm not sure," Judy said. "But I've noticed redness on his bottom. I've seen it a few times."

"Redness?" Debbie asked. "What kind of redness?"

"Around his anus," Judy said. "It started earlier in the summer...and now it's happening again."

"What do you think it is?" Steve asked.

Judy only shook her head.

Debbie was not overly concerned.

"Maybe he did something with a toy," Debbie speculated. "You know how kids experiment. He could've done something like that...right?"

Judy turned away.

"Maybe you should take him to the doctor?" Steve suggested.

But again, Judy shrugged. She did not tell them that she'd already taken Mitchell to a doctor who'd told her that the redness was most likely due to eczema.

* * * * *

Driving west, their backs to the morning sun, Judy and Steve's folks, Pastor Myrus and Helen Knutson, left Yucca Valley, a small desert community near Joshua Tree National Park, a two-hour drive to the coast. They were anxious to get to Manhattan Beach, a reunion with their entire family. Yet their thoughts and prayers were dedicated to Mark.

Mark had always been their special gift, their first grandchild who, in spite of his fatal illness, never lost hope. In fact, through his battle to survive, Mark had become even more spiritually adept—forgiving and selfless, a "true child of faith," the pastor said.

Nonetheless, Mark's disease devastated his grandfather.

Years before, when Pastor Knutson first got the call about Mark's inoperable condition, he rejected the notion that it was simply part of God's plan—for why, the pastor asked, would the good Lord use this horrible disease to wreak havoc upon his family time and again?

Regrettably, in 1956, Judy and Steve's natural mother, Delores, died from an accelerating form of cancer. Judy, twelve at the time, dedicated herself to seven-year-old Steve, nurturing him through his formative years. She dressed him, cooked his meals, and kept their home immaculate out of respect for their mother's memory.

Two years after Delores's death, Pastor Knutson, the leader of a parish in Hancock Park, found love in the arms of Helen Gregson, the pretty woman in the front row of the choir. They shared a brief courtship, and he surprised her with a marriage proposal.

At first Judy objected, angry at her father for trying to replace her mother. But, over time, she accepted his choice, his need for a companion, and Judy came to love Helen for the person she was.

Like most parents, as their children grew into adults, the pastor and Helen offered guidance to both Judy and Steve—and yet Judy's life, long before Mark's illness, had been filled with drama and setbacks. Her ongoing marital crisis was a prime example.

Brad's decision to leave Judy in the midst of Mark's treatment had bothered Pastor Knutson, but it didn't surprise him. The pastor didn't care much for Brad, a strict agnostic. "He wouldn't have been my first choice," the pastor said.

Brad's lack of faith had long been a point of contention within the family, and Pastor Knutson was appalled that Brad had kept his children from their relationship with God. As an adult, Brad had the right to make his own decisions, to chart his own destiny. But to seal the fate of his dying son was, in the eyes of the clergyman, indefensible.

When the pastor and Helen arrived at the Johnson home, they were greeted by smiling faces. Mitchell wrapped his arms around his grandfather's leg, while Mark slowly approached, embracing him warmly, burying his face into his grandfather's chest.

Pastor Knutson kissed Mark's forehead, unable to take his eyes off the hole in the side of the boy's head, the scar over which his hair would never re-grow.

They all went inside, huddling in the tiny living room, the seven of them, reminiscing, as close as they'd ever been.

* * * * *

The Knutson family reunion lasted three days. On the morning of Friday, August 5, both couples packed up and returned to the blistering heat of their desert homes.

Coincidentally, the climate in Manhattan Beach would not be much better. The forecast for Los Angeles called for a measurable increase in temperature. That day hovered around 81 degrees, but by the next afternoon, it rose to 97.

The heat wave put Mark at grave risk. Judy found him in his bedroom, lying on his mattress, breathing slowly and heavily. He had a high fever. Their home did not have air conditioning, so Judy placed Mark in a lukewarm bath with a cool compress over his forehead. She stayed by his side for three days.

On her calendar, on August 7 and 8, respectively, Judy wrote "Mark Gets Pneumonia" and "Pneumonia." She circled "NEW MOON," also known as a *dark moon*, as she prayed for his fever to break.

CHAPTER 3

Thursday, August 11, 1983

Just after 10:00 a.m., Ray picked up Virginia outside of her beachfront home. They headed south on Highland Avenue, enjoying the peaceful mood along the commercial strip. Shoppers gawked at window displays as joggers ran in place at the traffic light. The first wave of beachgoers flocked to the strand.

Typical of beach town traffic, they moved slowly, a constant stop and go. They stopped.

"Good morning, Virginia," came the voice of a young girl.

Virginia turned and recognized the child right away. Cynthia Charles, a 1977 graduate of McMartin, by then an eleven-year-old headed into the sixth grade at American Martyrs Parochial.

"Well, look who it is," Virginia said. "I hardly recognized you, you got so big."

Cynthia blushed and smiled. Her mother, Jane, stepped out of the shop and waved to Virginia.

"How's it goin'?" Jane hollered.

"It's goin'...gettin' younger by the day," Virginia replied, as Ray pulled ahead.

That morning, like every other, they cruised along. Ray, the family's unassuming black sheep, proudly chauffeured his Gram through the quaint streets of Manhattan Beach, a revered woman living out her golden years.

Virginia, born Virginia Steely in 1907, was a native Angeleno whose family had relocated to Los Angeles from El Paso the year before. She'd lived in Manhattan Beach since 1931, back when "Manhattan" was little more than an undeveloped stretch of white dunes pushed up against the shore. Virginia and her husband, Charlie McMartin, arrived with their two youngsters, Peggy and Glenn, and found a modest settlement of Southern and Midwestern migrants, a down-home feel that suited them well.

In 1946, however, to Virginia's shock, Charlie left her for a younger woman. Heart-broken at thirty-eight, and with her best years seemingly behind her, Virginia had to start over. She went to work at Metlox, painting household ceramics to keep her head above water while she took college courses at night.

One spring, while helping out at a church nursery, an administrator recognized Virginia's "love and understanding for children" and told her she should pursue it as a career. Virginia heeded the woman's advice, enrolling in several child education courses while working part-time at Miss Dawn's Nursery in Manhattan Beach, fixing lunches and running errands.

After a few years, Miss Dawn announced that she would be selling the school, and Virginia jumped on it. Peggy fronted her enough cash for the deposit, and a savings and loan backed the rest. Peggy, also interested in child care, agreed to run the school with her.

Thus, in the fall of 1956, at the age of forty-nine, Virginia opened the doors of The McMartin Preschool.

The buzz about McMartin became infectious—a "special place" for kids to learn—a warm family setting, just like home—and its prestige was cemented. By 1966, with such high demand, Virginia and Peggy opened School II, the site at 931 Manhattan Beach Boulevard, and they ran both schools for ten years, until they closed School I as Virginia neared retirement.

Over that twenty-year stretch, between the two sites, the McMartin Preschool taught more than 5,300 students and employed nearly thirty instructors—the undisputed core of Manhattan Beach's early-education base.

The community, recognizing her commitment and longevity, paid homage, lauding Virginia with four awards for "outstanding community service"—the President's Award from the Chamber of Commerce, an Award of Merit from the Coordinating Council, the Super Booster Award from the students of Mira Costa High School, and the Rose &

Scroll Award, the city's highest honor. Virginia became the first and last citizen of Manhattan Beach to achieve such a level of commendation.

The McMartin name, and those associated with it, symbolized more than local daycare. They were, by every definition, pillars of the community. They represented a mindset that had been ingrained into Manhattan Beach for decades: The notion that family, Christ, and education were the clearest path to their children's future—the essential virtues of a planned community.

Because of that, Manhattan Beach had developed into a sleepy little seaside town tucked below LAX, a setting more reminiscent of Savannah and Charleston than Malibu or Venice. Twenty miles from the bustle of downtown Los Angeles, and well outside the growing violence of South Central, some considered it the "best kept secret" in LA County.

Ray stopped abruptly at the red light, the intersection of Highland Avenue and Manhattan Beach Boulevard—the heart of the community—where its two main throughways came together. Virginia glanced right, looking toward the ocean, where the famed Manhattan Beach Pier extended out into the water. Fisherman cast their lures into the crashing tide as boys and girls ran circles around its Roundhouse Aquarium.

Overhead, from light post to light post, city workers were hanging the banner for the Old Hometown Fair, the annual event held each October, a Southern California harvest festival. Like a rural township in the Midwest, the event had a three-legged race, pie-eating contest, chili cook-off, salt water taffy, and a kissing both, all highlighted by a Saturday night street dance where sarsaparilla was served.

Ray looked left and recognized a guy, standing in front of The Kettle, a twenty-four-hour diner and hotspot for locals. Ray had played beach volleyball with him the day before.

"What's happenin'?" the guy said. "See ya later, right?"

"Oh, yeah," Ray said. "I'll be there."

That late-summer morning, with Labor Day just around the corner, The Kettle had a line out the door, a hungry flock ready for a hearty brunch before hitting the sand. Somewhat of a landmark in town, The Kettle offered a real taste of Americana. Its menu, an artful sketch of a Woodie Wagon with surf boards jutting out the back, had "Welcome to Manhattan Beach" printed across the top, as if eating there was more than a meal.

Like Ray, most residents had patronized The Kettle at one time or another, but everyone knew where to find it. Its distinct marquee—a large black cauldron over a bed of scalding flames, a simmering crucible on the verge of boiling over—hovered high above the busy walkway.

* * * * *

Ray and Virginia arrived at the school minutes later. He escorted her into the office where she sat for a few minutes before heading to the yard. Those summer sessions were relaxed, more daycare than education, with only two of the four classrooms in use.

Around noon, most parents arrived to pick up their children. Peggy drove Virginia home—they lived only one street apart—and their workday was done.

Ray and Babette stayed with the handful of afternoon students. Some napped while others colored or played.

Around 3:00 p.m., Fran Gammer arrived to pick up two kids whose parents needed care until 6:00 p.m. Fran and her sister, Mary Lou Briesler, ran home babysitting services a few blocks away, and they'd worked with Virginia and Peggy over the years, providing care into the early evenings for the dual-income families.

Babette walked the children out. "How are ya, Fran?" Babette asked.

"I'm good," Fran said, signing the sheet, "just making my rounds."

The children stepped out as Babette swung the gate shut and flipped the latch.

"See ya, Babs," Fran hollered, waving over her shoulder and prodding the children to do the same.

The clock showed 3:45 p.m. Ray counted the minutes, looking to get down to the beach. The children, too, were a bit riled up, anxious to go home.

"Settle down, now," Ray said. "Everyone settle."

The kids giggled even louder.

"Do as Mr. Ray says," Babette warned—and they did, subduing into a soft chatter.

Ray, content not to be the enforcer, stepped back. In his periphery, he noticed movement. He turned and saw a blond woman outside the fence. He couldn't make out who it was. She waved nervously as she peered through the reflective bay window, trying to be noticed. She didn't come inside the gate, abiding by the preschool's strict rule that parents were not permitted on the grounds. Babette stepped over and recognized her immediately—Judy Johnson.

"Mitchell, let's go," Babette said. "Your mommy's here...time to go."

Ray grabbed Mitchell's carry bag, taking him by the hand as he opened the door and led him out. Ray was a bit surprised that Judy had arrived fifteen minutes early. She'd signed Mitchell in at 8:56 a.m., and had noted 4:00 p.m. as his pick-up time. It wasn't a big deal, but the preschool had a structure they liked to follow, and if Judy had showed up on time, they would've had Mitchell ready.

Moreover, Ray knew Judy's history of unexpected behavior—the way she'd secretly dropped her son off three months earlier. Ray could still picture Mitchell standing in the yard with a bag at his side, confused by the unfamiliar place. Ray knew his mother to be a forgiving woman, but he was rather surprised she had allowed Judy Johnson to enroll her son after what Judy had done.

Since Mitchell started at McMartin, Ray's contact with the boy had been minimal. Mitchell had attended Tuesdays and Thursdays, usually mornings, except on the three occasions he'd stayed until 4:00 p.m.—this day being the third. Mitchell wasn't in Ray's class during the morning sessions—Betty Raidor was in charge of the two-year-olds. In total, Mitchell had attended McMartin about a dozen times, and there hadn't been any problems. This was Ray's first face-to-face meeting with Judy.

Ray walked Mitchell along the concrete path—the six-foot-two man bending down to hold the boy's hand. They approached the fence where Judy waited, straight-faced, not pleased that she had to wait several minutes to be noticed.

Ray opened the gate and Mitchell walked out.

"He's a very nice, helpful boy," Ray said to Judy. "Have a nice day." Ray turned and stepped away.

Judy guided Mitchell along the sidewalk, but she kept her eyes intently on Ray. From Judy's perspective, Ray was the only teacher working, not having seen Babette.

Judy took Mitchell home.

Around 7:00 p.m., Brad came by the house to pick up Mark and Mitchell. He drove them to Straw Hat Pizza, where they ordered their food to go. Then they went directly to Brad's apartment.

After they'd eaten, in response to Mitchell's noticeable discomfort,

Brad examined the boy's anus. He noticed redness. Aware of Mitchell's recent diarrhea, Brad applied zinc oxide to the surface.

Brad returned the boys to Judy at 8:30 p.m.

* * * * *

The nights were quiet since Brad had left. Judy sat at the small kitchen table, alone. Vengeance flooded her mind.

Hours earlier, while giving Mitchell his bath, Judy again noticed redness on his bottom, the fourth instance since late-June. This time, alas, it all seemed clear. Judy knew precisely what had happened to her boy: He'd been violently raped.

The image left Judy stewing, a boiling anger that she had to purge—so she wrote down her thoughts.

Judy pictured him, the monster, man-handling her defenseless child—a baby writhing in pain. The vision pierced her subconscious. Judy stopped writing.

Tucked away in their bunk beds, Mark and Mitchell were fast asleep. Judy stepped around the corner to peek in on them. She stood in their doorway, admiring the peacefulness of their slumber. Mark was on top, lying on his side, while Mitchell slept below, curled up against the cool surface of the wall, so precious, so innocent. *How could he have done this to my sweet angel?* The thought of it brought her to tears.

Judy rushed back to the table. She grabbed her calendar, turning the pages, and glared down upon the small box of August 11. She took her pencil and drew a thick, darkened square around the number 11, then shaded in the box, marking that date as one to remember.

* * * * *

The light of dawn delivered Judy a new mood. Her anger had morphed into diligence. Her distress had given her cause.

On the steps outside the rectory of Trinity Lutheran Church, Judy sat with her pastor, Reverend David Brostrom, seeking counsel to guide her next step. The pastor, a Lutheran minister like her father, held her hand. They prayed.

Mitchell played with the other children in the yard. Judy and her pastor watched him closely. They admired his joy despite the trauma he'd endured.

The pastor told Judy that, although the coming days would be trying, she had a responsibility to all of the children within the grasp of that evil man. Sometimes, the pastor inferred, the Lord requires us to take action against the wicked, to stand with a righteous voice to help the helpless.

The pastor stepped away, returning to the rectory.

Sometime thereafter, Judy wrote of that fateful moment:

> *With the police investigation, would it further traumatize him? The minister talked of social obligation, something already burning a hole in my psyche. I sat on the porch after he left, watching Mitchell jump off a small brick garden wall. How could a man's adult penis penetrate such an angel? There were lots of angels still at that school. I began to feel my blood boil. This madman must be stopped. I called Detective Hoag. I will take my child to the police. She was to accompany me to the general hospital.*

CHAPTER
4

Friday, August 12, 1983

Manhattan Beach Police Detective Jane Hoag sat at her desk, staring at the blinking light of her phone. A voice came over. "Judy Johnson, line one."

After eleven years on the force, Hoag was the department's expert on child sexual abuse. Since November, the number of cases reported to the department had increased by more than five-hundred percent, and the conviction rates had nearly tripled. Hoag had recently closed a case where a father had been accused of molesting his three daughters, charged with one count against the youngest, while the other two were taken into protective custody.

The topic, the crime, had become something of an epidemic, with awareness at an all-time high. Some of the nation's top experts had found a home in the South Bay—pediatricians, clinicians, psychotherapists—and it had become routine within Manhattan Beach that whenever a child made a disclosure, the case wound up in the hands of Detective Jane Hoag.

According to the police report, Judy Johnson's call came in at noon on Friday, August 12.[1]

"This is Hoag," she answered.

---

[1] All information regarding Judy Johnson's initial complaint and the investigation that followed is found in the official police report, D.R. No. 83-04288. According to Noreen Noel, Judy's social worker, Judy knew Jane Hoag prior to the complaint, and that Judy had periodically gone to the department to report random incidents—the proverbial Good Samaritan.

"Detective Hoag, this is Judy...Judy Johnson." Judy's voice quivered as she struggled to find the right words.

"What's going on, Judy?" Detective Hoag asked.

"I need to file a complaint...child molestation," Judy said, pausing for a beat. "My son just told me that he was molested by Ray Buckey, his teacher at the McMartin Preschool."

The phrases "child molestation" and "McMartin Preschool" created a distasteful vortex when spoken in the same sentence. Having worked in Manhattan Beach for more than a decade, Detective Hoag was well aware of Virginia McMartin and what she meant to the community. The thought of a sexual abuse investigation into Virginia's preschool left Hoag uneasy. She had to move cautiously.

Before Judy bothered coming to the station, Hoag wanted her to get Mitchell examined by a doctor, a specialist.

"I want you to take him to the Pediatric Emergency Department at Harbor General," Hoag told Judy. "You need to go right away."

"But I've already arranged to have him examined at Kaiser," Judy said, "by Dr. Scott McGeary."

"Judy, I highly recommend you take him to Harbor," Hoag said. "They're the best. I can call right now and arrange an exam at the Marion Davies Clinic."

UCLA-Harbor Medical Center was the most highly regarded pediatric institution in the area. To build a case, nothing was more vital than a qualified, indisputable physical examination by a specialist whose testimony would hold up in court. From Hoag's perspective, UCLA-Harbor was the only choice.

But, again, Judy declined.

"It's your call," Hoag said. "But I need you to come down to the station. We have to initiate an investigation."

Judy arrived at the station at 4:15 p.m. without Mitchell. Detective Hoag took her to a private room, where Judy laid out the events of the past seven weeks, how Mitchell began attending on Tuesdays and Thursdays, usually in the morning with the exception of a few afternoon sessions. Judy said that, from the beginning, she noticed redness on Mitchell's anus.

"A few weeks ago, I discussed it with my brother and sister-in-law," Judy said, "but none of us could figure it out. Then, yesterday, I went to pick him up at the school. He stayed late, until four o'clock. When I got there, Ray was the only employee on site. They left him *alone* with the children. Ray walked Mitchell out, and he told me, 'He's a very nice and helpful boy.' Later, when I was giving Mitchell his tub, I noticed it again."

"So why do you think it was Ray who did it?" Hoag asked.

"This morning, I asked him, 'Did Ray ever put his penis in your anus,' but he said, 'No, no, Mommy. Ray takes my temperature.' Then I asked, 'Do you play doctor at school, Mitchell?' But he just said, 'Ray takes my temperature.' Then, a few hours later, I talked to Mark, my thirteen-year-old, and he said that Mitchell told him, 'Ray hurt me.'"

Judy told Hoag that "sometimes the boys shower together," so she asked Mark, "Did you *ever* put your penis near your little brother's anus," but Mark said, "No, absolutely not."

Judy also said that, in her opinion, Ray acted inappropriately with the children.

"He lets those kids crawl all over him," Judy said. "I just don't like it."

Detective Hoag scheduled Mitchell's police interview for a later date, not wanting to subject him to questioning right before he underwent a physical exam. Hoag asked Judy to bring Mitchell back to the station the following Tuesday—five days after the alleged abuse.

"Do not discuss this with anyone," Hoag instructed. "Not the patrol officer and not Sergeant Samuel."

Sergeant Brian Samuel, a friend of the McMartin-Buckey family, had a daughter currently attending the preschool, and, like most parents, was part of Virginia's network of trust. If Samuel caught wind of it he could undermine Hoag's inquiry.

Hours later, just before 10:00 p.m., Detective Hoag took a call from Dr. Scott McGeary at the Emergency Room at Kaiser Hospital in Harbor City.

"I just examined Mitchell Johnson," McGeary said, "and he appeared pleasant; he ran around the room, having fun. All of his vitals are normal: eyes, ears, nose, and throat. His mother said there's blood around his anus, and that she thinks he was sexually molested. She wouldn't tell me the name of who did it. Just that it was one of the instructors at his preschool."

"What's your determination?" Hoag asked.

"Well, I examined the anus, and it's not tightly closed. There's definitely redness around the circumference, which is concerning. He could've been sodomized or penetrated by some type of object. So I'm preparing a report of *suspected child abuse*."

In Detective Jane Hoag's police report, however, she noted that Dr. McGeary's finding was "inconclusive," that he [McGeary] was "not a specialist in sodomy," and therefore did not have enough experience to make a diagnosis.[2]

* * * * *

Four days later, on August 16, Judy arrived at the Manhattan Beach Police Department with Mark and Mitchell. She informed Hoag that, since the previous Friday night—after returning from his exam at Kaiser—Mitchell suffered from diarrhea. Judy was "certain he did not have diarrhea on Thursday [August 11], the day she noticed the redness."

Detective Hoag interviewed Mitchell privately. In a somewhat mumbled dialogue—the verbal sophistication of a two-and-a-half-year-old—Mitchell said he had his "temperature taken in his anus," and that he'd "seen Ray's and Mark's penises." Hoag noted in her report that Mitchell became restless and inattentive.

"What did Ray use to take your temperature, Mitchell?"

Mitchell did not immediately respond, but then blurted, "I showered with Mark."

Detective Hoag concluded the interview with Mitchell, as it appeared "his attention was drifting from the subject of the investigation."

Judy had been watching through a glass window from the adjacent room. Hoag motioned her inside, hoping she could ease Mitchell's anxiety. In Judy's presence, Mitchell added that "Ray had taken a picture of him without his clothes on."

Judy related a series of statements Mitchell had told her prior to the interview. "Mitchell told me that Ray pulled him from his cot and took him into the bathroom. He put a *hair dryer* on his head. He said Ray rolled him over and 'poked him in the anus.' "

Detective Hoag asked to speak with Mark, alone. Mark entered and sat in a chair next to Hoag. He admitted that he had "occasionally showered with Mitchell," and that his little brother had "touched his private

---

[2] This contradiction between Dr. McGeary's sworn testimony and Detective Hoag's official police report was never reconciled. Dr. McGeary testified: "I don't feel this [police report] states my opinion."

parts," but said that he'd never engaged in any kind of sexual activity with Mitchell, "not even touching."

Hoag knew from an earlier conversation with Judy that Mark's parents had been separated since April.

"When was the last time you saw your father, Mark?"

"Last Thursday," Mark replied. "Thursday night we went to his place for pizza."

"Last Thursday night? What time?"

"I don't know. I think he picked us up around seven," Mark said. "We got Straw Hat and took it to his apartment."

"What time did you get home?"

"Around eight-thirty, maybe. I'm not sure."

"Was there any time while at your dad's place that Mitchell was alone with your father?"

"No, no way. Mitchell was with me the whole time."

Hoag concluded the interview.[3]

The Johnsons left the station just before five o'clock. Twenty minutes later, Judy telephoned Detective Hoag, highly animated.

"Mitchell just told me that Ray made two other children cry. He said, 'Holly' and 'Matthew,' but he doesn't know their last names."

Detective Hoag hung up and ran a background check on Raymond Charles Buckey: white male, twenty-five years old, six-foot two-inches tall, one hundred seventy-five pounds, with brown hair and hazel eyes; D.O.B 5/24/58; he lived at 117 16th Place, Manhattan Beach, the owner of a 1968 Volkswagen Bus. He had a criminal record—an arrest on January 18, 1980, by the Hermosa Beach Police Department for Possession of Marijuana for Sale.

Detective Hoag called Judy.

"I want Mitchell to be examined again," Hoag told her. "But this time it needs to be done by a specialist. Do I have your consent to set it up?"

---

[3] According to the police report, Detective Hoag, having discovered that Mark and Mitchell had spent the evening of Thursday, August 11, with their father, did not ask Judy why she'd failed to disclose that fact. Since the boys had spent an hour and a half in the sole company of their father, Ray Buckey was not the last man to be in the care of Mitchell from the moment he left the McMartin Preschool to the time Judy filed the complaint. Instead of pursuing that potential lead, Detective Hoag proceeded with her investigation as if Ray Buckey was the only possible suspect.

"Yes," Judy said. "Please make the appointment."

The following day, August 17—six days after the alleged abuse—Mitchell was examined at UCLA-Harbor's Marion Davies Clinic by Dr. Jean Simpson, attending physician, and Dr. Linda Golden, resident pediatrician, both members of the clinic's Child Abuse Team.

Just as Dr. McGeary had noted five days earlier, Dr. Simpson confirmed that the opening was "quite lax" and "gaped open." She also found "redness, excoriations (broken skin), and yellowish-brown bruises" at the lower edge of the rectum.

After the exam, Dr. Simpson called Detective Hoag.

"It appears the boy's anus was forcibly entered several days ago. I definitely believe he's been sodomized." [4]

As a result, in her official report, Detective Hoag identified Raymond Charles Buckey as the lone suspect in the sexual abuse investigation of Mitchell Johnson, a crime categorized as a "major injury or rape." The report stated that Ray Buckey had "inflicted injury, bound and gagged his victim, and committed forcible sodomy" while on the premises of the Virginia McMartin Preschool in Manhattan Beach.

Detective Hoag contacted Judy Johnson and informed her of the findings.

The next morning, Judy rushed into the station, distressed.

"Mitchell said Ray took nude pictures of him, Holly, and Matthew. He said he was tied up. He used Mark's scout rope to demonstrate it."

Judy described other recent changes in Mitchell's behavior, things she had not told Hoag during the first five days of the investigation.

"The other night he had a terrifying nightmare," Judy said. "I found him crouched on his bed, face down with his butt stuck up in the air. He was whimpering and saying, 'Get away. Get away'...like he was being attacked by an imaginary figure. He said that Ray was putting a hair dryer on his head."

Judy said that since attending the preschool, Mitchell had made a

---

[4] Dr. Jean Simpson later testified that, at the moment of the examination, she ruled out the possibility that diarrhea or hard stools could've caused Mitchell Johnson's trauma, though her report did state that it could've been caused by "rubbing or penetration." Moreover, despite Detective Hoag's insistence on having a "specialist in sodomy" conduct Mitchell's second physical examination, Dr. Simpson later testified that her diagnosis of "sodomy" in respect to Mitchell Johnson was the first of her professional career.

reaction to every noise, fearfully asking, "What's that noise?" He had a loss of appetite; he did not want his mother to carry him; he had red body marks and rashes on his inner legs and around his mouth; he had a red anus, a swollen face; he constantly picked at his blanket; he had an extreme fear of men; he would cling to her then run and hide for long periods; he had a fear of all strangers; he was restless in his sleep; he had irritable tantrums, a loss of urine control, an inability to sit still; he pushed with his feet, sucked his thumb, and was afraid of "monsters in the dark."

Detective Hoag, seeing that Judy had become frantic, pulled her aside as she prepared to leave.

"Judy, I know you're upset, but you can't discuss this with *anyone*," Hoag instructed. "No one can know about this investigation."

Judy did not look Hoag in the eyes. "I'm sorry," she said, "but I've already spoken to a few people."

"Who?" Hoag asked. "Who did you speak with?"

"I talked to Ron and Cheryl Crass," Judy said. "They live around the corner from us. Their son, Kevin, he's three years old. He was in Ray's class, too."

"Oh, no, Judy, you should *not* have spoken with them. You shouldn't have mentioned this to *anyone*."

"I know...but listen, their son was in Ray's class," Judy said, "and they started noticing problems with him at the exact same time I started seeing problems with Mitchell. Cheryl may know other families who had kids in Ray's class. You need to speak with her."

Three days later, Detective Hoag did just that.

"I spoke to Kevin," Cheryl told Hoag, "but he said nothing happened to him, only that he didn't like going to McMartin."

"Did he say why?"

"No. Not really. He just started crying once they put him in Ray's class, so I took him out of the preschool."

"Well," Hoag said, "thank you for your help. But please make sure you keep this confidential. You can't discuss this with *anyone*."

An unnerving silence hung between them.

"Mrs. Crass? Do you understand?" Hoag asked. "Do you understand that you can't discuss this with anyone?"

"Well, I'm sorry, Detective, but I didn't know that."

"Who have you spoken to?"

"Well," Cheryl said, "my husband spoke with Neil Stedman about it. The Stedmans have two children that go to McMartin, a boy and a girl."

Cheryl Crass named four additional McMartin families, all members of American Martyrs Catholic Church, who, because of their close relationships with the Stedmans, had more than likely become aware that a "child had accused Ray Buckey of molestation" and that a pediatrician at UCLA-Harbor had "confirmed that the child had been sodomized."

* * * * *

Speculation about Ray Buckey spread faster than evidence could be collected. Detective John Dye, an associate of Detective Hoag, contacted several families of children who'd been in Ray's class. All of these families were members of American Martyrs Catholic Church, and before he'd reached them, they'd been talking amongst themselves. A few of them had spoken to "the mother of the little boy who'd been abused."

Detective Dye told each parent that "the investigation was highly confidential, and if they were to divulge anything, it could seriously jeopardize the direction of the case." Dye never mentioned the suspect by name, but, according to his report, most assumed it was Ray. Several of them said they "thought it was strange that Ray was teaching a class at the preschool."

Within days, someone told Peggy of the allegations, and she called the station.

"This is ludicrous!" Peggy shouted at Detective Dye. "Why didn't you come to me first?"

"I can't discuss this with you, ma'am," Dye said. "It's confidential."

"Confidential? How can you say it's confidential? You've already contacted half a dozen people."

"I can't talk about the case. I'm sorry."

"Will you at least tell me who the complaining child is?"

But Dye gave her nothing.

Days later, Peggy called back, asking for Detective Hoag. "The way you're handling this is really foolish," Peggy said. "Are you going to force me to call every parent at my school to find out who filed the complaint?"

"I'm sorry, Mrs. Buckey, but the case is confidential and no information can be released."

"You know, my mother is a long-time friend of Chief Kuhlmeyer, and I can't imagine he approves of this."

Detective Hoag ignored Peggy's subtle threat and changed the subject.

"Do you know the whereabouts of your son?" Hoag asked.

"Ray's out of town. He left three days ago with his sister. He's hiking in South Dakota."

"Really?" Hoag asked. "He left the state?"

"He planned this trip months ago. You can check his flight arrangement if you'd like."

"That's not necessary," Hoag said. "But when he gets home, make sure he sticks around."

Hoag hung up, contemplating her next move.

Detective Jane Hoag, to the well heeded folks of Manhattan Beach, embodied the stereotype of a police woman—a strict professional with a dry persona whose aura resembled her look. If "plain Jane" were ever duly applied, the case of Jane Hoag fit the bill—as if her name and countenance had inspired the cliché. She was stout but solid, medium height, and pulled her hair into a tight bun. She wore light makeup, modest attire, and wasn't known for her endearing smile. In fact, Hoag held the classic scowl of a law enforcer, a reminder to all that she meant business.

Hoag had joined the Manhattan Beach Police Department eleven years earlier, in the fall of 1972. With an AA degree from Los Angeles Valley College in 1969, she earned a BA in Police Science Administration two years later from California State University, Los Angeles. She spent fifteen months as a deputy in the San Bernardino Sheriff's Department before heading to this quiet, low-crime setting. When she arrived, she had no specific training in the area of sexual abuse.

Since then, however, she began building her resume, attending various seminars, including a three-month course at the University of Southern California's Delinquency Control Institute, which dealt with "juvenile investigation and child abuse." She also attended a handful of forums on child abuse and sexual assault investigations, as well as a one-week course at the College of the Redwoods on the exploitation of children.

Most importantly, though, Detective Jane Hoag had attained hands-on experience through her "great many years working in the field," where she interviewed "several thousand children" of which more than "five hundred" had been abused.

Detective Hoag had learned much about the typical pedophile—the textbook definition being "lover of children"—and the ways they stockpiled child pornography, rarely disposing of their explicit material. Hoag knew that pedophiles often used Polaroids for instant gratification and avoided film-processing centers. Some had photo-developing labs within their homes; others used post office boxes as fronts, not only for delivery but for secret communiqués.

Hoag knew how to identify pedophiles, and she was confident she had pinpointed Ray Buckey—a twenty-five-year-old who lived next door to his parents, a man who spent his days with small children. None of that, of course, was a crime—but it fit the profile.

Detective Hoag suspected that Ray Buckey had stashed the evidence, the kiddie porn, once he became aware of the investigation. Instead of coming down to the station to discuss it—like an innocent man would do—he had his mother do his bidding while he quietly flew out of the state.

Hoag was convinced she understood his mindset. Even on the verge of being caught, she suspected that Ray refused to destroy the pictures. They were far too precious. Without hesitation, he traveled a thousand miles northeast to the Wind Cave National Forest, deep within the Black Hills of South Dakota, where he buried the photographs. One day, he would return to retrieve them, and if not, just knowing they were there would keep their memory alive.

Ray's mother said that his trip had been scheduled well in advance, which may have been true—a lucky break that the investigation of Mitchell Johnson coincided with his preplanned trip to South Dakota. But had it not, he could've hidden the photos in any one of the canyons or caves within the mountain ranges of Southern California.

Hoag figured Ray had not been able to gather every piece of evidence, every token or souvenir of his past crimes. He was young, careless—his vile acts against Mitchell Johnson proved as much—and he'd likely missed something in his rush to make that flight.

With Ray out of town, Detective Hoag acted quickly, preparing a request for search warrants. In it, she asked for a broad reach—a three-block section of small homes and apartments just off the Strand, as well as the premises of the McMartin Preschool. She identified the homes of Ray Buckey (116 17th Street), Peggy and Chuck Buckey (117 16th Place), and Virginia McMartin (112 16th Street), as well as their vehicles and storage spaces.

Hoag asked to "seize school records of all students in attendance at the McMartin Preschool from 1980–1983," including employee records to determine who was working when Mitchell Johnson attended, explicitly naming items that would've been used to bind up Mitchell, such as rope and cords, and the make-up and hair dryer the boy had spoken of.

Hoag listed all items she hoped to recover: cameras, videotapes, video equipment, slides, prints, movies, undeveloped film, diaries of the suspect—and she even stated that evidence of "simulated sexual activities between human beings and animals" may be uncovered.

Four days later, on Friday, September 2, Judge Mark Wood granted Detective Hoag's request. He also issued an arrest warrant for Ray Buckey.

* * * * *

A convoy of squad cars left the Manhattan Beach police station, headed for the beachfront. With it, the community simmered, an unsettled energy that had been brewing for weeks. The police entered the narrow streets—essentially throughways for beach access along the strand—where the three residences were located. The three sites were just a minute's walk from each other, as the three generations of McMartin-Buckeys had remained neighbors.

A crew of six officers entered each location with warrants in hand, leaving their squad cars blocking the roadway. Being a busy afternoon on the beach, the Friday before Labor Day weekend, it caused a stir as people stepped up to see what the commotion was about.

The police searched Virginia's home, confiscating her personal files. She sat, her chin held high, disgusted by it all. Next, the police moved west onto 16th Street, then north up Ocean Avenue. They went through the homes of Ray and his parents, grabbing any items they deemed fit.

Once the raids were complete, the squad cars headed south on Highland Avenue and turned inland up Manhattan Beach Boulevard, stopping at the vacant lot next to the McMartin Preschool. The officers parked their vehicles and entered the premises.

On that preholiday Friday, with many locals working half days or not at all, the scene at 931 Manhattan Beach Boulevard turned heads along the commercial strip. Some drivers slowed to get a better look.

Inside the classrooms and around the yard, police searched for pictures, photographic equipment, publications depicting nude children, and any correspondence relating to pedophilia. The process took more than three hours—but the police uncovered nothing incriminating.

Among the items confiscated: a three-foot piece of rope, a Playboy magazine tucked underneath Ray's mattress, and a pair of boxer shorts with a large banana printed on the crotch. The police took possession of all volumes of the McMartin Preschool's records, as well as Virginia's personal diary.

* * * * *

Five days later, on the morning of Wednesday, September 7, detectives Jane Hoag and John Dye returned to the preschool. Chuck Buckey stood behind the fence, getting the property back in order after the raids had left everything pulled apart and overturned. The school was scheduled to open the following Monday.

"Mr. Buckey, we need to speak with your son," Detective Hoag said.

"My son's at home," Chuck replied. "But you should know that we've acquired an attorney, Donald Kelly, so you'll need to talk with him. I can call home and see if Ray's there."

"No, that won't be necessary," Hoag replied.

As they prepared to leave, the detectives spotted Ray Buckey walking east on Manhattan Beach Boulevard toward the preschool. They confronted him and asked him to identify himself, which he did.

"Ray Buckey, you're under arrest. You have the right to remain silent…"

Ray was handcuffed and transported to the Manhattan Beach Police Department, and placed in a cell. Ray sat for hours, waiting to be booked, still puzzled as to which child had accused him of molestation.

But the anticipated interrogation never took place. At no time did the detectives question Ray about the alleged sodomy of Mitchell Johnson.

Ray's attorney, Donald Kelly, called the station and spoke with Captain John Wehner. Kelly complained that he'd pre-arranged with Detective Hoag for Ray to turn himself in.

"Hoag's a liar!" Kelly charged. "She reneged on our deal. She knew *exactly* what she was doing. She wanted to arrest him in public, right there on the boulevard. She wanted to humiliate him. She's trying to turn people against him. This is bullshit!"

Captain Wehner conveyed Kelly's complaint to Detective Hoag, but she claimed to have never spoken to Kelly about such an arrangement.

Either way, as Ray waited in the cell, his parents posted $5,000 for his bail—but it was refunded within minutes.

Ray Buckey was released for lack of evidence.

The next morning, Thursday, September 8, the Manhattan Beach

Police Department expanded the investigation to hundreds of current and former McMartin families, some of whose children had graduated more than three years earlier, well before Ray Buckey began teaching at the preschool. From the police perspective, without additional victims—other students to corroborate the crimes, preferably older children who could better articulate how the acts had occurred—Ray Buckey would continue to walk the streets.

Thus, in an aggressive move, the police drafted a "Dear Parent" letter, which was mimeographed and mailed to more than two hundred households. The letter was accompanied by a four-page questionnaire for parents to fill out and return. The exact wording and format of the letter is as follows:

POLICE DEPARTMENT
City of Manhattan Beach
420 15th Street
Manhattan Beach, CA 22252

September 8, 1983

Dear Parent:

    This department is conducting a criminal investigation involving child molestation (288 P.C.). Ray Buckey, an employee of Virginia McMartin's preschool, was arrested September 7, 1983, by this Department. The following procedure is obviously an unpleasant one, but to protect the rights of your children as well as the rights of the accused, this inquiry is necessary for a complete investigation.

    Records indicate that your child has been or is currently a student at the preschool. We are asking your assistance in this continuing investigation. Please question your child to see if he or she has been a witness to any crime or if he or she has been a victim. Our investigation indicates that possible criminal acts include: oral sex, fondling of genitals, buttock or chest area, and sodomy, possibly committed under the pretense of "taking the child's temperature." Also, photos may have been taken of children without their clothing. Any information from your child regarding having ever observed Ray Buckey to leave a classroom alone with a child during any nap period, or if they ever observed Ray Buckey tie up a child, is important.

    Please complete the enclosed information form and return it to the Department in the enclosed stamped return envelope as soon as possible. We will contact you if circumstances dictate same. We ask you to keep this investigation strictly confidential because the nature of the charges and the highly emotional effect it would have on our community. Please do not discuss the investigation with anyone outside your immediate family. Do not contact or discuss the investigation with Raymond Buckey, any member of the accused defendant's family, or employees connected with McMartin Preschool.

THERE IS NO EVIDENCE TO INDICATE THAT THE MANAGEMENT OF VIRGINIA MCMARTIN'S PRESCHOOL HAD ANY KNOWLEDGE OF THIS SITUATION AND NO DETRIMENTAL INFORMATION CONCERNING THE OPERATION OF THE SCHOOL HAS BEEN DISCOVERED DURING THIS INVESTIGATION. ALSO, NO OTHER EMPLOYEE OF THE PRESCHOOL IS UNDER INVESTIGATION FOR ANY CRIMINAL ACT.

Your prompt attention to this matter and reply no later than September 16, 1983, will be appreciated.

HARRY L. KUHLMEYER, JR., Chief of Police
JOHN WEHNER, Captain

PART II
Changing Society

CHAPTER 5

On the first day of the fall semester, Grace Shelby, an American Martyrs parishioner, the mother of Jennifer, a four-year-old McMartin student who'd been in Ray Buckey's class the year before, closed the mailbox outside of her home in the Tree section. As she sifted through the stack, a particular envelope caught her eye—the one with the emblem of the Manhattan Beach Police Department. She opened it and began to read. Moments later, unable to manage her emotions, Grace rushed into the house. Her husband, Bill, sat in his recliner, newspaper opened wide.

"Look at this," Grace said, forcing the letter upon him.

"What is it?"

"Read it!"

Bill read the first paragraph—*a criminal investigation involving child molestation*. His brow lowered when he came to the second paragraph about the oral sex and sodomy that may have occurred during nap time.

Grace didn't wait for him to finish. She went to the den where Jennifer sat on the carpet, playing with her Cabbage Patch kid.

"Jenny," Grace said, gently pulling the doll away and setting it to the side. "Do you remember last year…last year at the preschool? Back when you were in Mr. Ray's class?"

Jennifer nodded. "Yeah."

"Did Mr. Ray ever do anything bad to you? Did he ever touch you… anywhere on your body…like on your privates?"

Jennifer shook her head.

"Never? Are you sure?" Grace asked again.

"No, never. I like Mr. Ray. He's nice."

Grace stood and stepped back into the living room. Bill had just finished reading the letter. He handed it back to her, stupefied. He exaggerated his expression as he spoke.

"This is unbelievable," Bill said.

Grace read over the letter a second time, line by line, agitated by the thought of Ray, a grown man, doing such things to small children.

"I'm calling Peggy," she said, grabbing the phone and dialing frantically. Peggy answered.

"Peggy, I got this letter from the police—"

"I know all about it," Peggy said. "I can't believe they sent a letter like that. It's horrible."

"Did Ray really get arrested?"

"Well, they arrested him last week, but they let him go. They had to. There's no evidence. Nothing."

"But how can they send out this letter if they don't have any evidence?"

"I have no idea what they're doing. They won't even tell us which child's accusing him," Peggy said. "You should've seen what they did to our homes and the preschool. They came in and turned everything upside down. They tore everything apart."

"But why? Why would they do all of this if they don't have anything?"

Peggy was silent, somewhat perturbed by the implication.

Grace spoke softly, easing back into a more cordial place. "Well, we talked to Jenny, and she said nothing happened. That Ray was nice to her. And that's what we're going to tell the police," she assured Peggy. "Okay? I just want you to know that."

"I appreciate that," Peggy said, her voice quivering. "I can't tell you what this is doing to my mother."

"Please send her our love," Grace said, then hung up.

For Peggy, that conversation repeated itself throughout the night and over the following days. Most parents refused to believe it—the whole story was so over the top. Yet, there were some, a small group, who were concerned that Ray "had been arrested," that he'd been accused of "fondling, sodomy, oral sex, and pornography." If the police believed it, which apparently they did, there had to be something to it.

Thus, each morning, with the beginning of the new semester, as mothers left their kids at the preschool, Peggy sensed their apprehension, as if they did not want to let go of their children the way they once had. Ray was no longer on campus—his attorney had advised him to stay away from children until the matter was settled—so the students were in no immediate danger.

Still, Ray or no Ray, the McMartin Preschool had lost a bit of its sheen. Most of the mothers, the longtime friends of Virginia and Peggy—the faithful—swore to stand by them.

Yet there were others—the vigilant—who kept a watchful eye. And they made no promises.

* * * * *

Ray Buckey, who'd never been in any serious trouble, could only wonder how things had come to this. How he had gone from a simple preschool instructor to having more than two hundred families in his community suspecting that he may have molested their children.

Born and raised in Manhattan Beach, Ray had grown up with the Pacific Ocean as his backyard. He'd spent most of his time playing sand volleyball and jogging the shoreline, and he'd recently taken an interest in rock climbing. He viewed his family as the "Ozzie-and-Harriet type," a wholesome, old-fashioned clan where no one cussed, drank, or smoked. The Buckeys attended church regularly, as members of the Church of Christian Science. His father, an engineer at Hughes Aircraft, was a quiet man who never stopped working, while his mother was a personable character, known for her kindness and empathy. His sister, Peggy Ann, naturally pretty and highly respected, had always been a pillar of virtue.

Through high school, Ray stayed close to Peggy Ann, feeling most comfortable within her circle of friends. In fact, Peggy Ann's high school boyfriend, Steve Bartlett, became Ray's best friend. They were all clean-cut athletic types, teenagers who liked to party, but nothing out of control.

In time, however, as energetic as Ray had been about recreation, he developed into a rather lazy fellow. In 1976, at eighteen, following his graduation from Mira Costa High, his parents made it clear that he needed to either "get a job or go to college." Ray, of course, gave them an affirmative nod, a show of respect, but he spent the next two years working odd jobs, not serious about his future. Peggy and Chuck, although frustrated, did not pressure him.

Two years passed, and Ray entered Northrup University to study airplane maintenance. He dropped out within three months.

Not long afterward, Ray had his first run-in with the law—an arrest for drunk driving. He spent the night in jail and paid a significant fine.

Months later, he and a friend decided to smoke pot in a car that had a dead battery, not realizing that they were parked directly behind the Hermosa Beach police station. "I wasn't too bright," Ray later said. "I would've pled guilty—because we were—but it never went to trial."

For the next two years, Ray continued to work part-time jobs in Manhattan Beach. He was a stock boy at Harry's Market, a delivery boy for a local drugstore, and he volunteered as a nursing assistant at a convalescent home on weekends. Ray enjoyed helping the elderly, but found it depressing. "I couldn't stand to see people suffer," he said.

In the fall of 1980, at the age of twenty-two, Ray moved away from home, enrolling in San Diego State University, a two-hour drive south. Midway through the semester, though, unable to adjust or make close friends, he became homesick and returned to Manhattan Beach.

It was then, in the new year of 1981, that Ray began to see his family's preschool as a potential career move. "For the first time in my life," he said, "I looked at the preschool and saw why my family was so involved with it, and why they enjoyed it so much. It was a very happy, uplifting atmosphere to be in."

That January, Ray began working at the preschool as a part-time teacher's aide. Enamored by the "zest for life" that the children exuded, Ray found it "contagious." But mostly, he said, it was easy, that "watching children play all day isn't hard work." Ray began to contemplate the notion that he could make the preschool a third-generation family business.

Once given his own class, Ray's daily interaction with the children was rather uneventful. The students would sit on the rug in a circle, where they were encouraged to bring something to share, or they would do various arts and crafts before going outside for juice and crackers in the yard. Once back in the classroom, Ray said, "I'd read them a story, clean up the room, and by that time, it was noon—time to go home."

Through his day-to-day experience, Ray began to see his future. He believed he had an innate connection with the kids.

"You gotta love children," Ray said of the experience. "You have to understand that they do things wrong but don't mean to." Children, Ray believed, were driven by their innocence, and thus, they were often misunderstood—much like him.

With that in mind, despite the general consensus that Ray was a *good guy*, there was, long before the "police letter," an underlying mood amongst certain parents that was far less welcoming to the college dropout.

Manhattan Beach was a small town—a uniquely cliquish community—where a man's reputation, warranted or not, had a way of becoming the discernible truth about his character.

Hence, in the case of Ray Buckey, in parallel with the rosy narrative of the McMartin Preschool's "next generation," an unseemly tittle-tattle had made its way around the local beachgoers who found his presence at the preschool to be an odd career choice—something that seemed even more peculiar once he'd been accused of such heinous crimes.

* * * * *

Five days after the letters had been postmarked, Ray Buckey's attorney, Donald Kelly, called the station. He unloaded on Captain John Wehner.

"You guys have really screwed this up from the beginning," Kelly argued. "Not only have you failed to give me a copy of the police report, but now you're trying to turn the community against my client by spreading lies. I shouldn't have to remind you that Ray Buckey has constitutional rights."

"Peggy's the one calling around town, harassing parents for information," Captain Wehner replied.

"Oh, give me a break," Kelly shot back. "That letter did all the damage that could be done. That was way out of line."

Kelly told Captain Wehner he didn't trust Detective Hoag's objectivity, that she was building a false case against Ray Buckey. Kelly cited a series of child sex abuse cases that Detective Hoag had spearheaded in the past, cases in which some of his colleagues had represented one of Hoag's suspects.

"This isn't the first time Hoag has used *creative writing* to stir up prejudice against the accused."

According to Hoag's police report, at the end of his tirade, Kelly warned, "If Jane Hoag turns up with two broken legs, it's because I put out a contract."

* * * * *

Bob Currie, a businessman, a middle-aged father of three, looked out the window of his office unit on Manhattan Beach Boulevard, across the street and down the block from the McMartin Preschool. From his desk, Currie had a bird's-eye view of the preschool's entrance, where mothers delivered their children each morning.

Currie had acquired an impressive list of properties near his home on Monterey Boulevard in Hermosa Beach. He had rented this space to take advantage of the booming market in Manhattan Beach, keeping his eyes open for fresh opportunities.

In his hand, Currie held the police letter. He glanced over it a second time, not particularly worried that any of his three kids—all former McMartin students—had been abused by Ray Buckey since his youngest, Gary, had graduated from McMartin well before Ray began working there. None of the Currie children had ever been in contact with Ray.

Currie and his wife, Angela, were members of American Martyrs Catholic Church, and all three of their children currently attended American Martyrs Parochial, as did the children of most of their friends. The Curries were active in the community. Bob, an ambitious fellow, had been considering a run for the city council, while Angela, an active member of The Sandpipers, had a philanthropic drive.

When the initial rumors of the investigation spread through the parish community, Bob Currie didn't think much of it. Unlike the previous spring, when he'd rushed into the rectory at American Martyrs, confronting Monsignor Robert Deegan about the crimes of Clement Renaud, the pedophile janitor, Currie treated the case of Ray Buckey with more skepticism.

"The way I heard it," Currie said, "Ray got accused of playing with some kid's butt. As far as I could tell, it really didn't make it over the believable hump."

When they received the police letter, Currie discussed it with Angela, who hadn't formed a strong opinion, but she was somewhat guarded.

"Don't you think it's strange that a grown man would work at a preschool?" Angela had asked him.

"I don't think so," Currie had replied. "They're probably just getting him ready to take over the business when his elders pass away. That's a nice little thing they got going there."

But Angela remained suspicious, an intuition that fit the sign of the times. In an era of fashion and booming wealth, where twenty-something men cruised around in sports cars trying to score women, a guy like Ray Buckey was an anomaly—a soft-spoken man still living under the wing of his mother, spending his days with little children. Once whispers of Ray being a "child molester" moved from home to home, the profile began to make sense, at least to some.

Currie could see Angela's point—that Ray had a strange air about him—but that wasn't enough to accuse him of being a pedophile. Actually, Currie had figured Ray to be gay. It was something in the way Ray carried himself—the nuance of his speech. Ray had a gentle nature, an awkward innocence underscored by a subtle lisp. Never noticeably flamboyant, Currie thought Ray's mannerisms and lifestyle evoked the portrait of a homosexual man suppressing his orientation.

That day, according to Currie, a late afternoon in the second week of September, his office phone rang. He answered to hear the distressed voice of Peggy Buckey.

"Bob, this is Peggy," she said. "Ray is in trouble. We need some help."

"What can I do for you?" Currie asked.

"I need to get a loan of about fifty thousand dollars. I need money for Ray's bail. Can we get together?"

"Sure, I'll be right down."

Currie, a forty-five-year-old former Marine, was medium height with short brown hair, stout but not fat. He wore a thin, well-trimmed moustache. A long-time friend described Currie as "a man who will do anything to get what he wants," labeling him a *Bastard Teddy Bear*. "Half the time you're calling him a 'bastard,' but the other half of the time you just want to give him a hug." Currie was known to get vocal at city council meetings, causing a raucous over civil matters, usually real estate development.

Currie said that he left his office and walked toward the McMartin Preschool, about one hundred yards west. He went through the front gate and stepped into the school's office, where Peggy greeted him with a nervous smile. Virginia sat in a chair, looking rather upset.

Currie sat down and Peggy described the injustice her family had endured—the false allegations leveled against her son, which resulted in Ray's arrest, followed by the police letter. He said Peggy told him they needed money to get Ray out of jail and to pay for an attorney.

Currie, after hearing Peggy's plea, gave it to her straight.

"Listen, Peggy, I know that Ray's gay, and, honestly, to me, it's no big deal. There are a lot of gays in the world these days, so I don't hold it against *you* because your son's a homosexual."

To Currie's surprise, Peggy became enraged. She stood over him, leaned in and stuck her finger in his face, raising her voice. "You don't know what you're talking about. My son is *not* gay. Don't you say that about Ray. Don't you say that."

Currie was stunned. He'd known Peggy for many years and that was the first time he'd ever seen her angry. Currie remained seated, unsure how to respond. Then, he said, she stepped back, turned, and walked toward the restroom, a small half-bath connected to the office. It had no door, so Currie could see her clearly. She wore a long, loose flowery dress, and she pulled it up as she entered the bathroom. Currie noticed that she wasn't wearing underwear. According to Currie, Peggy sat down on the commode, in plain sight, and began urinating.

Currie, dumfounded, turned to Virginia, who glared at him.

"Bob," Virginia said, "you're a very tenacious young man."

Currie agreed with her. "When I was a boy, my mother told me to fight hard for everything I believed in. I always have and I always will."

Before Peggy returned from the bathroom, Currie's decision had been made: He would not loan any sum of money to the McMartin-Buckey family, regardless of Ray's guilt or innocence. Currie stood up and left the premises without saying another word.

That story—Bob Currie's recollection of his meeting with Peggy and Virginia in mid-September 1983—differed greatly from their version.

As Peggy recalled, Bob Currie came by the preschool that day unannounced, not at her request to seek a loan to post bail. She didn't need bail money, she noted, "because Ray was released the same day he was arrested."

Seeing Currie approach did not concern Peggy, as he would drop by from time to time in the years after his kids had graduated. He would stand outside the gate and converse with her, usually updating her on his family. In fact, Currie stopped by often enough that Virginia would tease Peggy, saying, "I think he has a crush on you, Peg," which made Peggy blush. "Oh, Mother, don't be silly," she would say, embarrassed but flattered all the same.

That day, as Peggy recalled, Currie was visibly agitated. He told Peggy that he was offended by the police letter. He'd come to offer his assistance. He complained that the letter was "irresponsible and tasteless," and he told Peggy and Virginia that he planned to make his feelings known to the Manhattan Beach Police Department. Currie told them that he didn't believe a word of it, and he assured them of his loyal support.

CHAPTER
6

The fresh air of autumn had arrived, a rather dry Indian summer, the back end of a grueling El Niño that had hammered Southern California with immense rainfall. Within Manhattan Beach, befittingly, a tempest was brewing, an ominous sentiment that moved from home to home, like a slow wind sifting through the trees.

Amongst the families who'd received the police letter, the notion that one little boy had been molested had sunk in—but it seemed to have ended there. Hundreds of children had been questioned by their parents, and not a single child had come forth to say they'd been abused.

Despite that simple truth, however, some parents chose to remove their children from the preschool. It had become a rather negative atmosphere, one that dampened the spirit of what preschool was all about. The name "Raymond Buckey"—the things he was said to have done—left an unfavorable image in the minds of some, opening the door to other subliminal effects.

Simultaneously, in that first week of October 1983, the evening news did just that, tracking the formation of a Category 4 hurricane in the eastern Pacific. Each night, weather reports led with the ferocious event—"a gale of 145 miles-per-hour wind with its well-defined eye"—a massive display of nature's force. The deadly storm, the strongest ever recorded in the region, came to be known as Hurricane Raymond.

With Raymond raging 800 miles off the California coast, holding its peak intensity for two days, a small group of McMartin mothers continued to press their children about "Mr. Ray," looking for any emotional signs that indicated past abuse.

Within that brewing turmoil, Judy lay in bed, longing for rest, but the night sounds from the street kept her awake. She went to the window and carefully pulled back the shades.

Ten weeks had passed since she'd filed the complaint, and her identity, she assumed, had been revealed. Someone—likely the mother of a McMartin student—had informed Peggy that Judy Johnson was the accuser. The Buckeys had many lifelong friends throughout Manhattan Beach, some of whom lived close to Judy. They had her address; they knew where to find her. It was only a matter of time before the hounds were unleashed.

From the far end of Vista Drive, a car sped toward the Johnson home. It slowed as it neared. Judy watched it pass and pull away. Its taillights faded in the distance. She went back to bed, lying motionless, listening as another car approached. Its engine revved. Judy jumped up and stood at the window, peering out, but it too cruised by and vanished in the dark.

Again, Judy lay down and closed her eyes, allowing her peaceful fatigue to take her away. She fell into a relaxed state of consciousness.

"Maaaa! Maaaa!"

The shrill of Mitchell's scream lifted her upright. She leapt from her bed and rushed to his room. Mitchell shook in terror, his body pressed against the wall.

Mark climbed down to console him, but Mitchell kept screaming.

"Maaaa! Maaaa!"

"Oh, baby...come here, baby, Mommy's here," Judy said, reaching out to him as he lunged into her arms.

"Are you having nightmares again? Are you having those bad dreams?"

"Uh-huh," Mitchell cried. "Yeah."

"It's okay," she said, rocking him gently. "Everything's going to be okay. It's just a dream. Mommy's here now. Don't be afraid, baby. Don't be afraid."

Judy lay down with Mitchell in her arms, pulling the blanket over them. Mark leaned down and kissed his mother's forehead. He climbed back up top.

A few hours later, the morning light offered a new direction, a sign of hope and renewal. Despite her fear that many McMartin parents were pulling back, Judy remained vigilant.

On Wednesday, October 5, Judy met with Detective Hoag.

"There's another student, a little girl named Tamra Morgan," Judy said. "Mitchell saw her in the bathroom. She was naked. This happened at the preschool, in front of Ray."

The next day, Judy called Hoag again.

"Ms. Betty was absent in July because her daughter died. *That's* when Mitchell went into Ray's class. *That's* when I started seeing the redness on his bottom."

Judy also began to associate with a specific group of McMartin parents—the women of American Martyrs Catholic Church—who were open to the possibility that their children, too, might have been abused by Ray Buckey. Janet Rogan was the first.

Janet Rogan and her husband, Dave, a stock broker, lived with their seven-year-old son, Austin, on 21st Street in the northwest quadrant of the Tree section. Austin, who was in the second grade at Martyrs Parochial, had attended the McMartin Preschool from fall 1978 through summer 1981, spending his last six months in Ray's class.

Upon receiving the police letter, the Rogans sat Austin down and asked him if he'd been molested at the preschool.

"No," the boy said. "Nothing bad happened to me."

Still, his parents persisted. They asked Austin to think back to his preschool days, to think about "Mr. Ray." The thought of Ray—the tall man with glasses who used to watch over him—was a hazy image, but Austin remembered his former teacher, and his parents could see that his memory had struck an emotion.

"You remember him, don't you? *Mr. Ray?*"

Austin nodded. He was somewhat apprehensive.

"Did he do anything to you, Austin? Did he ever touch you?" his mother asked.

But Austin said nothing more. He shook his head and turned away.

Janet, a homemaker during Austin's preschool years, had recently begun a career in child therapy. She'd been working part-time at the South Bay Center for Counseling (SBCC) in Manhattan Beach, logging hours to earn her license. Janet worked under the tutelage of Dr. Cheryl Kent, a well-known child psychiatrist.

Concerned that Austin may be hiding a secret, Janet brought Austin to SBCC to have him examined by Dr. Kent, her mentor.

But the interview produced nothing. Austin continued to deny that he'd been molested.

At that time, as Janet began to suspect that Austin may have been abused, she came in contact with Judy Johnson.

At the top of her October 1983 calendar, Judy wrote, "South Bay Co. Center." Within the date-box of Friday, October 7, Judy wrote, "STATEMENT—Janet calls Melvin Belli"; on October 18 she noted, "Pete called Dan Dunbar 6:00"; and on October 27 she wrote a reminder to "Call Dunbar."

Daniel Dunbar, a Torrance-based attorney two years out of Loyola Law School, was an associate of the Beverly Hills legal offices of Melvin Belli, the famous personal injury lawyer who'd made his name defending Lee Harvey Oswald's assassin, Jack Ruby, and gained further notoriety in 1969 when he took part in a televised phone call with a man who claimed to be the Zodiac Killer.

Evidently, a handful of McMartin parents—Judy and Janet included—asked the Belli firm to explore the potential of suing the McMartin Preschool for damages.

Filing a multi-party civil action, however, would be difficult without more evidence. Additional victims were needed.

Thus, Janet spoke to some of her friends, mothers of former McMartin students, fellow parishioners at American Martyrs, telling them that Dr. Cheryl Kent was interested in interviewing their children, to look for "indicators" of past sexual abuse. A small group of parents agreed to bring their children to SBCC.

But again, after a series of independent therapy sessions, each child denied having been abused at the McMartin Preschool. The investigation seemed to have hit a wall.

However, someone in that group—either a parent or one of the professionals at SBCC—contacted Jean Matusinka of the Los Angeles District Attorney's Office, who in turn recommended another facility in downtown Los Angeles—Children's Institute International (CII), a private company seeking government funding for its research and development.[5]

Within CII, a nationally recognized expert, Kee MacFarlane, had been hired as the institute's director. Touted as an innovator, a new-age specialist with the ability to obtain a child's disclosure, she had the skill to gather evidence in a manner that would hold up in court.

---

[5] Dr. Cheryl Kent of SBCC was married to Dr. James Kent, an executive at Children's Institute International. Although not officially confirmed, it is likely that through the Kents' personal relationship the correspondence was facilitated.

A small group of parents agreed to meet with Kee MacFarlane.

* * * * *

On Friday, October 28, in the living room of a Tree section home, five couples awaited the arrival of Kee MacFarlane, praying that she would bring clarity to what they'd come to believe was their children's "mysterious behavior." Although every child had continued to deny being molested, something wasn't right. Their children seemed withdrawn, as if they had a deeper reason for avoiding the subject.

"I don't want to talk about it anymore," one girl had screamed.

"No, no, no," another boy yelled, shaking his head with his hands firmly over his ears.

To their parents, the children appeared more afflicted than annoyed. Moreover, many of the parents were displeased with Jane Hoag's interviewing techniques, her abrasive style. To some, it seemed, Hoag was interrogating their children with the strong arm of a cop, not the kid gloves of a therapist.

That night, a cool evening three days before Halloween, the parents agreed to keep an open mind, to listen to the words of an expert. In the foyer stood Detective Jane Hoag and Deputy District Attorney Jean Matusinka, head of the DA's Planning & Training division on child abuse, a woman instrumental in forming the Los Angeles County's Interagency Council on Child Abuse and Neglect (ICAN). Matusinka and Kee MacFarlane were long-time friends and colleagues.

Once Kee MacFarlane arrived, Matusinka led her into the living room and introduced her. MacFarlane, thirty-six, an attractive woman with blond hair and blue eyes, spoke of her background—her tenure at Arizona's Children's Association in Tucson, where she'd witnessed the growing epidemic of child maltreatment. From Arizona, she headed to Washington, DC, where she became a lobbyist for the National Organization for Women and a grant writer for the National Center on Child Abuse and Neglect.

MacFarlane had relocated to Los Angeles a year earlier, primarily for the purpose of co-authoring an article with Dr. Roland Summit, the nationally recognized physician based out of UCLA-Harbor Medical Center who was preparing to publish his groundbreaking "Child Sexual Abuse Accommodation Syndrome."

Soon thereafter, MacFarlane was hired by Children's Institute

International, where she and her colleagues employed new methods of extracting disclosures from potential child victims—the concept of using videotape to capture a child's statement to validate its authenticity.

"Historically," MacFarlane explained, "the process of obtaining a child's disclosure has been flawed. It requires a victim to recant their abuse multiple times to multiple parties—to therapists, physicians, police investigators, prosecutors, and then to a jury.

"Each interview," she said, "in succession, whether medical, clinical or for other legal purposes, forces the child to retell a story that is frightening and guilt-invoking. It causes the child extreme anxiety...and it happens over and over again."

MacFarlane described how she and her colleagues had developed a far more comforting process—a *victim-centric* approach. They used "anatomically correct dolls" to create a friendly, child-like setting. These dolls—essentially puppets with genitalia—enabled children to re-enact their experience in a playful manner. The video camera would capture the child's description of the abuse, like testimony—whatever it may be—giving the parents an objective view and the opportunity to reach their own conclusions.

If, regrettably, a parent came to believe that their child was a victim, and if the parent was determined to pursue criminal charges, allowing their child to testify, the district attorney could use the videotape as evidence.

"If your child was abused at that school," MacFarlane explained, "then they are suppressing their memories. They don't want to confront it. They don't want to relive it. They may even be fearful of what could happen to them if they told...afraid of being called a *liar* by their parents who aren't equipped to deal with the truth."

In order to be certain, MacFarlane concluded, she would need to interview their children privately.

When the meeting ended, each parent agreed to bring their child to CII.

Three days later, on Tuesday, November 1, the first child was interviewed.

CHAPTER
7

Mid-November 1983
The Manhattan Beach Community Church

Reverend John Calhoun stepped through the rectory, holding a fresh cup of coffee. He moved faster than normal, rushing back to his office desk to take the call of a woman on hold. His secretary had just informed him that Nancy Peters, one of his most dedicated parishioners, had an emergency.

"She's frantic, hysterical," his secretary had told him. Nancy would not say what it was about, only that she "needed to speak with Reverend Calhoun now, right now."

Reverend Calhoun picked up the receiver before sitting down.

"Nancy? Are you okay?" the reverend asked.

"Reverend...I need to see you," Nancy said, weeping as she struggled to speak.

"What's wrong? What's happened?"

"It's Michelle..."

The reverend closed his eyes—a reflective prayer for Nancy's precious daughter, presuming that she may've been injured or diagnosed with a dreadful illness.

"We just returned from the therapy center downtown," Nancy cried. "They told us that Michelle was sexually molested, that horrible things happened to her back when she went to the McMartin Preschool."

Nancy told Calhoun the whole story: How they'd just returned from CII, where Michelle, a five-year-old, had spent ninety minutes in a video-taped interview with a child abuse expert. During the session, Michelle had finally admitted that she'd been abused. After the interview, Michelle underwent a physical examination by a pediatrician who confirmed the abuse.

"They showed me the video. I saw her say it. I saw her say that she was molested," Nancy wailed. "And when the doctor examined her genitals, they found scarring. She was abused so bad that she has scars."

Nancy desperately needed counseling and spiritual guidance. Reverend Calhoun told her to come to the rectory at once.

Over the following weeks, Calhoun received dozens of calls from other parishioners sharing the same nightmare—the shocking discovery that their children had not only been molested, but they'd been concealing their secrets for years. Overwrought with anger and despair, they sought revenge.

"Please stay calm," Reverend Calhoun told each of them. "Please come to the church. We can work through this together, with Christ at our side. Please come to the Lord's house."

The Manhattan Beach Community Church, a large, suburban, Protestant church in the southeast section of town, had a congregation of nearly one thousand members, people from all backgrounds. More liberal and relaxed than other South Bay Protestant churches, the preaching of the gospel was open-ended.

Reverend John Calhoun had been the acting preacher since 1975, a pleasant man with an inviting disposition and an engaging smile. By that third week of November, his rectory was so overrun by parents of former McMartin students—those who had come to believe their children had been victimized—that he began holding group meetings in the sanctuary. As the pews filled to capacity, Calhoun said, "a state of confusion set in," as the parents were not prepared to deal with this subject matter.

Such uncertainty led to fear, anxiety—and, as Calhoun put it, a "disruptive climate" began to formulate within Manhattan Beach.

"When the news came from CII," Calhoun explained, "a lot of parents were naturally upset because they believed what they'd seen on the videotapes and what they'd been told by the therapists—that their children, in fact, had been molested.

"As the numbers grew and as more children were interviewed," he said, "the word around the community was that maybe children had been molested for many years."

According to Calhoun, none of the parents believed the stories until they'd gone to CII and spoke with Kee MacFarlane. After interviewing a child, MacFarlane would inform the parents that their child had been "hiding a dark secret of sexual abuse." Still, many were not convinced, not until MacFarlane showed them a video recording of their child disclosing specific acts of molestation.

Once they watched the tapes, most parents agreed to let their child be physically examined by CII's pediatrician, Dr. Astrid Heger, who, in more than 90 percent of the children she evaluated, found genital scarring "consistent with a history of sexual abuse."

"So you had this scenario," Calhoun said, "that as people went to the institute, by and large, most came to the conclusion that the story was true."

At that point, he said, the parents accepted that the crimes had occurred. The therapists at CII stressed the need for them to support their children's claims. It was hard enough on their children to admit what had happened, but it would be further traumatic if they didn't receive their parents' undying loyalty.

Most troubling, though, was that the parents felt compelled to do something, to take action against the people who'd raped their children—but they couldn't. The investigation was ongoing, so they were instructed to stay out of the way, to let the authorities do their job. Not surprisingly, many parents refused, choosing instead to mobilize.

Reverend Calhoun aided these families through the process, organizing group meetings for church members whose children were said to have been abused, providing a forum for wide-open discussions. They started with random gatherings, then, as more families returned from CII, they held weekly meetings.

"In the beginning," Calhoun explained, "we only let the people who were members of the Community Church attend. There were rumors that some people within the parents' group may've been involved in the cover-up. This type of information was floating around."

* * * * *

Martin Burns, a twenty-six-year-old investigative journalist a few years out of Occidental College, stood at the corner of Walnut Avenue and Manhattan Beach Boulevard—the vacant lot adjacent to the McMartin Preschool. He had his eye out for Ray Buckey.

It was mid-morning, well after parents had dropped off their children.

Burns knew that Ray was no longer working there, but some believed that he'd been returning to the school during the day to molest the students. The rumor was that his mother, Peggy, was facilitating his crimes, giving him access to the kids, all part of their family conspiracy. And if that were the case, in the minds of some, the other teachers were likely involved.

Ray Buckey didn't appear.

Burns headed toward the beach, turning right on Highland Avenue, passing the black cauldron of The Kettle, where a small group of mothers conversed at the corner, a rather animated discussion. He turned left down 16th Street and parked along the curb, the same illegal spot he'd used the morning before. Burns had a clear view of Ray Buckey's apartment.

In the second-story window, Burns saw a man: a tall figure that he assumed was Ray. The man moved closer to the glass, motionless, surveying the neighborhood as if he was on the lookout. Not wanting to be spotted, Burns pulled away, avoiding eye contact.

Burns had been following this story for nearly ten weeks, since late August when he and his associates at Community Information Project (CIP), an independent investigative news agency, got a tip from a child abuse hotline about a major investigation into a "reputable preschool" in the South Bay.

"There were no specifics," Burns said, "just that a monstrous molestation crime was being investigated. We sniffed around but came up with nothing, at first. But then, a few weeks later, we got another tip that it was a preschool in Manhattan Beach. We had friends inside their police department, and they spoke to us on the condition of anonymity. They told us that they were investigating a male teacher at the McMartin Preschool."

CIP put a team on the ground. Once the police letter went out, everyone knew that Ray Buckey was the suspect. CIP was so interested in the story that Dan Leighton, CIP's founder, moved into a local apartment to investigate full-time.

"We conducted stakeouts, did background checks on all the teachers, and knocked on doors, asking people if they'd ever seen anything," Burns said. "We started swapping information with the Manhattan Beach Police. They were in way over their heads; they just didn't have the manpower to follow up with all those families.

"We searched one end of Manhattan Beach to the next. We drove to San Diego State to meet with one of Ray's professors. We spoke with one of his old neighbors. We even broke into his old apartment looking for clues. But all we ever got was that 'Ray was strange' or that 'Ray masturbated,' but nothing that indicated he was a pedophile."

According to Burns, Manhattan Beach simmered with suspicion and anger, an unspoken agitation that intensified by the day. The general belief that "Ray molested one boy" developed into "Ray molested a bunch of kids," and eventually, there was widespread consensus that "the entire staff at the McMartin Preschool must've been in on it."

Parents demanded answers, but the police—particularly Detective Jane Hoag—offered them nothing. Dozens of children had revealed their secrets of being abused, and yet the school remained open. Ray Buckey continued to walk the streets as if he'd done nothing wrong, strolling along Highland Avenue or hanging out on the boardwalk, within reach of many children.

"Why is he not in custody?" the father of an alleged victim asked Hoag in the lobby of the station. "You're just gonna let him keep doing it?"

"There's nothing I can do," Hoag replied. "At this point, it's up to the DA. You're going to have to be patient. Just stand down and wait."

But some ignored her directive, choosing instead to take matters into their own hands.

Of all the parents, according to Martin Burns, one man stood out— the outspoken landowner, Bob Currie. "As we hit the streets," Burns said, "running a parallel investigation with the police, we kept bumping into Bob Currie. He was kind of a wannabe detective, poking around, trying to break the case. But ultimately, he was just a pain in our ass."

Bob Currie, despite the fact that his kids had never been in Ray's presence, began to wonder if there was more to the story. He knew several families who'd been told by therapists that their children had been brutally raped and left scarred. If that were true, then a far more sinister crime was at hand.

The Curries contacted CII to have their children interviewed, only to find that hundreds of families were ahead of them—many of their friends from American Martyrs. The Curries were placed on a two-month waiting list.

In the meantime, Bob Currie embarked on his own investigation, conducting the same kind of surveillance as Burns and his team at CIP.

For Burns, though, Currie's presence was problematic, as he kept spooking parents before CIP could get authentic information. It was a distraction Burns didn't need since he already had a formidable competitor on the ground—KABC-TV investigative reporter Wayne Satz, an award-winning journalist who seemed to have an inside track.

"Wayne Satz definitely knew about the investigation and wanted to break the story," Burns said. "Satz had his own connection in the Manhattan Beach Police Department, and we thought he was going live with it based on Ray Buckey's arrest in September. We wanted to break it, too, but the police were telling us to stand down, that making it public would interfere with the broader investigation, which was in the hands of the district attorney."

Like CIP, Wayne Satz got a tip about the probe into Ray Buckey, but instead of venturing into Manhattan Beach, he headed to UCLA-Harbor General to meet with Dr. Roland Summit, the nation's foremost expert on child sexual abuse, and a close colleague of Deputy DA Jean Matusinka. Satz knew that if the DA was involved, Dr. Summit, their top consultant, would certainly know about it.

* * * * *

In the fall of 1983, Dr. Roland Summit had been promoting his recently published "Child Sexual Abuse Accommodation Syndrome," which explained why a child would "accommodate" their ongoing sexual abuse. Considered the most enlightened and comprehensive analysis of child sexual abuse ever written, Dr. Summit's "Accommodation Syndrome" was a progressive roadmap for the next generation of clinical and legal professionals.

For years, Dr. Summit had lectured throughout the South Bay of Los Angeles, a virtual guru who voiced a new sense of urgency—the notion that America's children were more vulnerable than ever before. That fact had been on display in a case that he and his colleagues had recently worked: the McCuan/Kniffen case in Bakersfield, California, the burgeoning oil and agricultural community two hours north of Manhattan Beach.

The two couples, the McCuans and the Kniffens, had been convicted in a daycare sex ring involving their four children—the first "multi-victim, multi-offender" child sexual abuse indictment in North America. Dr. Summit had consulted the prosecution in that case, who used Summit's "Accommodation Syndrome" to prove why so many children had continued to be brutally victimized without coming forth.

According to Dr. Summit, Wayne Satz contacted him about a report he [Satz] was doing on "Agency Indifference and Incompetence on Child Sexual Abuse." Satz didn't mention Ray Buckey or the McMartin Preschool during their meeting, but as they conversed, Dr. Summit gave up the information Satz had been looking for—the name of Kee MacFarlane, the DA's expert.

Satz turned his focus to CII.

Shortly thereafter, on a morning in mid-November, Wayne Satz stood in CII's lobby, a small area packed with parents and children waiting for their videotaped interviews. Satz asked the receptionist to speak with Kee MacFarlane, who, knowing that he was with *Eyewitness News at 6*, came out to greet him.

Satz told MacFarlane that he'd "dropped by" to discuss a general story he was doing on child sexual abuse—but while there, he'd "stumbled onto the McMartin case."

"I can't talk to you about this case, Mr. Satz," MacFarlane said. "This is a confidential investigation."

"I understand," Satz said. "But it sounds like these kids were molested by their preschool teachers, the McMartin Preschool in Manhattan Beach. Is that was this is about?"

"Like I said, I really can't discuss it."

"Can you at least confirm that your investigation is about McMartin?"

MacFarlane paused, thinking of a careful response.

"I can say that we are in the middle of conducting interviews with McMartin students," MacFarlane confirmed. "But that's all I can say."

* * * * *

Kee MacFarlane returned to the room where four-year-old Tina Wilkes, a former McMartin student, sat at a table playing with dolls. MacFarlane had given her a few minutes to get acclimated before they got started.

An American Martyrs parishioner, Tina was the third of the Wilkes's children to go through McMartin—Kristen and Billy had graduated in 1978 and 1980—and they were students at American Martyrs Parochial. Tina's mother, Sharon, was one of the first parents the police had contacted in August when the investigation broke. At the time, Sharon had been adamant that none of her children had been abused at the preschool. Sharon had long considered herself a close friend of Peggy and Virginia, and she was certain that she would've "noticed something" had any of her children been abused.

Through the fall, however, Sharon's opinion changed. She'd listened to Kee MacFarlane on that night before Halloween, and MacFarlane's logic made sense—maybe Tina was too afraid to tell the truth. Sharon decided to take Tina to CII.

The first hour of Tina's interview moved rather slowly. MacFarlane questioned Tina about her experiences at the preschool—but Tina repeatedly denied that anything improper took place. MacFarlane asked her if, while at the preschool, she had "taken off her clothes"; she asked Tina to identify male and female genitalia on the anatomically correct dolls she placed before her; she asked Tina about "naked games" she might've played; and she even asked her if she'd "taken a picture of a naked horsey," which prompted Tina to reply, "Are you crazy!"[6]

MacFarlane told Tina that she'd been "talking to some of her [Tina's] friends" to figure out "some of the things that happened" at the preschool, back when "Mr. Ray was your teacher."

"I don't want to tell," Tina said.

"Do you think something *bad* will happen to you?" MacFarlane asked. Tina nodded.

"Ray will stick his nails in my back...his fingernails," Tina said. "He'll slug me if I tell."

"That's not true," MacFarlane said. "You're never going to see him again."

"I know that Ray's sick," Tina replied, as if she'd already discussed Ray's *problem* with her mother.

MacFarlane continued her questioning. She told Tina that it was "real important" for her to help "figure out what Mr. Ray did," as well as what "Ms. Peggy" may have done.

But after several minutes of explicit questioning about Peggy, Tina repeatedly denied that "Miss Peggy had touched her," or that she'd "seen Peggy's boobies," or that she'd ever been taken "away from the school in Mr. Ray's van or car."

"No?" MacFarlane challenged. "I thought you told your mommy you did [leave the school in Ray's van]."

But again, Tina answered, "No"—then held up the naked black male doll and said, "I'm a nigger."

---

[6] The information regarding the interview of Tina Wilkes is taken verbatim from the official transcripts of her videotaped session, as well as the testimony of her mother, Sharon.

Concerned that Tina was too uncomfortable to speak of her abuse to a stranger, MacFarlane invited Sharon to join them.

MacFarlane turned off the video camera and left the room. When the video came back on, Tina was sitting next to her mother at the table. They were looking at a TV screen that showed them being taped.

"There's Mommy," Tina said, pointing to the screen.

"Oh, my goodness," Sharon said, "you can see me."

"See," MacFarlane told Tina. "I told you we'd put mommy on television."

"See," Sharon said, "now I can watch you. And then you can watch me afterwards. After you talk, okay?"

MacFarlane looked at Tina. "Okay?"

"Okay," Tina said.

MacFarlane said it was "real important" that Tina "told the truth this time" so that they could get this all straightened out.

For the next five minutes, MacFarlane asked her questions about Ray "not wearing underwear," about whether she'd seen him naked or taking his clothes off, and about the things that had happened "in the bathroom" with "Ray and Ms. Peggy."

Eventually, Tina nodded, affirming that Ray and Miss Peggy had their "clothes off" at the preschool, and that Peggy had been naked within her own classroom.

"You're not going to go back to that school," Sharon assured her daughter.

"You mean Virginia McMartin's?" Tina asked.

"You're never going back to Virginia McMartin's," Sharon replied. "So you can say whatever you want."

"Because Ray's never going to see you again, okay?" MacFarlane added.

"You're never gonna see Ray," Sharon said, "and you're never gonna see Miss Peggy."

Before concluding, MacFarlane made a deal with Tina—if she could "think of anything else," she would promise to tell her mother. Tina agreed.

Tina said it was time for everyone to get ice cream, followed by, "Okay, now let's play Barbies."

CHAPTER 8

Standing over her kitchen table, Judy Johnson pushed the papers aside, making room for her cocktail, a blend of rum and Coke on ice. She took a sip and placed it down.

Thanksgiving approached, Judy's first holiday season without a man in the house, a reality that had crept upon her like the subtle chill of that autumn night. Judy took another sip, a heartier gulp, refreshed by the warmth as it moved through her chest. Alcohol had become her friend, a loyal companion that helped her escape.

Judy sifted through the stack, the random notes she had scribed over the past six months since Brad had left, a scattered diary that spoke of their estranged union:

> *He called me a slut & freeloader—won't see kids until I work— if I work he wants adjustments in his payments even tho I must pay sitter fees.*

In her desolation, as she sat alone, finishing her cocktail and stepping to the kitchen to mix another, she had no choice but to accept that Brad had moved on, that he had found a younger woman, a nurse named Gloria who didn't depend on him for support. Brad loved Gloria; he loved her the way he had once loved Judy, long ago.

Since leaving in late May, Brad continued to hound Judy about reaching a quick settlement, to get ahead of that fourteen-year alimony requirement—but Judy balked time and again. At first she stalled, mainly out of spite. Then, once she had filed the complaint against Ray Buckey, formally ending their marriage had been the least of her concerns. Judy had no money; she had no job; she had a dying teenager; and, adding to her woes, she had a two-year-old suffering from the post-traumatic stress of having been sexually abused.

Still, with such weight to carry, Judy forged ahead, maintaining a sense of normalcy. Her November calendar showed how she kept her daily life in order, filling the date-boxes with her activities. She wrote "Library," "Nautilus," "Books Due," "Movies," and "Oil Change." She referenced her trip to Yucca Valley to see her father—"Leave for desert"—as well as her weekly counseling with "Joy" every Monday at 5:00 p.m. Judy went to various doctor's appointments—"Dr. Kim" and "Dr. Segal"—and, notably, she attended a meeting on Tuesday, November 22—"Roland Summit Meeting 8:00"—where Dr. Summit had come to Manhattan Beach to consult with parents.

On a loose piece of paper, on the back of the same page she had written her retrospective about stopping the "madman," Judy wrote:

Ask Your Children:
Has anyone ever taken off your clothes?
Does anyone take your picture without Mom there?
What games do you play at school?
Possible red lights—
Movie Star Game, Alligator, Candy Bar, Baby,
Ring Around the Rosey
Be extremely cautious about pre-school in general
No one is going to care for your child like you will
Guilt—Good
Molding of children—6 years of age and under
Changing Society
Power of women

Despite her outspoken advocacy for the child victims, though, Judy did not reveal Mitchell's abuse to the people closest to her—not her father, nor her brother, not even her best friend and neighbor, Gayle Schaeffer. As the story ran rampant through the small town, Gayle had no clue that Judy was the mother who'd filed the initial complaint. Moreover, Judy hadn't even told Brad.

According to Gayle, Judy kept Mitchell's abuse, as well as her role in the case, a *complete* secret.

Looking back, Gayle said, Judy had become extremely suspicious and paranoid that someone might be out to harm her; she "freaked out" when an unfamiliar car drove through the neighborhood or when a stranger lurked near the corner. At the time, Gayle figured Judy was insecure because she no longer had a man in the house, but it worsened as winter neared and the darkness of night arrived earlier.

Keeping this news from Gayle, Pastor Knutson, and Steve was one thing, but not telling the boy's father—not making him aware that a pediatrician had confirmed that his son had been viciously raped—was inexplicable.

"Judy didn't tell Brad anything specific," Gayle said. "She only told him, 'I've done something really good...something that will make you very proud of me.'"

Evidently, despite Judy's disdain for Brad, irrespective of the pain he'd caused her, she was inspired by the thought of pleasing him.

* * * * *

On the morning of Wednesday, November 30, Judy placed a call to Detective Jane Hoag—their twenty-third conversation since the investigation had started. Judy was belligerent, militant.

"Babette stepped on Mitchell's stomach," Judy said. "She made him vomit. He described an *old fat woman*...she came to the school and held his feet down while he was sodomized."

Judy told Hoag that Mitchell was forced to perform oral sex on Peggy, that Peggy made him "kiss her private parts," and that she didn't wear underwear.

"Mitchell said they took him to some kind of ranch, far away," Judy said. "That's where he rode naked on horses."

At the ranch, Judy said that Mitchell saw the same old fat woman and that he'd seen Ray taking pills.

"Ray gave himself a shot," Judy said. "He killed a dog and dumped a cat in hot water."

Three weeks later, on Monday, December 19, Judy made her twenty-fourth and final phone call of 1983 to Detective Hoag.

"Mitchell said Ray wore *costumes* while he molested him—a policeman, a fireman, a clown, and a priest. Once he even dressed up as Santa Claus," Judy stressed. "He said Ray chopped up rabbits, and that Peggy put some kind of *star* in his bottom."

That statement was uniquely compelling to Detective Hoag. For years, rumors had circulated amongst sexual assault investigators that children had been the targets of satanic ritual abuse, where the occult molested them as part of their ceremony.

Judy's reference to the "star" invoked images of a pentagram, which Hoag knew to be a symbol of the Church of Satan.

* * * * *

Five days before Christmas, in the midst of interviewing former McMartin students, Kee MacFarlane received a telephone call from KABC-TV reporter, Wayne Satz.

"I know all about Ray Buckey," Satz told her before saying hello. "I know he was arrested in September for sodomy, and I know there's a medical exam to back it up. I know the police let him go because they had no evidence, and I know that they sent out a letter, because I'm holding it in my hand."

He waited for her response, but she said nothing. Satz continued. "I know that dozens of kids have already said they were molested, and that other teachers may have been involved."

MacFarlane remained silent.

"I've got a story here, and you know it. The whole town is going crazy over this. You know I can get people to talk. You got some *very angry* parents out there. They're all wondering what the DA's gonna do. I could go live with this right now, just on the fact that Buckey was arrested. You know I can. So why shouldn't I?"

"Please don't do that," MacFarlane pleaded. "That will ruin this investigation. It will destroy everything we are doing here."

They conversed a while longer, and they agreed to meet personally to discuss it.[7]

---

[7] In the months that followed, Kee MacFarlane and Wayne Satz developed a romantic relationship. It's unclear when exactly their association progressed from friends to lovers, but by spring 1984, they were openly dating. Irrespective of where their liaison led, their relationship began in the winter of 1983—a professional arrangement where MacFarlane granted Satz exclusive access to confidential information in respect to the ongoing McMartin investigation.

MacFarlane hung up the phone. She turned to her colleagues, her fellow therapists who sat nearby, listening.

"He knows everything," she said to them. "Everything."

* * * * *

Christmas had passed. The reverence of the Nativity scene calmed the mood of the angry crowd gathered in the courtyard outside the Manhattan Beach Community Church. Unlike Sunday mornings, when parishioners arrived with smiling faces, ready for another inspiring homily by Reverend John Calhoun, this particular Wednesday evening was different. These folks, a deeply afflicted group, conveyed the stirrings of a revengeful mob.

Reverend Calhoun tallied them as they came through the door, an assembly that had grown larger and more intense by the week. More than one hundred mothers and fathers were packed into the pews, subduing their rage, yet tempted by the thought of vigilante justice.

These weekly meetings were, if anything, a chance for the parents to purge, to rid themselves of their unbearable guilt, the realization that each day, as they had gone off to run errands or play tennis, they'd unknowingly hand-delivered their children to their abusers. They could not get the images out of their heads: the thought of Ray Buckey and the staff of elderly women violating their little ones.

Most agonizing, of course, was that they, the parents, were not free from blame, for it was they who'd allowed it to happen. For years, as the rape and sodomy continued, the parents had been oblivious. That fact could not be ignored. They had no excuse, no rebuttal to their dereliction. It was unfathomable that it had gone unnoticed for so long, inconceivable that their children had come home, taken baths, dressed and undressed each day, while routinely visiting their general practitioners, and all the while not one parent had enough of an emotional connection to their child to realize the torture they were being subjected to.

Some couples turned on each other, accusing their spouses of being so selfishly immersed in their own lives that they'd failed to see the pain their children had endured. Some wondered if other parents may have been involved—for this could have never continued without a conspiratorial link.

With suspicions running rampant, with feelings of betrayal penetrating deeply, the parents had no means of reconciling their emotions. They wanted blood.

On that December night, as Reverend Calhoun walked up the aisle, stopping short of the altar where he prepared to speak, the crowd took command.

"We should burn that place down," Brian Gallatin yelled. His daughter, a five-year-old, had allegedly been raped and sodomized by Ray, while Peggy and Betty had danced around naked, taking pictures and singing songs.

"I'm gonna hang that son-of-a-bitch by his balls!" Dave Middleton threatened; his son, also five, had described graphic sex with Ray, while "strangers" filmed them.

Parents yelled indiscriminately, one drowning out the next, loud reverberations that swirled about the sanctuary. Most came to their feet to decry their revenge.

Reverend Calhoun tried to keep order. "Please…everyone. Please!" Calhoun said, raising his voice. "You must sit down. You must control yourselves. Be calm, please!"

"How can you ask us to be calm?" Heather Corbin replied, a parishioner he knew well.

Reverend Calhoun looked upon her with sympathy, an expression of remorse, knowing that he was about to ask her to do the impossible, to suspend her hatred for those who'd done unspeakable acts to her child.

"I know none of this makes sense, that none of it seems possible," he said to her, slowly walking down the aisle. She sat with her arms folded. Her anger changed to stoic sadness.

"I know you're in pain. I can't imagine what you're going through," he continued, putting his hand on her shoulder, then looking around at everyone, "what you're all going through. But the only way to get justice for your children is to let the professionals do their jobs, and for all of you to stick together, to have faith."

Heather Corbin, tears running down her face, shook her head, surrendering to her worst impulses. "Father, you know what they did to my girl. You know!"

"Yes, I do," he replied. "I know what they did to her."

"She'll never be the same," Heather said. "Never."

Reverend Calhoun had no response worth offering.

"I want them to suffer for what they did," she said. "That's all I want. That's all that I'll ever want. They should die for what they did."

Reverend Calhoun could only shake his head, not condemning her anger, but pitying her condition. This was not a consultation to bereave loss, but an ongoing crisis of pain, where the aftermath of a great disaster had left droves of children physically and psychologically devastated. Their parents, their loving parents, could do nothing to protect them from what they'd already endured. They could only provide treatment, a way to acknowledge what had happened and to deal with it over time, like an incurable disease that they would have to live with for the rest of their lives.

"I don't have an answer for you," Calhoun said softly. "I can only plead with you, for the sake of your children, to think rationally."

The loud voice of a man came from the back, a man Calhoun did not recognize.

"Is that why we're here, Father? Are we here to talk about how *calm and rational* we should be, while these people are walking the streets?"

Another woman, Amy Colbert, spoke. "The school is still open, Father. They still have kids going there. I spoke to one of the mothers, and she doesn't believe any of it. She thinks we're all crazy. Nothing is going to happen to these people."

The man in the back stood and headed toward the door.

"Please don't leave," Reverend Calhoun called out to him. "You're welcome to say whatever you want. You don't have to leave."

Stephen Tibbs, the father of a young girl, knew the angry man well. "He just got the news today. He needs some time," Stephen told the group. "We just need to give him time."

CHAPTER
9

Monday, January 9, 1984
The first day of the spring semester

The New Year brought little hope to the McMartin-Buckey family. On a day when students normally returned with the joyous spirit of Christmas, anxious to talk about their gifts from Santa, there simply were not that many kids left. They were down to six boys and five girls, just the families who'd vowed to "stand by them to the end."

The story was no longer a rumor, but a real and ongoing event. From every corner of Manhattan Beach, people spoke of it—*the monsters at the preschool who had slaughtered animals to keep the children silent*. No one had been charged, not yet, but word on the streets was that something was about to go down.

Virginia and Peggy had received several prank calls over the past month, violent threats against their teachers, so they let go of everyone but Babette.

On that morning, just after 9:00 a.m., Virginia and Peggy conversed near the preschool's entrance. Peggy glanced east on Manhattan Beach Boulevard and noticed Bob Currie walking toward them.

"Good morning, ladies," he called out, stepping closer.

"Good morning, Bob," Peggy said.

He shook his head in frustration. "I gotta tell ya," Currie said. "I went to a meeting last night…a meeting of parents, and it doesn't look good."

"What do you mean?" Peggy asked.

"There are a lot of people coming after you, a lot of people that want to take legal action. They want to destroy your family."

"Oh, Bob, that's silly," Peggy replied. "Who would want to do that?"

"I'm tellin' ya, Peggy, you better wake up," Currie said. "I listened to these people for hours, and they're looking to take you for everything you own."

"And how are they going to do that?" Peggy asked. "And why? Why would they want to do that to us?"

"Peggy, you have no idea what's going on behind closed doors," Currie said. "The district attorney was at this meeting...the district attorney! They're in control of the investigation, and they got a bunch of kids sayin' they were molested, and that it happened *right in there*," Currie said, pointing to the classrooms. "The parents believe it, and they're mad as hell. They wanna take you down. I'm tellin' ya, they're comin'."

"And what do you believe, Bob?" Virginia asked.

A bit uneasy, Currie paused before responding. "Look, I'm your friend. I've known you for how long? What...ten years?"

"Yeah, about ten years," Virginia confirmed.

"Right...and you know that I don't have a dog in this fight. My kids graduated way before Ray was here, so I'm not havin' that conversation with ya. I'm just telling ya, as a friend, that what I saw last night was about two steps shy of a lynch mob."

Virginia and Peggy weren't sure what to believe, not privy to what was happening behind closed doors, yet they'd heard enough to know that something serious was brewing.

They believed Currie when he said he didn't have a dog in this fight, because he didn't. Nevertheless, many of the parents rumored to be pursuing the case were American Martyrs parishioners, all of them close friends of the Curries, and all their children were classmates of the Currie children at American Martyrs Parochial. It was hard to believe that the Curries had no opinion on the matter, even if they didn't believe their children were victims.

As their conversation ended, Currie made a suggestion. "You know, it's pretty clear the school's falling apart, regardless of what happens. Have you thought about selling the property?"

"We have no intention of letting this school fall apart," Virginia replied, "and we certainly aren't selling it."

Currie knew that this parcel—931 Manhattan Beach Boulevard—had nearly doubled in value in the past ten years, a prime commercial lot on the main thruway in a booming Southern California beach town.

"Well, I'm just sayin'. If you get to where you're ready to sell, gimme a call," Currie said. "I'm looking for a spot to build some office spaces."

"Bob," Peggy said, "we have no interest in selling. Not now, not ever."

According to Peggy, Bob Currie didn't react positively to their refusal to sell. Even though he'd shown up that day declaring his loyalty, by the time he left, he seemed offended.

* * * * *

Later that evening, ABC Theatre aired a two-hour special on incest titled *Something About Amelia*. Sixty million viewers tuned in.

The movie, starring Ted Danson and Glenn Close, depicts an upper-middle-class family living in an affluent neighborhood. The father, played by Danson, secretly molests his young teenage daughter. The girl suffers from depression and becomes helplessly withdrawn. Her mother, played by Close, denies that the abuse occurred and rejects her daughter for telling such a horrible lie. In the end, it's determined the girl told the truth.

The incestuous father isn't characterized as a demon; instead, the plotline condemns his behavior, his sickness. The moral of the picture conveys that incest isn't exclusive to the lower-classes or the uneducated, presenting the theme that child sexual abuse happens everywhere.

Something About Amelia became one of the highest-rated made-for-television movies of the decade, and it won an Emmy Award for then-fourteen-year-old Roxana Zal, the youngest-ever award recipient for a prime-time feature.

The following week, more than five thousand people called abuse hotlines—the outreach numbers for victims had been displayed at the movie's end—as people from around the nation reported how they, too, had been sexually abused in their youth.

Something About Amelia was considered a "groundbreaking media event" that made the sexual abuse of children a marketable topic. As one reviewer wrote, it "took enough stigmas off the subject for the national media to discuss it."

The evening after *Amelia* aired, Virginia sat in her rocking chair. The phone rang. She let it ring many times, assuming it was just another prank. It had gotten worse in the past twenty-four hours, a barrage of calls that Virginia tried to ignore, but eventually she answered.

"Hello?"

"We're gonna cut Ray's balls off," the man's voice said, a deep, growling disguise intended to scare her.

"Who is this?"

"We're gonna hang you for what you did to those kids."

"Who is this?"

"You better shut that school down, bitch. You better shut it down or your whole fuckin' family's gonna die."

The caller hung up—but the phone continued to ring.

Consequently, four days later, on Friday, January 13, 1984, after twenty-seven years of proudly serving the families of Manhattan Beach, fearing for the safety of her family and staff, Virginia voluntarily shut down the McMartin Preschool.

* * * * *

One week later, Judy Johnson again went to see Detective Jane Hoag. "Mitchell said they took him to a car wash," Judy told the detective. "They molested him there. They stuck him in the trunk of a car."

Hoag took notes as Judy relayed Mitchell's words.

"There's a guy at Nautilus...*Kurt Walford*...he used to work in Las Vegas. He hurt Mitchell, he and James, the manager. They both hurt Mitchell. He named them both—*Kurt* and *James*."

For Hoag, Judy's allegations were growing increasingly bizarre—and yet, if the entire staff at McMartin had been in on the scandal, as many had come to believe, then there could very well be other people within the small community—like the guys at Nautilus—who were part of the conspiracy.

Still, at least according to her official report, Detective Hoag made no effort to follow up on Judy's claims. Hoag never interviewed "Kurt" and "James," nor did she run surveillance on the Nautilus facility.

Following her meeting with Hoag, Judy left the station, driving her VW van, cruising through the neighborhoods of Manhattan Beach, searching for evidence. She started at the McMartin Preschool, then drove to several other locations, timing the duration of travel—to and from the Red Carpet Car Wash, and to and from Barnaby's Hotel. Both were locations Mitchell had identified. As she drove by them, Mitchell pointed, affirming that he'd been there.

In less than thirty minutes, Judy surmised, the crimes could've happened—driven from McMartin, taken inside, disrobed, molested in numerous ways, all of it photographed or filmed, then brought back to the preschool.

Judy drove east on Manhattan Beach Boulevard, crossed PCH, turned right on North Aviation, and right on 10th Street. She parked on the north side of the street, one lot east of the "zoo" that Mitchell had talked about, the name he'd given to the Manhattan Ranch Preschool, located about a mile west of McMartin.

Judy turned off the engine and waited patiently. It was almost five o'clock, the time he—the young male teacher's aide—normally left. Sure enough, there he was, right on schedule, an athletic sixteen-year-old, hopping onto his moped. He rode west.

The next morning, Judy called Detective Hoag. "Mitchell said he was taken to the Manhattan Ranch Preschool. It's at 1843 10th Street, right down Manhattan Beach Boulevard, this side of Aviation."

Detective Hoag knew of the school.

"Mitchell said Ray took him there," Judy added, "and that Ray picked up other children from Manhattan Ranch."

* * * * *

Friday, January 27, could not have come soon enough for Bob and Angela Currie. They'd waited anxiously for six weeks to have their three children interviewed at CII, stuck on a waiting list that continued to grow.

Contrary to what Currie had told Peggy and Virginia just weeks before—that he was "coming to them as a friend," a neutral bystander—he'd actually been counting the days until his CII visit.

Currie had listened carefully to what had been alleged, and, if there was any truth to it, the scope of the crimes went far beyond what the other parents had conceived.

For months, Currie had been running his own investigation, piecing together clues—his son's fascination with morgues and dead bodies, and a doctor's visit years before, where a long dark hair had been discovered wrapped around his son's penis. No one could ever explain it.

Currie's visit to the preschool in mid-September was his first attempt to feel them out, to see how Peggy and Virginia were reacting to the investigation. But they'd stayed pretty cool, maintaining that Ray had been wrongly accused.

Later, in January, while the community mobilized against them, the women didn't flinch—in fact, they were brazenly standoffish.

To Currie, it seemed peculiar that they'd refused to sell the property, especially with the business having already lost its value. The preschool would never recover from this scandal, and they must have known that. Still, there they stood, unrelenting.

Maybe, Currie wondered, they didn't want anyone else getting a hold of the property. Maybe they were concerned of what may be uncovered, what lay beneath the surface.

That Friday, when the Curries arrived at CII, they were greeted by Sandi Krebs, an associate of Kee MacFarlane who'd been taking on some of the workload. She escorted them into a waiting room and handed them a CII Intake Form—a fifteen-page questionnaire regarding "unordinary" symptoms they may have noticed in the past.

While the first Currie child was escorted away, Bob and Angela spent forty-five minutes filling out the forms. An hour and a half passed before their next child was examined.

After five hours, all three of the Currie children had been interviewed. Sandi Krebs guided the last child into the waiting area and motioned for the Curries to join her inside.

The Curries sat at a table next to a television and VCR. Sandi played the tapes one by one, fast forwarding to segments of each child's interview where the child made disclosures: explicit claims of sexual abuse.

The videotape revealed that Currie's youngest son, Gary, did not want to talk about it. He, like his older brother and sister, repeatedly denied being molested.

"He had to be tricked," Currie said later, "by the use of anatomically correct dolls."

But once Gary began to talk, he didn't stop, providing a detailed account of a group sexual endeavor where Ray Buckey performed a ritual that was assisted by all of the women.

"He described robes and candles," Currie said, an organized activity where the children "chanted" and witnessed "dead bodies" and other morbid practices.

Gary's disclosures led Currie to one conclusion—that his son had been forced to take part in a satanic ritual.

Currie thought of his past conversations with Peggy and Virginia, and he suspected that every encounter had been part of a "master deception," their way of placating the Curries before secretly molesting their children, an insidious game that had left so many families shattered.

But Currie wasn't like the other parents. Despite the shocking discovery, he and his family took it in stride, leaving CII with a positive attitude. "The day we won was the day we found out that our kids had been molested," Currie said, "because that's when we started doing something about it."

Bob Currie viewed that day as one to commemorate.

"We went to McDonald's that night and had ice cream sundaes," Currie said later. "I had a feeling that we were the only family that went out to celebrate. Everybody else, I think, went home and cried. But we had ice cream sundaes because the kids talked. I wanted to show them that nothing bad happened to them—we're all still alive, and *you* just had an ice cream sundae.

"Now to a kid," Currie said, "you can't feel any better than that. And we did it right after they talked. They weren't bribed beforehand about getting ice cream sundaes. The secret was out and the victory was ours."

PART III
Only the Beginning

CHAPTER 10

Thursday, February 2, 1984
KABC-TV newsroom, Glendale

Wayne Satz prepared for his broadcast. He'd waited weeks to break this story, something he would've never done in the past, but this report was unlike any other. It would be his first in a series of ongoing "breaking news events."

Wayne Satz had worked at KABC-TV Channel 7 since 1974, specializing in provocative investigations. His most notable work earned him a Peabody Award in 1977—interviews with a masked Los Angeles police officer who claimed that many of his colleagues were racists, that they had a tendency to "shoot first."

Satz had a reputation of being a sensational journalist long before the term "sensationalism" was in vogue. *Los Angeles Times* television critic Howard Rosenberg wrote that Satz was "one of the last of the city's old-fashioned reporters who knew how to report aggressively as well as interpret. He was rough and sometimes stepped over the line, but he was also a genuine journalist, a TV breed almost extinct."

That night, February 2, marked the beginning of the Nielsen sweeps, the industry's audience tracking system that drives the buying and selling of media advertising time. The evening news—not technically prime time—set up the rest of the night.

Jerry Dunphy, the iconic anchorman, and his co-anchor, Christine Lund, the highest-rated broadcast team in Southern California, sat in the studio, flanked by Wayne Satz.

Dunphy, with his stark white hair and trusting persona, opened the broadcast with his traditional greeting: "From the desert to the sea, to all of Southern California, good evening, this is the latest at six.

"In a case which has been described as one of the most bizarre and shocking ever to involve young children, the district attorney has a team of six investigating the allegations of more than sixty young children that they were sexually assaulted, photographed, and terrorized into silence while in the care of a prestigious preschool in Manhattan Beach.

"Reporter Wayne Satz has held up this story for more than three weeks, and is being told that the report might jeopardize the ongoing investigation. But he is now able to bring you this extraordinary exclusive story. Wayne."

Wayne Satz, a handsome man in his late thirties—thick brown hair with a well-manicured beard—appeared on the screen. He wore a serious, saddened look, as if reporting this dreadful story was a traumatic burden, where more than sixty children from the McMartin Preschool had been keeping the grotesque secret of being sexually abused, that they were made to appear in pornographic films and forced to witness the mutilation and killing of animals as a means of scaring them into silence.

* * * * *

Ray Buckey sat motionless, staring at the screen. His family gathered around him—his mother, father, sister and grandmother—tears streaming down their faces. Ray, too, began to cry.

As Wayne Satz reported that "small animals had been killed," cute little bunnies appeared on screen, feeding in their pen, which led to a wide screen shot of the McMartin Preschool. The camera closed in on the preschool's handmade wooden sign. The point of view was through a circular lens, as if being surveyed from across the street through a pair of binoculars.

Satz described the McMartin Preschool as "the place" for upper-income beach residents to send their small children—"owned by one of Manhattan Beach's most honored citizens, Virginia McMartin."

The picture changed to Satz standing next to the Manhattan Beach Pier as young children ran about.

"It started out here in Manhattan Beach, looking like an isolated incident," Satz reported. "One mother noticed that her young son was having nightmares and difficulty sitting down, with *redness* on his bottom. Authorities would later conclude that her two-year-old son had been sodomized. That was last summer. In the months since, the number of possible victims has multiplied, to say the least. Authorities now believe that at least sixty young children were victimized, and that the ultimate number could be much greater."

Satz spoke of the letter sent to parents by the police, asking them to question their kids, and how each child had said nothing happened. "The parents did not know then," Satz reported, "that their children had allegedly been terrorized into staying silent."

Kee MacFarlane appeared on the screen. She wore a hand-puppet and used it to playfully speak to a child. Satz identified MacFarlane as the "nationally recognized expert" the district attorney had employed to "unlock the secrets" the children had been suppressing.

Satz reported that scores of children had told MacFarlane that they had been taken to locations away from the school and filmed, and the films were sold, presumably as kiddie porn. Satz also said the children had been sexually abused in every imaginable way.

The children were terrified, Satz said, because *guns* were allegedly brandished in front of them, and because they'd witnessed the maiming and killing of small animals as a warning that "such would be the fate of the child's parent if the secrets were not kept."

The broadcast continued, eventually naming Ray Buckey, "the only person the authorities have arrested in this nightmarish case."

The picture cut back to Satz concluding his broadcast from the studio desk.

"As it stands now, no one involved with the McMartin Preschool has been charged with any crime. What we are reporting here is simply that a large number of children have, in separate sessions, made extraordinary allegations, which, in turn, have led to one arrest, several lawsuits, a warning to parents from local police, and, a few weeks from now, a full-scale grand jury investigation."

* * * * *

The impact of the broadcast shook all of Los Angeles. The fascination, the sheer terror, crossed every demographic, as no one had ever heard such a report. This wasn't the alarm of the Manson murders or the mystery of the Hillside Strangler, nor the far-away tale of the ghastly serial killer, John Wayne Gacy, or even the unthinkable butchery of Theodore Frank, the child-predator who'd struck so close to home. The story of the McMartin

Preschool invoked a new level of dread and disgust—the day that the people of Southern California began to wonder if there was any place their children would be safe.

By the next morning, Manhattan Beach became the epicenter of a media frenzy. Every major network put a team on the ground.

That night, around 5:50 p.m., KABC-TV ran a teaser—"the latest on the McMartin Preschool child sexual molestation case, coming up at six."

Down at the strand, at Peggy and Chuck's 17th Street home, the family gathered. Ray sat on the sofa next to his sister; his father stood behind him, his hand on his son's shoulder. Peggy and Virginia sat near the television, waiting.

Out on the sidewalk, reporters and news vans huddled, hoping for a statement from the accused. Cars drove up and down Ocean Avenue, drivers laying on their horns. "Molesters!" one driver yelled. "Creeps!" cried another. A pair of bicyclists rode along the boardwalk, pointing to the address and shouting, "That's where they live. Right there!"

Inside, the Buckeys had disconnected the phone; it hadn't stopped ringing since the night before. They were, in every sense, trapped.

Six o'clock came. The *Eyewitness News* logo appeared, along with the opening music. Jerry Dunphy went through his standard intro before, once again, conceding the platform to Wayne Satz, who recapped his report from the previous night.

On the screen, for the first time, a picture of Ray Buckey appeared—a disheveled, awkward-looking man. He wore thick-rimmed glasses and gave an intimidating glare, as if, in that moment, he didn't want the image captured.

Ray shook his head slowly, aggrieved that such an unflattering photograph had been used. His face reddened.

"Could they've used a worse picture?" he said aloud. "That doesn't even look like me. That looks like a psychopath."

On the screen, Kee MacFarlane emerged, seated in a comfortable setting—a private interview she'd taped with Satz.

"How could it be," asked Satz, "that kids would keep secrets of this nature for so long?"

"Children are taught to trust and obey adults," MacFarlane explained, "especially very young children…to believe what adults tell them, especially threats. And children will go to great lengths to protect themselves and to protect their parents.

"I don't think that the depth of terror put into a child should be underestimated," MacFarlane warned. "In my thirteen years of working in this field, I've never seen a situation that compares with this one."

"Why would a kid open up and tell you something when he or she wouldn't tell his or her own parents?" Satz inquired.

"Often it's not the children who tell me," MacFarlane said. "It's my puppets that tell me."

The video changed to footage of MacFarlane with a hand-puppet—a character reminiscent of Sesame Street—as she interacted with a small child. "For the children," she said, "that gives them a measure of safety. Also, if the children have been threatened, I'm not someone they were warned not to tell."

Ray couldn't watch any longer.

"Turn it off," he yelled. "Turn it off, please."

Peggy came to him, her eyes red from crying, trying to console him. He was shaking.

"I'm going to jail. I'm going to jail because of that lady and her puppets. That's what's happening, right?"

"It's going to be okay," Peggy said, embracing him—but he slumped to the floor and wept.

"How can this be happening?" Ray asked his mother. "How can they do this to me?"

But it wasn't just Ray under the microscope.

By the next night, the story had grown in scope and magnitude.

"Now," Satz reported, "older children are telling authorities that they were sexually abused when they were little toddlers at the preschool. These incidents allegedly occurred as far back as 1974. Ten years ago."

Satz described Manhattan Beach as a community divided between "those who believe" and "those who don't." He said that many parents could not accept that the celebrated McMartin family could have been involved in such depravity.

"Others do believe," Satz countered.

A woman came on the screen, a blond who appeared to be in her thirties, surrounded by a large group of supporters. "There is no doubt in my mind, or anybody else's mind, that my son was sexually molested," she said. "He could *not* have made *any* of this up. No way!"

The scene had a hint of revolution, as if times were changing in that very moment—a real-life drama acted out on television, for all of Los Angeles to see.

Chuck Buckey turned off the TV. His family sat speechless—the silence of a wake.

Peggy stepped to the window and pulled back the shade. A crowd had gathered on 17th Street, right below their home. The entrances at both Ocean and Highland Avenues were blocked by onlookers walking about, conversing, and enjoying the grand spectacle that had placed their small town on the national stage.

Peggy spoke to herself, but loud enough for the others to hear. "They're coming for us," she said. "They're coming for us all."

CHAPTER 11

Thursday, February 16, 1984

With the onset of the night, Judy sat at her table, slightly buzzed, sipping her drink as she wrote down her thoughts.

Hours before, until dusk, Judy and her intimate group of McMartin parents had scoured the neighborhoods of Manhattan Beach, doing the job they believed the police had failed to do. Judy, Bob Currie, Ron and Brenda Gantry, and Andrew and Jessica Lankton were the regulars—all of them convinced that a conspiracy was at play, one that personified evil.

Their latest theory: Someone inside the Manhattan Beach Police Department had to be in on it—an officer, maybe even the chief himself. They suspected that other parents—some of their closest friends—were likely covering it up. *How else could this have gone unnoticed for so many years?*

Bob Currie was particularly suspicious, insisting that they were not just dealing with a child molestation ring, but that an "underground satanic cult" was at play, a secret society out to destroy the next generation.

"That's how Satanists operate," Currie told the group. "They conceal their identities. They lull you into a state of comfort, and then they move in for the kill."

Currie's demeanor—and particularly his graphic language—turned many people away, but not this group. They knew he was on to something. "Fondling, oral sex, rape, and sodomy are the first step," Currie said. "Then you get into things like torture. You know, there's nothing like making a dog or cat squeal. You have to inflict pain, excruciating pain—but you have to keep the victim alive while you're doing it. The object is not to kill them. The object is to make them fearful. It gives you power. You can feel power. And this is a crime of power. Satan worship is the fear of power."

Currie's intuition, as eye-opening as it seemed, was not a recently conceived concept, for the subject matter had been influencing American society for some time. Several books published in the 1970s described how witches, druids, and the Illuminati were covertly running world politics and the mainstream media—but the audience was primarily the members of fundamentalist churches.

By the late 1970s, however, it had morphed into a message that cut across the heartland. With the growing interest in backward masking of satanic messages in rock music, heavy metal was whispered to be the occult's recruiting ground. That led to bizarre stories of human sacrifice, and tales of "devil worshippers breeding children for ritualistic murders."

In 1980, a popular book, *Michelle Remembers*, co-authored by Michelle Smith and Lawrence Pazder, written as a true account, documented Smith's experience as a young girl. The book told the story through Smith's "recovered memory" during therapy sessions. She claimed that the Church of Satan had taken possession of her when she was five years old, forcing her to take part in an "eighty-one-day ritual where the devil had been summoned." Smith alleged to have been raped, tortured, and locked in cages, where she witnessed several murders. She claimed to have been smothered with the body parts of dead babies.[8]

Fearing that the Church of Satan had found a home in Manhattan Beach, Judy sat Mitchell down for a talk that Thursday evening. She asked him to describe the satanic ritual he'd been subjected to.

Later, with Mitchell fast asleep, Judy transcribed his words:

> *the three women are witches. The man poked him. Peggy, Babs and Betty are dressed up as witches, too…*

Judy continued to write, drinking her cocktail between sentences:

---

[8] In retrospect, *Michelle Remembers* was discredited, determined to have been pure fantasy. But in the early 1980s, it was considered to be the most highly accepted autobiography of a satanic ritual abuse survivor. Some of the social workers involved in the McCuan-Kniffen case in Bakersfield, CA, had attended a seminar where *Michelle Remembers* was offered as "training material."

> *Peggy gave Mitchell an enema...staples were put in Mitchell's ears, nipples and tongue...Babs put scissors in his eyes...she chopped up animals...*

Judy went on and on, documenting every detail of the account as if she believed its literal meaning:

> *Something awful would come in the window. Ray made small babies cry...Mitchell describes having communion in a church. A prayer similar to the Lord's Prayer...a <u>Goat</u> climbed higher and higher...*

Judy's handwritten account, a 421-word diatribe of Satanism and group sex ended with the bloody sacrifice of an infant:

> *Ray poked Peggy at the altar. Lots of candles...Ray pricked his pointed finger. It bled. Ray put it on the goat's anus...Old grandma played the piano...a real baby...the head was chopped off...brains were burned...Peggy killed the baby...Mitchell had to drink the baby's blood...on the altar...Mitchell's bottom was bleeding...Ray put a Tampax up his bottom to stop the bleeding...then he took it out...*

The next morning, Judy contacted Detective Hoag.
"I need to see you. I need to see you, now," Judy said.
"What's wrong?"
"I spoke with Mitchell again. You need to hear what he's saying."
Judy arrived at the department and gave Detective Hoag the complete document.
Five days later, on Wednesday, February 22, Detective Hoag delivered Judy's letter to the DA's investigator, Tim Tyson, who had a follow-up telephone interview with Judy, where she provided another account that Tyson transcribed:

> *Mitchell feels that he left LAX in an airplane and flew to Palm Springs area... At the armory there were some people wearing army uniforms...The Goat Man was there...a ritual type of atmosphere... At the church Peggy drilled a child under the armpits...atmosphere was that of magic chants...Ray flew in the air.*

* * * * *

Three weeks later

The morning of Tuesday, March 6, Judy struggled to get dressed. Balancing herself with her hand on the dresser, she prepared to head downtown for her grand jury testimony.

Days before, while carrying a load of laundry in the garage, Judy stepped on a baseball bat, falling sideways onto the concrete. She already had a weak femur from a near-fatal car accident as a teenager, and this impact resulted in a fracture.

"Judy gave me a call after she tried contacting Brad," Gayle Schaeffer said, "but he refused to help her. He wouldn't take her to the hospital."

When Gayle entered Judy's living room, she found Judy sitting on the ground, sobbing. "She seemed so abandoned," Gayle said, "like her world had fallen apart."

Gayle took Judy to the hospital, where her leg was fitted with a cast.

That morning, the day of her testimony, Judy asked Gayle if she would take Mitchell to his preschool class at the Trinity Lutheran Church, then come back and drive her downtown. "She didn't want to be seen," Gayle recalled. "She was afraid of being followed by the press, and having them find out she was going to testify that day. She needed help, but she couldn't get around on her own. She definitely couldn't drive. I was all she had."

On Gayle's way to Trinity Lutheran—with Mitchell sitting innocently in the backseat, oblivious to it all—a news report came over the radio: "Police raid eleven locations in association with the McMartin Preschool case—the cities of Manhattan Beach, Torrance, Rowland Heights, Newport Beach, and Riverside County—a collection of homes and private businesses."

On her way back, Gayle drove along Valley Drive and turned left toward Highland Avenue. She came upon the Manhattan Beach Police Station and noticed that a small crowd had gathered, a scrum of reporters and cameramen vying for position in front of the entrance.

"The atmosphere was electric," Gayle said. "It was as if something was going to happen, something historic, like a major event."

About an hour later, Gayle and Judy arrived at the Los Angeles County Court Building, pulling into the underground entrance. They parked and waited until an armed policeman arrived to lead them in. "With his gun drawn," Gayle said, "he escorted us to an elevator. It was a very long walk, especially for Judy on her crutches, but we eventually came to the office of Jean Matusinka, the DA working the case."

Standing outside of Matusinka's office, a group of people—parents and professionals, all of the key players involved with the case—huddled in a conversation.

"They were having an intense discussion," Gayle said. "Ron and Brenda Gantry, Dr. Roland Summit, and Kee MacFarlane were there when we arrived." Gayle recognized the Gantrys, people who'd been investigating with Judy prior to her accident.

According to Dr. Roland Summit, "Jean [Matusinka] was having a tough time keeping everyone organized." He described it as a "zoo"—that everyone had their own opinion; each of them wanted to be heard, but only so much could be put before the grand jury.

Dr. Summit said that Judy, in particular, seemed distressed; it appeared to be something less obvious than her broken leg, something internal. Summit had met with Judy a few weeks earlier—a therapy session where, he said, she was well-grounded and lucid—but at that moment, at least from his perspective, she was noticeably disturbed.

It wasn't long before Judy was summoned into Jean Matusinka's office, where Matusinka prepped Judy for her testimony.

"They spoke for about twenty minutes and I stayed outside," Gayle said. "And then Judy poked her head out and asked me to come in, which kind of surprised me. They talked a little about the McMartins, how they always asked the parents, 'When are you going to pick up your child?' and how they always made the parents *feel so good*."

Once prepped, Judy and Gayle were escorted down a hallway and into a different elevator. "They took us to an underground tunnel that led to the courtroom located across the street," she said. "We ended up in a tiny room adjacent to the courtroom."

One by one, people were called in to testify. Judy and Gayle waited.

After an hour, Judy was called in.

As Gayle sat, praying for it to be over, she worried about Judy. Judy had been nervous for days, and she seemed even more anxious during their drive down, on the brink of tears, as if she didn't want to relive the experience. It made sense to Gayle—the pain and guilt Judy was going through—but it seemed like something more, something Judy didn't know how to express.

"Then, just minutes after she went in," Gayle said, "Judy came rushing out, crying uncontrollably. She kept saying, 'They're not listening to me! They're not listening to me!' So I put my arms around her and tried to calm her down. She felt so betrayed, demoralized. She'd been waiting for that moment to tell her story, and it just didn't happen."

Like most grand jury proceedings, Deputy DA Jean Matusinka had limited Judy's line of questioning. Judy, though, had been eager to tell her story, the whole story—her bizarre account of the human sacrifice that Mitchell had witnessed.

But Matusinka wasn't going there—and she made that clear to Judy during their prep session. Matusinka didn't want to hear about Mitchell's trip to the "ranch" or his experiences at the "car wash." She had no interest in the "old grandma" who'd played the piano while Mitchell received "communion in a church," and she certainly didn't want the grand jury to hear about the "Ritual of the Goat Man."

Matusinka focused Judy's testimony on specific dates and times—the happenings of August 11 and 12, 1983—the moment Judy came to believe her son had been sexually abused at the McMartin Preschool.

For Judy, it was a catastrophic let down. The district attorney seemed to believe that Mitchell was simply molested when, in fact, he'd been tortured and indoctrinated by the occult.

Gayle guided Judy back to the car, where they drank a glass of wine and shared a tear.

"I really think that was the turning point in Judy's paranoia," Gayle said. "That's when she stopped trusting people."

CHAPTER 12

Ray Buckey waited in his parents' living room. The police were on their way. His mother and father sat with him, unsure if they, too, were about to be arrested. The sound of blaring sirens grew louder.

Just before 9:00 a.m. on Thursday, March 22, two squad cars, accompanied by Wayne Satz and his *Eyewitness News* crew, arrived at the Buckeys' home. Two officers approached the porch. The lead officer knocked loudly.

"I have arrest warrants for Ray Buckey and Peggy Buckey. Open up, please!"

Chuck Buckey opened the door cautiously, and the officers pushed their way in. They found Ray and Peggy standing side by side.

"Turn around and put your hands behind your back!"

Ray and Peggy did as the police said. They were handcuffed, read their rights, and led out to a squad car, a humiliating walk as neighbors and other spectators gathered. Wayne Satz stood with his crew near their news van; his cameraman walked alongside the officers as they ushered the Buckeys to the squad car, capturing every step.

At the opposite end of Manhattan Beach, another squad car sped through the Tree section, screeching to a stop at the home of Babette Spitler. An officer pounded on her door, ordering her to step outside. She did. Babette was cuffed, Mirandized, and taken away.

After six weeks of nightly news reports, where a vast conspiracy was being contemplated, Babette and her husband, Don, had feared that Babette would be arrested. More concerning was that their three children might be taken into protective custody. Thus, that morning, Don began hiding their kids. He left their baby grandson, Daryl, a two-year-old whom they were in the process of adopting, in the care of a neighbor, and took Justine, thirteen, and Carl, eight, to relatives in San Diego County. They were enrolled in new schools under assumed names.

Don returned home sometime thereafter. The neighborhood was packed with traffic from squad cars and news vans. When he stepped inside, Babette was gone. An arrest warrant lay on the kitchen table. Don was not named.

In Torrance, seven miles southeast, Betty Raidor was apprehended in her home. The sixty-four-year-old stumbled as police escorted her down the steps, gently pushing her head down as they guided her into the backseat of the squad car. Too confused to cry, Betty closed her eyes and dropped her head as the door slammed shut.

Five miles south, in Palos Verdes Estates, Maryanne Jackson, a fifty-four-year-old who hadn't worked at McMartin for three years, was arrested in the same manner—handcuffed and placed in the back of a squad car while her home was raided. Maryanne was dazed, unsure if the police had confused her for someone else. From the back of the squad car, she watched investigators carry out boxes of confiscated items. Then the car pulled away.

Forty-five minutes east, in the burgeoning community of Santa Ana, the heart of Orange County, Peggy Ann Buckey stood in front of her class of special-needs students. She was distracted when two officers came through the threshold. They approached her calmly, not wanting to frighten the children, and, just as they'd done with the others, handcuffed her while they informed her of her rights.

The police could not locate Virginia McMartin—but she'd been informed through her attorney that a warrant had been issued for her arrest. She headed downtown to turn herself in.

* * * * *

At the Los Angeles County Courts building, Virginia staggered into the courtroom where she joined the other six. The group would come to be known as the *McMartin Seven*.

The seven defendants stood before Superior Court Judge Ronald George, each wearing their own expression of confusion and torment.

The courtroom filled to capacity. Reporters from every major news agency lined the walls with video equipment. Outraged parents crowded the pews, some shouting violent threats. At one point, the room had to be cleared while officers conducted a search for weapons.

Sitting at the counsel table, Los Angeles District Attorney Robert Philibosian looked on as his chief prosecutor, Deputy DA Jean Matusinka, read the list of charges.

"Your Honor, we have a total of one hundred and nine counts of felony child molestation involving more than one hundred students over a ten-year period."

Matusinka pleaded with Judge George to consider an extraordinarily high bail for each of the seven, arguing that all of these women had facilitated Ray Buckey's perverted activities and, on many occasions, had taken part in the molestation.

"They have nothing to lose, Your Honor," Matusinka argued. "At this point they have every reason to follow through with their threats against these children and their families."

Judge George took a moment to consider her request. "Bail will be set tomorrow," he said, slamming down the gavel.

The crowd jeered and mocked the defendants as they were led away.

Later that evening, KABC-TV's *Eyewitness News at Six* led with another exclusive report by Wayne Satz—his live video of the arrests was over-dubbed with his narrative of the Buckeys being hauled away.

The screen cut to District Attorney Robert Philibosian giving a prepared statement on the steps of the Criminal Courts building.

"We are alleging," Philibosian announced to the crowd, "that approximately one hundred children were sexually molested at the school over the past ten years. To obtain their silence, these people told the children that their 'parents would be harmed.' And in order to back up those threats, small animals were actually slaughtered in the children's presence."

Philibosian looked over the scrum of reporters, pausing for a moment to punctuate the severity of the charges. "These are considered 'lewd and lascivious acts on children under the age of fourteen.' That's the Penal Code definition. We're talking about such acts as rape, sodomy, oral copulation, and fondling."

Satz continued. "The grand jury investigation is over, but the DA's investigation is not. That's important news for the group of affected parents represented by this woman, who read from a prepared statement this afternoon."

The camera cut to the parents' spokesperson, Colleen Mooney, the co-director of the South Bay Center for Counseling, where most of the alleged victims were receiving post-traumatic psychotherapy.

"Although parents feel some sense of relief," Mooney announced, "it should now be made clear that these indictments don't go far enough. Dimensions of this case still need to be more closely explored. There remain many suspects of crimes against these children that have not been exposed."

The picture came back to Wayne Satz in studio with Jerry Dunphy and Christine Lund.

"The district attorney refused to acknowledge whether kiddie porn was involved in this case," Satz said, "but we have reported that kids have claimed to have been photographed pornographically, and we stand by that story.

"On the charges of child molestation, Ray Buckey could face a maximum sentence of one hundred and fifty-six years, and his mother thirty-six years. They and five others will have their bails set tomorrow morning, and of course, we'll be there."

The next day, in the same hostile forum, The McMartin Seven stood before Judge Ronald George, who set their individual bails: Chief defendant Ray Buckey, charged with seventy-five felony counts of child molestation and conspiracy, received a bail of $1 million; Peggy Buckey was jailed under a $350,000 bail; and the bails of the other five women ranged between $50,000 and $100,000.

Bradley Brunon, Virginia's public defender, requested that her bail be waived due to her age and her ailment, arguing that the brutal conditions of the Los Angeles County Jail were a risk to her health.

But Judge George declined. He ruled that because of the violent nature of the allegations, she and the others posed a threat to the community of Manhattan Beach, and therefore all of their bails would remain in effect for at least two weeks, until their arraignments on April 6.

Moments after the bail hearing, lost in a barrage of cameras and microphones, District Attorney Robert Philibosian went again to the courthouse steps. "This office has just uncovered the largest conspiracy ever to involve the sexual abuse of children, with links to pornography and organized crime."

Philibosian confirmed that the investigation was ongoing, that there was an abundance of evidence linking these seven people to a conspiracy that stretched from Manhattan Beach across the South Bay.

"We believe this school was involved in a large-scale, clandestine operation."

Within days, guided by that premise, Philibosian's team widened its investigation into Lynwood, a middle-class community five miles east of Manhattan Beach, the lower edge of South Central Los Angeles. Twenty-three-year-old Henry Anthony Lawson was arrested on a felony charge involving a four-year-old boy at the Little Angels Day School Center. Following Mr. Lawson's arrest, his three-year-old son was placed into protective custody and named as a potential victim.

Hours later, Philibosian held another news conference, announcing that a "search warrant had been issued" for a third local preschool—the Hickory Tree Preschool in Torrance—where a male employee had been interrogated, but no arrest had been made.

"These recent cases of alleged molestation have resulted in widespread calls for more scrutiny of day care centers," Philibosian declared, "and a greater public awareness of the signs that may indicate abuse."

In an aggressive move, Philibosian requested that the FBI be assigned to scan the cities of the South Bay in an effort to uncover the McMartin conspiracy. [9,10]

* * * * *

For the DA, determining a motive was imminent, a reason these elderly women would've taken part in such a repugnant scheme. The most

---

[9] Danny Davis, the newly appointed attorney for Ray Buckey, filed a motion to disqualify District Attorney Robert Philibosian. Davis accused Philibosian of being "intensely zealous" in his efforts to "promote the case for political publicity"; that he "presented himself to the public in close association with the prosecution of the case, choosing to seat himself at the counsel table during the most highly publicized aspect of the case," making no statement, just sitting "in front of the audience and television cameras"; and that after the court proceeding he had "conducted an informal press conference outside the courtroom."

[10] Robert Philibosian, two months away from a special election in June, was not a popularly elected politician. He'd been appointed by the Board of Supervisors after former District Attorney John Van de Kamp had been elected Attorney General. Philibosian was a long shot to retain his job, polling well behind City Attorney Ira Reiner. Back in September 1983, Philibosian hired political consultants to guide his election effort. His advisors determined that he lacked name recognition, and that he would be well served to "publically identify himself with a criminal prosecution involving child molestation or abuse charges."

plausible explanation: an underground child pornography ring—a cash incentive.

That narrative linked McMartin to another criminal network the DA had been investigating for some time, the case of Catherine Stubblefield Wilson, the largest distributor of child-pornography in the greater Los Angeles area.

Since the mid-1970s, Catherine Wilson, an attractive, middle-aged black woman—known by sexual assault investigators as "Black Cathy"—had operated a lucrative business out of her northeast Santa Monica home. She was said to have the "worst product available": hard and soft porn, sadomasochistic, bestiality, and other fetishes.

Cathy was not a producer, just a distributor. She had developed an intricate mailing system that federal investigators could not trace. She had an associate who managed her post office box in Copenhagen, Denmark, where her orders were originally sent, after which they were forwarded back to various post office boxes under different names in a handful of California cities, mainly San Diego, Los Angeles, Bakersfield, and Fresno.

Cathy's methods were discreet. Married to a local musician, she had three children, so she carried on her domestic lifestyle while she made her drops. Cathy had been arrested once before—but the evidence was confiscated without a warrant, so she walked.

As diabolical as it seemed, however, in the late 1970s when Cathy's business flourished, crimes of obscenity were not a priority. The DA wanted to nab the producers, the people forcing children into the world of pornography, not the shippers and handlers. Cathy was strictly a businesswoman, and her acuity had kept her legally unscathed for years—that is, until March 1984.

Midway through the McMartin grand jury hearing, a search warrant had been issued for Cathy Wilson's home. Nothing significant was confiscated, but enough to make an arrest.

Considering the statements children had made at CII, the DA was exploring any connection between Cathy Wilson and the McMartin Preschool.

During her interrogation, though, Cathy Wilson said she had never come across the names McMartin or Buckey within her network of child pornographers.

While incarcerated in the county jail, Cathy was placed in the cell next to Peggy Buckey.

"We had several conversations," Peggy said later. "She was a very nice woman. She thought the district attorney and the police were out of their minds. She kept saying, 'I don't know you people. What do they want from me?'"

* * * * *

On Friday, April 6, the McMartin Seven stood again before Judge Ronald George to be individually arraigned.

Much had changed in the past two weeks. Jean Matusinka had left the case—appointed to a judgeship—and Deputy DA Lael Rubin took over as lead prosecutor. Rubin, thirty-seven, a litigator, had just come off the Catherine Stubblefield Wilson case. A rising star in the department, Rubin was aggressive, holding nothing back in her debut appearance.

"This district attorney will be filing an additional three hundred and ninety-seven counts," Rubin announced, increasing the count total to more than five hundred.

Since the bail hearing, forty-three more children had been examined at CII, all of whom were said to be victims. The prosecution had rushed to bundle these charges so Judge George could see the growing magnitude of the evidence. Because these added counts had yet to be filed, they were considered "uncharged crimes."

Rubin pointed to a chart that outlined the specific charges against each defendant.

"Your Honor, our latest reports from CII indicate that the children were drugged into drowsiness by the use of a pink liquid pill," she said. "I would respectfully ask that *none* of these defendants be freed on bail, for it would cause the children to endure great psychological trauma, just knowing that their former teachers were back in the community."

Rubin quoted Kee MacFarlane, who said she had seen, "sheer terror in the children" and that "an entire generation of children" had been affected.

Judge George looked over the courtroom; the pews were jammed with parents. Their expressions, their enduring pain, left him little choice.

"If there was ever a non-capital case where there should be no bail," Judge George said confidently, "this is the case."

Judge George revoked the bail of five of the seven, leaving only Virginia McMartin and Maryanne Jackson free. Each defendant pleaded not guilty.

Following the arraignment, reporters packed the corridor outside the courtroom, as District Attorney Philibosian made a surprise announcement—the re-opening of a long-running cold case that some McMartin parents believed had a connection to the preschool.

"This department is now reviewing the unsolved murder of Karen Ann Klaas," Philibosian said, receiving applause from a small section of the crowd.

Eight years earlier, on Friday, January 30, 1976, Karen Klaas, the mother of a McMartin student, had been brutally murdered in her Hermosa Beach home in the hours after she'd dropped off her five-year-old son at the preschool. The case had gained notoriety because Klaas was the ex-wife of Bill Medley, a member of the famed singing duo The Righteous Brothers.

The morning of Klaas's murder, unable to contact her by phone, a few of her friends entered her home through the sliding glass door in the back, and were startled by the dark image of a man running across the living room and out the front door.

On the floor, Karen Klaas lay naked and unconscious. She'd been raped and strangled with her pantyhose.

Days later, Klaas died in the hospital.

On this day, with the district attorney standing atop the courthouse steps in front of a gathering of reporters and enraged parents, many speculated that Klaas may have solved the mystery long ago, that she'd discovered what was happening at the McMartin Preschool, but, before she could contact the police, was executed in her home—the first piece of evidence to support the children's claims of murderous threats.

* * * * *

Before midnight, the sound of broken glass woke Trevor Preston. He jumped out of bed and ran to the window.

Trevor lived in an apartment down the street from the McMartin Preschool, and he had a clear view of the property from his bedroom window. He peered out, trying to bring it into focus. Shadows moved across the grounds. An object crashed. Fire ignited. Flames spread. Trevor called the police.

The next morning, Trevor stood on the sidewalk, surveying the damage. Police and firemen gathered information. Trevor gave his statement.

Along Manhattan Beach Boulevard, cars passed slowly, viewing the unsettling portrait. Every window in the McMartin Preschool had been shattered; the interiors of the classrooms were charcoaled from the flames of a Molotov cocktail; and on the large, open wall that faced the street, the caricature of a "hangman" had been spray-painted, an unartful representation.

Next to it, the vandals warned: "ONLY THE BEGINNING."

CHAPTER 13

The sanctuary of the Manhattan Beach Community Church filled to capacity with nearly five hundred McMartin parents, the largest crowd to date. The church, an A-frame with an earth-toned interior—a classic 1950s suburban design—ran twenty-two rows deep. An exquisite pipe organ sat atop the rear balcony, where the choir sang.

This night, the parents were visibly agitated, some hysterical. They had come from all over the South Bay, wanting to hear from the experts, the professionals who'd convinced them that their children had been brutalized. Most were crammed into the pews, while others hung in the back, pacing in and out of the foyer, preferring not to sit.

Dr. Roland Summit, the evening's keynote speaker—a tall, slender man, slightly balding with a light complexion—stood before them. He shushed the audience.

The architect of California's doctrine on child sexual abuse, Dr. Summit had initiated a "call to action" five years earlier. In it, he stressed the "role of the community," the responsibility of each and every citizen to mobilize, to accept the reality of what was happening in society.

"When a child is sexually abused," Dr. Summit explained, "it's important that a qualified, experienced person investigate and make a determination as soon as possible. Fortunately, that is precisely what has happened in this case. But it doesn't end here. This is only the beginning. Now it's time for this community to take charge, for all of you to take an active role in bringing about awareness, to spread the word, and to keep this from happening to someone else's child."

Tammy Bristol, the mother of two children who were allegedly transported away from the preschool and molested by strangers—filmed in the act—was beside herself.

"How could this have happened, Doctor?" Tammy asked. "How could my children have been put through this, day in and day out, without me noticing anything? I never had a clue. Wouldn't I have seen something... *anything*? Wouldn't my children have shown some sign of being tortured like this? It just doesn't make sense. It doesn't seem possible."

Dr. Summit had seen this before, that moment when a parent discovers that they had failed to detect what should have been so obvious. He'd written about it in his "Child Sexual Abuse Accommodation Syndrome."

At the heart of his thesis, Dr. Summit stressed that children accommodated their ongoing or past sexual abuse through secrecy and delayed disclosure, and that they would ultimately retract their claims—that is, even though they'd come forth today, they may later take it back, saying that they'd lied, that they had "made it all up." It was easier that way.

Dr. Summit's message was simple: The trauma a child experiences from an abusive past is horrific, but the next phase, the stage of post-disclosure, would be even more demoralizing.

"Child victims of sexual abuse," Dr. Summit said, "face secondary trauma in the crisis of discovery...and while they attempt to reconcile their private experiences, they are most often *assaulted* by a society of adults and their disbelief, blame, and rejection."

"It's not that I think my son is lying," cried Carol Burkhart, the mother of seven-year-old Philip, who claimed to have remembered things that had happened to him three years before. "I definitely think he was molested, but some of the things he says are so incredible that I just can't make sense of it. He said he was molested at Harry's Market. I mean, we go there every day. My god, he said he flew on a plane. He said he went far away to a ranch. How? How did that happen? What airport did he fly out of, and how did he do that and make it back to the preschool before noon? And again, nobody—not one of us—ever saw anything."

Dr. Summit shook his head, a non-combative expression to ease her confusion. "With all due respect, it doesn't need to make sense to *you*. It may never make sense to you because you may never be able to accept that something like this has happened to your child.

"But you *do* need to understand that it's absolutely imperative that you *believe* your child." Dr. Summit panned the crowd. "Your children need to know that. They need to feel comfortable talking about their abuse, talking about what they've been suppressing for so long.

"If they don't have that safe place, if *you* don't provide it, then they will never be able to give a full account of their experience. They will never be able to identify all of the people who abused them, and of course, they will never begin to heal."

* * * * *

In the late afternoon of Friday, April 20, Judy packed her VW van, preparing for a trip to Yucca Valley, to the desert home of her father, Pastor Myrus Knutson, where the clean air and warm wind was the respite she longed for.

That day, nearly a year since she and Brad had separated, he formally filed for divorce.

Judy continued to stuff the van with personal items, preparing for an extended stay. Mark helped her, as Mitchell sat on the back patio playing with his Tonka truck. The boys were always excited to take a road trip, but Mark noticed that his mother was uniquely distressed.

On the kitchen table lay a letter, face up, dated that day, one that Judy had just read. It was from Brad. In it, he had tried to ready Judy for what was coming, the post-filing intricacies that had to be addressed. He expressed his concern with the way the boys were being affected by Judy's pursuit of Mitchell's abusers—the ongoing investigative work she was doing with Bob Currie and Ron Gantry. Brad was concerned that her priorities were out of place.

"Mark needs to be in an education program," Brad wrote, and he wanted Mark to remain in Manhattan Beach, where he had "many friends." Brad said Mark could go to school and "stay with me," which would give Judy more time for Mitchell.

Brad stressed that Mitchell needed therapy, and that if he received the right treatment, he would have "a very good chance to recover from this incident unscarred."

However, Brad warned, if he was "continually immersed in an atmosphere which focuses on the incident," he would not recover. Brad wanted Mitchell to live the life of a normal three-year-old, not a pawn in a criminal investigation who was "being rewarded for turning up new clues."

Brad wanted Mitchell to be in "a warm and nurturing environment, not one based on suspicion and revenge."

In the same letter, Brad told Judy to "decide *today* the method you would like to use to legally dissolve your marriage." Brad wanted to start the healing process, and he urged that they be compassionate toward each other. He did not want to "open any new wounds," and he explained in detail the exorbitant fees for divorce attorneys—that the retainer costs alone would bury them. He emphasized that they needed to prepare a budget, to start thinking about a child custody agreement and the type of support payments she would expect.

Brad tried to reason with Judy, to keep her focused—but, he could see, she was gradually coming unhinged.

According to her father, Judy began receiving death threats over the phone; rocks had been hurled at her house on several occasions, frightening the boys. It was far too risky to stay.

Thus, Judy and the boys headed to the desert, to the small community of Landers on the northern outskirts of Joshua Tree National Park. With its mix of wildlife and hiking trails, it was the perfect spot for naturalists and outdoorsy-people, just as Judy had always been.

For that brief period in the spring of 1984, Judy and the boys moved into a small cabin behind her father's home, a modest abode, yet out of harm's way.

* * * * *

Later that day, the Manhattan Beach Police Department, working with social workers in San Diego County, entered the grounds of two separate schools—a junior high and an elementary—where Justine and Carl Spitler were attending. Their mother, Babette, was incarcerated at Sybil Brands Institute for Women, awaiting a dependency hearing scheduled for the next day, April 21.

Hours before, social workers had tracked down Justine and Carl's baby nephew, Daryl, who'd been hidden away at the Spitler's neighbor's home in the Tree section. As the officers converged on Justine's and Carl's classrooms, Daryl had already been taken into protective custody and placed in foster care.

With warrants in hand, the MBPD removed the Spitler children from their classrooms and transported them to Los Angeles to be evaluated. The Spitler children were critical to the state's case—the only young children of any of the McMartin Seven defendants. If the allegations were true, the Spitler children would have likely been indoctrinated for many years, subjects of an unthinkable childhood at the hands of their parents and the McMartin staff. But several hours of interviews produced nothing: just two children pleading to see their parents.

Following the evaluation, the police took Justine and Carl to Sybil Brand penitentiary for a brief visitation with Babette. They were confused as they were processed through security, and even more horrified when they found their mother seated, slumped over and handcuffed to a table.

"My son kept asking why *he* was being arrested," Babette said later. "I was in jail, going out of my mind, and when Don [her husband] came to visit, I couldn't even touch him. We just sat there looking at each other through a plate of glass.

"I told him to divorce me," she said, "so he could keep custody of the children."

But that wasn't a viable solution. The next morning, the dependency court ruled that Don Spitler, too, was an unfit parent, that he should have known the type of woman he was married to. For that reason, he was at least guilty of poor judgment and blatant neglect.

Justine and Carl were taken to MacLaren Children's Center in El Monte, twenty minutes east of downtown Los Angeles, a youth facility for wayward and neglected juveniles. They would remain there until the state found appropriate foster care. They were not allowed to be in contact with their parents.

* * * * *

Two days later, on Monday, April 23, the California State Department of Social Services (DSS) received a phone call from Linda Jacobson. The mother of Jimmy, a six-year-old student at the Manhattan Ranch Preschool, a facility located a mile east of McMartin, Linda was looking to file a complaint against Manhattan Ranch, and specifically claimed that her boy had been "physically abused" by Michael Ruby, the sixteen-year-old teacher's aide.[11]

According to Linda Jacobson, about three weeks earlier, after noticing

---

[11] The information regarding the complaint of Linda and Jimmy Jacobson comes from the official police report, DR-84093, filed with the Manhattan Beach Police Department.

that Jimmy had developed a "nervous twitch," she and her husband sat the boy down for a talk.

Linda asked Jimmy about the afternoon a few months earlier when she'd arrived at Manhattan Ranch to pick him up, the day she found him wrapped in a blanket. His clothes were wet and in the dryer. A staff member told Linda that "Jimmy was accidently pushed into a puddle" by Michael Ruby, or Mr. Mike, as he was known to the children.

"Is that what happened, Jimmy? Was it an accident? Did Mr. Mike accidently push you?" Linda asked.

"No. No way," Jimmy replied. "He did it on purpose. He was being mean. He's always mean to me. He hates me. He pushed me on purpose, and then he dragged me through the water."

And that was not all that Jimmy said.

According to his mother, Jimmy claimed that Michael Ruby had "placed him in a large trash can and hung him from a tree," and that Ruby had tied his arms and legs to a tree. Jimmy said that Michael Ruby tied a hangman's rope around his neck, stepped on his finger until he cried, crushed a small snail, and held it on his [Ruby's] finger, and that he threw Jimmy over a wall and left him there for a long time, so long that Jimmy "cried until another teacher let him back in."

Jimmy further alleged that Michael Ruby "slugged him in the head with a closed fist," forced meat and bread down his throat until he gagged, stuck needles in his fingers until he bled, made him take off his clothes to play doctor, and that he [Ruby] would watch Jimmy pee.

"He made me call him Master," Jimmy told his parents. "He said he would beat me up if I told anyone. He said he would *beat me good*."

The DSS forwarded the complaint to its licensing division, where it came into the hands of Inspector Richard Furikawa.

For Inspector Furikawa, considering the rampant reports of preschool abuse over the past month, allegations once considered outlandish, like this, had become the new normal. He scheduled an inspection of the Manhattan Ranch Preschool for early May.

CHAPTER 14

Sunday, April 29, 1984

The front page of the *Los Angeles Times* told stories from around the world. An article from The Hague where Nicaraguan officials complained that the United States had violated international law by aiding antigovernment rebels, a story from Peking where President Reagan gave a speech "extolling the virtues of capitalism," a report from London where an eleven-day siege on the Libyan embassy came to an end, and at the bottom of the page, "McMartin Case: A Community Divided."

The report was balanced; it outlined the perspectives of the McMartin Seven, as if they'd been falsely accused. It gave positive character references for some of the female defendants, with one of their supporters saying, "They're all moral, gentle, God-fearing women. They are ladies."

In contrast, it stated the prosecution's case: how the children were allegedly raped, drugged, tortured, threatened, and filmed in the nude. An unnamed father of a former McMartin student declared, "We're dealing here with masters of deception. One of their roles is as upstanding citizens, and the other is as predators."

The general theme conveyed that the usually tranquil Manhattan Beach had been split into camps of believers and non-believers. There was no middle ground. One either stood by the children, no strings attached, or one did not, opening oneself up to fierce criticism, even suspicion.

Some tried to remain neutral—"I don't have an opinion," said a man who was a family friend of an alleged victim who happened to live across the street from one of the defendants. Had he supported the child, he would be accusing his neighbor, but defending his neighbor would be calling the child a liar.

Others simply had no choice—those who worked with young children: the preschool teachers, daycare providers, babysitters, and anyone else whose vocation required them to spend time alone with infants and toddlers. Once the trusted caretakers of their community, they were being looked upon differently, skeptically, as if a shadow had been cast over them, a darkness that obscured their true identity.

With it came uncertainty, a sense of dread and foreboding. Crimes against children were said to have been committed, crimes so revolting that, despite the need for a calm evaluation of the facts, the demand for retribution was preeminent.

* * * * *

Five days later, on Friday, May 4, 1984, Michael Ruby, the sixteen-year-old teacher's aide at the Manhattan Ranch Preschool, arrived at work. As usual, he pulled up on his moped and parked near the school's entrance. Medium height, stocky, with brown hair and green eyes, he strutted into the office. Michael was greeted by Lois Jansen, the preschool's director. Her concerned look reminded him that he was five minutes late—at least that's what he thought.

"Michael, we need to talk," Lois said.

"What's up?"

"Mrs. Jacobson filed a complaint with the Department of Social Services. She said you *physically abused* Jimmy. It's all here in the report." Lois handed him the document.

Michael's eyes widened as he read over it.

"I know with all this McMartin stuff going on, you might get a little freaked out," Lois said. "But this has nothing to do with sexual abuse."

Michael shook his head as he continued reading—the part about him "shoving raw meat" down Jimmy's throat and "tying the child to a tree."

"She can't be serious with this, right?" he asked. "I mean, this is stupid. It's like she's rambling on, talking gibberish."

"The DSS inspector just left," Lois replied. "He said the complaint's unsubstantiated, but he had to come check it out. Standard policy, I guess."

"Did you tell him the whole story?" Michael asked.

"Yes," Lois replied, nodding vigorously. "I told him everything."

The *whole story* Michael referred to wasn't included in the DSS report—the backstory of Linda Jacobson's estranged relationship with the Manhattan Ranch Preschool.

Since December 1983, Linda Jacobson had failed to pay her children's monthly fee on time. She'd always had an impassioned excuse for falling behind, which placated the preschool's directors—at first. But by the end of March, she was more than two months delinquent, and she made no commitment as to when the balance would be settled. When she showed up on Monday, April 2, she was told that her children—Jimmy and three-year-old Lisha—were no longer permitted on site.

Two days later, Linda Jacobson and her husband sat down with Jimmy—the moment he made explicit accusations against Michael Ruby.

Three weeks after that, Linda Jacobson filed the complaint with the DSS, which prompted the investigation.

Michael handed the report back to Lois.

"This is crazy," he said. "She got booted for not paying her bill, and now she's suing to make some cash. It's so obvious."

"I explained that to him," Lois replied. "Again, I don't want you to worry about any of this, but I thought you should know."

After work, Michael went home and informed his mother, Evelyn. She drove straight to the school and talked to Lois Jansen, who showed Evelyn the complaint—how Michael, on top of shoving raw meat down Jimmy's throat, had allegedly tied the boy to a tree, rolled tires at him, struck him repeatedly, and threw him over a wall.

"This is unbelievable," Evelyn said to Lois. "Does she even realize what she's saying?"

"I don't know," Lois said. "I really don't know what to think at this point. Only that the DSS has checked into it, and they don't want any part of it."

Evelyn went home, and she asked Michael if he wanted to quit, that working in that environment might be too much pressure.

"I'd look guilty if I quit," Michael replied. "And this is too crazy for anyone to believe. No one's gonna listen to this woman. She's a nut job."

Michael David Ruby was the second of four adopted children of Glenn and Evelyn Ruby. Born in a small town in Pennsylvania, he was three months old when they took him into their family, introducing him to his big brother, Glenn, Jr., a two-year-old.

Glenn and Evelyn, a devoutly religious couple, met at a church in

Chicago years before. Glenn, a youth counselor, and Evelyn, an aspiring nurse, fell in love with a shared vision of raising a family. But, to their dismay, they were unable to conceive. Knowing that God intended for them to be parents, they chose to adopt, taking in four parentless children.

After moving to Manhattan Beach, Glenn continued to spread Christ's message, forming Christian clubs on high school campuses around the South Bay. Glenn and the students would gather on the lawn after school for prayer sessions, discussing the Bible and other concepts of theology.

In time, Glenn chose to make it his full-time vocation. He incorporated the program Campus Outreach, eventually forming thirty-three satellites at schools as far away as Vista, Chatsworth, and Yucaipa.

As dedicated members of the Rolling Hills Covenant Church, Glenn fell into the role of youth pastor while Evelyn was a principal organist. Their children—Glenn, Jr., Michael, Linda, and Lisa—remained actively involved in the church, attending mass each Sunday and taking part in youth activities throughout the week.

When Michael was small, like most kids, he didn't enjoy going to church, mainly because it had been forced upon him. But by his early teens, that changed. Better versed on biblical scriptures than most kids his age, Michael took a leadership role, heading prayer groups and open conversations.

Still, for Michael, being the son of modest parents in an upscale town was humbling and somewhat disconcerting. The Rubys had placed their faith in God, on their spirituality, not on the tangible value of their possessions. They had all that they needed: a simple residence in the backlands east of Pacific Coast Highway, a station wagon to pack into each summer for a family road trip across the states, and most importantly, they had each other and their love of Christ.

With that in mind, in that summer of 1984, with Manhattan Beach at the epicenter of the material world, Michael Ruby found himself swimming upstream, a young man with limited means in the land of the privileged.

In his junior year, 1983–1984, Michael began to stray, drifting away from the church, more interested in drinking beer with his friends on the football team. He got a slightly punk haircut, not too radical, but well out of the mainstream.

"We were all football players and it was summer," Michael said. "It was nothing unusual, but my parents didn't approve."

Michael, a muscular guy, had always been bigger than the other kids, and he never ran away from a confrontation. From time to time, he'd gotten into trouble for fighting.

His freshman year, Michael started at tailback and linebacker, one of the better players on the football team. But that year, the fall of 1983, he decided not to play. He loved football, but he hadn't grown in two years, and he sensed that varsity was out of his league. His helmet gave him acne, and he'd become rather self-conscious about his looks. One morning, the head coach cornered Michael in the hallway and asked him to reconsider, but Michael's mind was made up.

An avid surfer, Michael got into the mod theme. He became close friends with Gregor Lawson, a talented artist. Michael had always been interested in drawing, and he and Gregor would sketch together, inspiring each other's work.

When describing their art, Michael said it was "rowdy and showed destruction," that they were "statements of non-conformity." Michael and Gregor listened to punk music while they sketched, including X, The Dead Kennedys, The Vandals, and Black Flag. Gregor gave Michael his first mohawk, and Michael did the same for him.

"I was looking for myself," Michael said of the time. "I was really struggling with my individualism."

As he got more into surfing, Michael bought a Volkswagen Squareback—what he called his "Manhattan Beach surf car"—and he needed money to keep it running. He needed a job.

In September 1983, Michael went to the Job Center at Mira Costa High School where they offered him a position as a playground aide at the Manhattan Ranch Preschool. He didn't like the idea of working at a preschool, but he took the job out of convenience. The hours were Monday through Friday from 3:00 p.m. to 5:30 p.m., and it was less than a mile from his house. He would make seventy-five dollars every two weeks, enough to keep the Squareback moving up and down the coast.

Once settled in at Manhattan Ranch, Michael anointed himself the "Commissioner of Discipline," inscribing that title on a strip of masking tape over a name plate. But to the kids he was "Mr. Mike."

Michael's job was relatively mundane. He watched over the children, keeping them in line. If they broke a rule on the playground, they got benched. If they made a noise while in the TV circle, the TV was switched off until they were quiet. If a child didn't obey his orders or showed him any disrespect, he turned the kid over to one of the adult teachers, and the kid's mother got a phone call. "That was the deal," Michael said. "It was my way or the highway, and those kids figured it out pretty quick. I wasn't messing around."

Michael confessed that he wasn't well liked by the children, but, he also admitted, he wasn't that fond of them either.

At a certain point, Michael said, he grew tired of being around the kids. Once in a while he snapped at them, perhaps unjustly. Sometimes, when Michael benched a child, the child would run away crying to one of the adult teachers, "Mr. Mike benched me!" But the teachers just smiled and said, "Do what Mr. Mike says," and the child would.

Despite those occasional episodes, however, the children were usually happy to see Michael when he arrived at work on his moped. They thought the moped was cool. They would run up to him yelling, "Mr. Mike's here! Mr. Mike's here!" They smiled and giggled, expressing their innocent joy.

Those were the subtle moments, Michael said, when he truly enjoyed the children, where he put down his guard and allowed the students of Manhattan Ranch to grace him with their unconditional kindness.

* * * * *

On Tuesday, May 8, four days after the DSS inspection of the Manhattan Ranch Preschool, Linda and Jimmy Jacobson arrived at the Manhattan Beach Police Department for an interview with Detective Patty Picker, an understudy of Detective Jane Hoag. Detective Picker had played an active role in the roundup and indictments of the McMartin Seven.

Linda Jacobson had come to report possible child molestation at Manhattan Ranch, naming the suspect as Michael David Ruby, a.k.a. Mr. Mike.

She went through the circumstances that led her to believe her son had been abused. She gave the brief history since early April, the day she and her husband "talked with Jimmy." She told the story of arriving at the school and finding Jimmy "wrapped in a blanket." She spoke of his nervous twitch that had become increasingly worse, and all of the other abuses that he'd alleged.

Detective Picker interviewed Jimmy privately.

"Mr. Mike was very mean to me," Jimmy said.

"How, Jimmy? How was he mean to you?" Picker asked.

"He choked me with his hands around my neck," Jimmy alleged, "and then he put a broomstick up against my throat and pinned me against a wall."

Jimmy reiterated some of the other claims, but said he was "embarrassed" to talk about the details.

Eventually, Jimmy revealed that Michael Ruby had taken him into the teacher's restroom and "tickled his hiney" and made him touch Michael's privates.

"He took pictures of me and two other boys," Jimmy said. "He told us it was for a picture contest."

Detective Picker ended the interview and took Jimmy back out to his mother, who informed Detective Picker that Jimmy had been in private therapy.

"Jimmy's been seeing a counselor," Linda said. "Her name's Cheryl Kent. She works at the South Bay Center for Counseling. He's told her many things."

Detective Picker knew of Dr. Cheryl Kent, that Kent was the psychotherapist working with many alleged McMartin victims.

The next morning, Wednesday, May 9, Detective Picker contacted Dr. Cheryl Kent, who informed the detective of the statements Jimmy had made to her in their last therapy session.

"Jimmy described semen coming out of Mike Ruby's penis," Dr. Kent said, "that it was 'white water, like pee.' He also said that Michael Ruby threatened to 'shove a lit cigarette down his throat if he didn't cooperate.'"

From Detective Picker's standpoint, Jimmy's allegations couldn't be ignored, especially since the MBPD already had the Manhattan Ranch Preschool on their radar. Four months earlier, on January 23, Judy Johnson had contacted Detective Jane Hoag and said that Mitchell had identified "other locations." Judy had specifically identified the Manhattan Ranch Preschool.

CHAPTER 15

Chuck Elliott, a columnist for the *Daily Breeze* in Torrance, the South Bay's largest publication, sat in front of his typewriter, surrounded by letters, notes, and stacks of his past articles. With the McMartin investigation widening, Chuck considered drafting a piece on preschool sexual abuse, maybe an exposé on a family affected by the case.

Chuck—a rotund man, medium height, balding with a thick goatee and an engaging laugh—was a likeable personality amongst his colleagues at the *Breeze*. He'd been writing his column since 1977, a mix of human interest stories from around the South Bay, where the voices of the community could be heard. Chuck was active in the beach cities—a frequent emcee or a judge at a chili cook-off—and he'd been given the title of "Mr. South Bay" by his loyal readers.

Known for his fun-loving persona, Chuck had received modest notoriety for his annual "Worst Joke Contest," collecting so many bad jokes that he'd recently published a book called, *The Best of the Worst Jokes I Ever Heard*. He'd been promoting the book on radio shows across the United States and Canada.

On that Friday, Chuck sat at his desk at the *Daily Breeze* when his phone rang.

"Chuck Elliott," he answered.

"Chuck, this is Jackie," said the crying voice of a woman.

"Jackie, what's wrong?"

"They just told me Julie was molested at McMartin," Jackie said, barely able to speak as she grasped for breath. "They said she was raped. They said she's one of the worst cases they've ever seen."

Chuck agreed to meet her at a laundromat in Manhattan Beach. Until that day, Chuck and Jackie hadn't met face to face.

"Jackie" was Jacquelyn McGauley, the winner of Chuck's 1984 "Worst Joke Contest" ("What did the female mushroom say to the male mushroom? You're a real fun-gi.")

"As first prize, Jackie earned a lunch date with me," Chuck explained later. "We hadn't set it up, but I started talking to her on the phone. We would talk for hours."

Through their conversations, Chuck learned that Jackie was a McMartin parent, that she'd enrolled her three-year-old daughter, Julie, into the preschool in September 1983, a few weeks after Ray Buckey was openly under investigation, but after Ray had stopped working there. Julie attended McMartin until Friday, January 13, 1984, the day Virginia shut the doors.

When the news reports broke in early February, Jackie told Chuck she "didn't believe a word of it" since her personal experience at McMartin had been so enjoyable. Jackie even kept a greeting card from Virginia taped to her refrigerator, a note thanking Jackie for her loyalty to the school through that unsettling time.

The note read:

> *Many thanks for your support, love, and understanding this school year. We do appreciate it. You are a fine person. Please keep in touch with us. We are always interested in your family.*
> *Loving you,*
> *Miss Virginia*
> *(Miss Peggy, too)*

But a few weeks after the story became a national headline, Jackie had an epiphany. One night, while she and Julie watched a Wayne Satz broadcast, Julie stared at Jackie blankly and said, "Die." It left Jackie uneasy. It made her suspect that Julie had been suppressing her true feelings, as if she had a dark secret.

The next morning, Jackie contacted CII and scheduled Julie for an evaluation. Julie was placed on a six-week waiting list.

Knowing the backstory, Chuck had anticipated Jackie's call to update him on the results of the examination—but he never expected to hear such devastating news. Chuck figured that since Ray Buckey wasn't at the school when Julie attended—a three-month period when police had conducted twenty-four-hour surveillance of both Ray and the preschool—it would have been impossible for Julie to have been abused. Chuck assumed that when Julie said, "Die," she was simply confused, or maybe she was influenced by the images she'd seen on television.

Chuck left the *Daily Breeze* and headed north on Pacific Coast Highway toward Manhattan Beach. As anxious as he was to finally meet Jackie—the faceless voice who'd been so enamored with him—the circumstances of their rendezvous couldn't have been more agonizing. Jackie's daughter had been brutalized, damaged in ways that would affect her for years. Chuck had no experience in dealing with such a tragedy.

As he drove, Chuck reflected upon their last conversation, an odd discussion where Jackie had asked him for a favor. According to Chuck, Jackie had told him that a few years earlier, back when she was pregnant with Julie, Jackie had met with a woman who called herself a "witch," an eccentric who gave horoscopes, read tarot cards, and offered other forms of clairvoyance.

"The witch told me, 'Your daughter is going to be famous one day,'" Jackie supposedly told Chuck. "I need you to help me find her. Can you help me track her down? I want to ask her if it's the McMartin case that will make Julie famous."

The whole story was a bit "loony-land," Chuck said, but, like a good reporter, he listened. Chuck had earned his chops in Washington, DC, in the early 1970s, working as a leg man for the legendary investigative journalist, Jack Anderson, conducting pre-Watergate surveillance of J. Edgar Hoover and his number-two man, Clyde Tolson—a story based on a lead that President Nixon wanted to replace Hoover. Chuck staked out Hoover's house, followed his limo, and he even watched them as "they ate lunch every day at the same corner table in the Rib Room at the Mayflower Hotel up on Connecticut." Chuck has a picture of those days, snapped by *ABC News*, the image of him standing over J. Edgar Hoover's trashcan holding a piece of meaningless rubbish. For whatever it was worth, Chuck Elliott was an old-school reporter, something he proudly admitted.

With such a background, Chuck was skeptical of Jackie's tall tales—that is, until he stepped into the laundromat and laid his eyes upon her. Jackie stood alone, a tall, thin beauty with long blond hair. She was sexy, out of Chuck's league on a normal day, but there was nothing normal about the situation.

Jackie recognized Chuck from the photo that adjoined his daily column, and she stepped toward him, embracing him and thanking him for rushing to be with her in her time of need.

"Frankly," Chuck admitted, "I'm a sucker for a damsel in distress. I guess I slipped into my Prince Charming Syndrome."

Chuck and Jackie spoke for hours, getting to know each other over dinner and drinks. That night, they slept together.

"Things moved fast, to say the least," Chuck confessed.

Chuck, whose marriage had been gradually falling apart, was already looking for an excuse to stray, which was why he'd spent so much time talking with the mysterious woman who'd won the joke contest.

"My wife, bizarrely enough, owned a preschool and had mismanaged the hell out of the funds," Chuck said. "In the process, she put us thirty-four thousand dollars in debt."

Chuck said they were forced to sell their home to pay the bills. "I was already unhappy in my marriage when Jackie came along, and then, on our first night out, we ended up in the sack."

Chuck's wry smile morphed into a blank stare as he took himself back to the experience. "I jumped out of the frying pan and into the fire."

Over the next six weeks, Chuck and Jackie's relationship grew stronger and more passionate. They both formally separated from their spouses—hiring the same divorce attorney for their independent cases—and they found an apartment in Hermosa Beach. Chuck, Jackie, Julie, and Darren, Jackie's eighteen-month-old son, became a family. Chuck's son, Max, a two-year-old, stayed with them every other weekend.

Chuck called the romance, "A Columnist's Fantasy Comes True," a love like no other.

"Have you ever been crazy in love?" Chuck asked as he thought back to his first days with Jackie. "I have, and I thought it would never end."

But for Chuck, the honeymoon ended before it started.

On the morning of May 13, the Sunday they moved into their new apartment, Chuck left unexpectedly. "I went looking for something of hers that I thought we'd left in the *Daily Breeze* truck that we'd used to move. When I returned to the apartment, I found her in a complete panic, doubled over, crying, incoherent, unable to talk and unwilling to be comforted."

According to Chuck, Jackie was hysterical, distraught that he'd left without explaining himself. From Chuck's perspective, he figured she would just continue unpacking and situating their new home. He hadn't given it much thought.

"Jackie feared that I'd left her," Chuck recalled. "She said, 'If you turn out to be like all the rest, I'll probably go crazy.'"

Chuck knew that Jackie had some emotional issues—a rough upbringing where she'd lost her father at a young age; and she'd given Chuck the impression that she'd been abused. When Chuck asked Jackie if her father had ever sexually abused her, she would only say that she "blanked out the details of her terrible childhood."

To Chuck, it seemed, because of that maltreatment and neglect, Jackie was constantly seeking affirmation.

About the time they were looking for an apartment, Chuck told Jackie he was thinking of writing an article about "The Ordeal of a McMartin Parent," and using her as the case study. There were so many couples, parents of McMartin victims, who were getting divorced. The reason, Chuck suspected, was that one parent would blame the other for allowing their child to be molested. Some of them, Chuck said, were using McMartin as an excuse for a divorce they'd long wanted.

Chuck's editor thought the story was an excellent idea and gave him the go-ahead. Within the piece, Chuck used a pseudonym for Jackie to protect her privacy. The article, a combination of the trauma of being a McMartin parent mixed with the backdrop of a yuppie couple living within Manhattan Beach, was compelling, but certainly not an accurate depiction of Jackie's life. It read more like the life that Jackie had always dreamed of, the life that had escaped her, coupled with the terrible realization that her daughter had been sexually abused.

Chuck completed the story, but it was never published. Being intimately involved with Jackie, Chuck could see his conflict of interest. As the live-in boyfriend of a woman whose daughter was an alleged victim, Chuck, too, had become a McMartin parent. Chuck's editor agreed.

Jackie, seeing the article as the first step in her daughter's fame—just as the witch had prophesized—was disappointed, particularly with Chuck. Her boyfriend, one of the most notable writers in the South Bay, would not support her long-term vision.

Chuck, however, felt he was filling a far more important role. Like a father dedicated to his daughter's recovery, Chuck attended Julie's therapy, nurturing her through her post-traumatic stress.

* * * * *

Meanwhile, Detective Patty Picker followed the Manhattan Ranch leads and the ongoing investigation of Michael Ruby. The district attorney had been exploring a theory of a conspiracy among preschools throughout the South Bay, and the case of Manhattan Ranch blended nicely into that portrait—a preschool just down the road from McMartin where another male teacher had been accused.

On Monday, May 14, six days after filing the complaint against Michael Ruby, Linda and Jimmy Jacobson arrived at the Manhattan Beach Police Department for a follow-up interview with Detective Patty Picker. Linda had been spending a lot of time with Jimmy, talking about his experiences, and he'd continued to attend therapy with Dr. Cheryl Kent at SBCC.

Detective Picker interviewed Jimmy privately.

"Mr. Mike took us into the bathroom," Jimmy said. "There was a bunch of us. He liked to do that, because that's where all his friends were. They were his *Ca-Ca* friends."

"What happened in the bathroom, Jimmy? What did Mr. Mike do?"

"He made us touch each other down there," Jimmy said, pointing to his groin. "And then he pottied on my hands."

Detective Picker asked Jimmy to "draw a picture" of Michael Ruby, what he looked like in the act. Jimmy drew a stick figure, a face with no delineation of a head, just big round eye balls with a small round nose between them. It had a wide open smile—a happy face—with stick legs and arms, asterisks for hands, and no body. Dangling in the center was a penis. It hung well below the knees, with a large ball at the bottom and a slit in the middle, like a urethra. The sketch of the penis resembled the pendulum rod and bob of a grandfather clock.

As she looked over the drawing, Detective Picker asked, "Why does Mr. Mike have such a big smile on his face, Jimmy?"

"Because he likes doing mean things to me," the boy replied.

Detectives Picker and Hoag discussed Jimmy's latest statements. It had become evident that, if Jimmy had been remotely honest, there were multiple victims and, in all likelihood, multiple abusers. If that were the case, the connection to McMartin was real.

The next morning, Detective Hoag met with Betsy Warren, an alleged McMartin victim. Hoag showed Betsy a photograph of the Manhattan Ranch Preschool.

"Do you recognize this place? Have you seen it before?"

"Yeah. I've been there before," Betsy said. "That's where Ray took me. He took me there a bunch of times."

"What happened when you were there, Betsy? What did you see?"

Betsy's eyes widened, and she recounted the events from years past. "That's where Ray killed the animals," Betsy said. "He drove us there, and that's when he killed the animals."

CHAPTER
16

By late May, Judy could see Brad playing nice—the fatherly approach—and she wasn't buying it. She knew what he was after; he needed to legally initiate their divorce by mid-June or it would cost him dearly. He'd acted as if he had the boys' interest in mind, but she knew he only wanted to move on, to begin a new life with another woman. By staying calm, by speaking from the heart, he may've thought that Judy would comply. He was mistaken.

Looking to separate their assets and liabilities, Brad asked Judy to give the bank permission to remove his name from their homeowner's insurance policy. Judy refused. He asked her to call their divorce attorney to schedule an appointment to mediate. Again, she made no progress and gave him no response.

On Thursday, May 31, Judy opened a letter from Brad, a short and concise note intended to assert his control.

"In an effort to move toward a meaningful dialogue," it opened, "I'm making some changes to our money arrangement."

The letter informed her that he would be decreasing the amount of money he deposited into her bank account over the next six weeks—"$175 on June 15…and $0 by June 30." Of course, it said, the decrease "could be avoided" if she simply contacted their lawyer and agreed to a date for mediation.

"Before you cry foul," it read, "remember…<u>You</u> are still in control of <u>Your</u> Bank Account…all <u>You</u> have to do is make the appointment prior to June 15, 1984 and <u>Show Up</u>."

Judy set the letter down, stepping into the kitchen to mix a drink.

This was a lonely time for Judy, one year since their separation, and the day found her more alone than ever. With Mark out of town for a few weeks, visiting Steve and Debbie in Bellevue, Washington, where they'd relocated with their newborn son, Johnny, it was just Judy and Mitchell.

Hours later, sometime after she'd contemplated Brad's letter, Judy sent Mitchell to spend the night with his father, a day earlier than their normal routine. Brad returned Mitchell the next morning. There were no issues.

Later that day, however, on Friday, June 1, Judy placed a frantic call to UCLA-Harbor Medical Center. She spoke with resident nurse Mary Logan.

"My son, Mitchell. He ran away while we were at the park," Judy said. "He was gone for several minutes, and when he came back, he'd been sexually molested!"

Judy didn't name a culprit, nor did she speculate how it could've happened in that setting. Judy only said that Mitchell had been abused while "out of her sight."

Nurse Logan instructed Judy to bring Mitchell in for an evaluation. Judy rushed to the facility, a twenty-minute drive to the eastern border of Torrance.

While there, doctors questioned Mitchell about his experience—the time period that he was "away from his mother at the park"—but Mitchell repeatedly denied that he'd been abused at the park. Instead, Mitchell said, it had happened "last night" while he was "in the tub at his father's house."

Days later, Judy took him to the station for an interview with Detective Hoag.

"Mitchell," Hoag asked, "why did you go to the doctor's last week?"

"I was hurt, poked," Mitchell replied, pointing to his bottom.

"How did you get hurt?"

"Got poked," he said. "The stick went in."

"Did Daddy ever hurt you?"

"Yes."

"How did Daddy hurt you?" Hoag asked. "And where?"

Mitchell pointed downward. "Daddy poked me with a stick."

Detective Hoag turned to Judy.

"You need to get him another exam, a second opinion."

"I've already scheduled him to see Dr. Richard Shearer," Judy said.

Dr. Richard Shearer, a pediatric oncologist at UCLA-Harbor Medical Center, had been treating Mark for his brain cancer.

Despite the fact that Dr. Shearer was not a specialist in child sexual abuse, and considering how adamant Detective Hoag had been ten months earlier when she persuaded Judy to take Mitchell to UCLA-Harbor General to see "experts" at the Marion Davies Clinic, Hoag allowed Judy to take Mitchell to Dr. Shearer, a pediatric oncologist, to conduct this critical examination for suspected sodomy—either an incompetent move or evidence that she did not take Judy's allegation seriously.

Nevertheless, on June 9, as a result of his examination, Dr. Shearer filed a "suspicion of child abuse report" against Brad Johnson.

* * * * *

Late in the evening of Wednesday, June 13, with Mark still away and Mitchell fast asleep, Judy sat at her kitchen table. On an unlined piece of note paper, Judy wrote in cursive:

> Brad,
> I have tried to contact you by phone and you have chosen not to return my calls. I have contacted Bonnie Neuman on June 7, 1984 as requested and am interested in this process. She was out of town and promised to return my call. If you have not processed your banking plan, as threatened, then all should run its course speedily. If you decide to play games and reduce $ for your children's welfare, it will be a costly, time consuming process as I must protect them. As you recall I signed the papers on the premise that this initial cooperation would be returned. As I just returned from a trip, I will call the bank in the morning to see what direction we will be taking.
> JAK

Judy signed "JAK," meaning Judith Ann Knutson, her maiden name, a sign of her independence.

Then, on a loose-leaf piece of lined paper, Judy wrote a summation of her life with Brad, highlighting his failures, as well as the emotional and psychological trauma she felt he'd put her through.

Judy scribed in cursive using a black calligraphy pen. She wrote how Brad had been "rejected from Med School & Law School," and how two years after they came to California, Brad's grandfather "finally kicked him out," calling him a "gigolo" and criticizing him for not having a job. She wrote of the "horrible 1-room apartment" he'd moved them into, and how she did "secretarial work" and "supplied food" while he was "fired many X's." She noted that they'd "been living off stock" that Judy was supposed to "keep as inheritance," and how he "begged to borrow" the money they needed for the down payment on the house on Vista Drive. She had "evidence of affairs" and wrote that she was "mentally" and "physically abused," to the point that she'd filed "3 incident reports" at the Manhattan Beach Police Department.

Brad, with his sights on a new beginning, had been tying up loose ends—the signatures and the final mediation. He had no idea that he was the target of a sodomy investigation.

Detective Hoag, aware that Brad was living nearby with a friend—just a two-minute walk from Vista Drive—did not want Brad to have access to Mitchell.

"Do not allow Mitchell to visit his father until this matter is resolved," Hoag instructed Judy. "I don't want him to be alone with Mitchell, not for a second. Do you understand?"

"Yes," Judy replied. "I'll keep him home, with me."

However, in the following days, despite her promise to Hoag, and without informing Brad of the investigation, Judy continued to send Mitchell to his father's home.

CHAPTER 17

By the middle of June, Chuck and Jackie's romance had all but ended. Once the knight in shining armor who'd rode into the laundromat to save her, Chuck had gradually become less prominent in her life. Jackie, an impassioned McMartin activist, spent her evenings with a small group of parents running a private investigation in and around Manhattan Beach, while Chuck immersed himself in his column. They were basically roommates, two single people cohabitating with their kids.

According to Chuck, Jackie's interest in the McMartin case had become an obsession. She clipped every article she could find. She taped the nightly news broadcasts and watched the segments over and over, jotting down notes and doing critical analysis, as she continued taking Julie to therapy and networking with other families. Jackie even formed a new group for "divorced McMartin parents."

"That was when Jackie first started to believe that there was a satanic cult behind the McMartin case," Chuck said. "That was about the time a certain man started coming by the apartment to pick her up."

A few nights a week, Chuck said, a car would pull up outside and honk. Jackie would grab her purse and run out, leaving him to watch her kids for hours on end. She usually would not return until after midnight. Finally, Chuck asked her where she was going and with whom.

"It's just another McMartin parent," Jackie told him. "A guy I'm working with. All three of his children were abused."

Jackie opened the door and spoke over her shoulder as she stepped out. "Don't wait up," she said.

But he did. He sat by the door, waiting beneath the dimmed light. Jackie returned home later than normal.

"You're pretty late," he said, startling her.

Jackie looked at her watch and shrugged. "Sorry, I didn't notice. We got caught up."

"So, who is this guy?" Chuck asked. "Do you have to meet with him every night?"

"It's not *every* night," Jackie replied.

"Who is he?"

"Why, are you jealous?"

"I'm definitely not jealous," Chuck said straight-faced, folding his arms. "I just want to know who he is. Don't I have the right to know?"

Jackie rolled her eyes. "He's just another McMartin parent that I'm working with."

"What's his name?"

"What do you care?"

"What's his name?"

"Bob," Jackie yelled. "Bob Currie."

* * * * *

When Bob Currie brought Jackie McGauley into his private investigative team with Judy Johnson, Jackie and Judy bonded right away. Jackie's daughter was the same age as Mitchell, so Jackie would take Julie to Judy's house for play dates. Judy and Jackie grew close, confiding in each other—two women recently separated, both dealing with the aftermath of their child's abuse.

More so, though, they had a mutual suspicion that Manhattan Beach had been infiltrated by a satanic cult, that their children had been subjected to rituals and forced to witness human sacrifice—the theory that Bob Currie had cultivated.

Currie admitted that the lure of money—the kiddie porn network—had played a factor in the conspiracy. But he was convinced that the true passion behind the crime was an unholy devotion to undermine Christian society. The profits simply funded the cult's endeavor, the proverbial means to an end.

"The DA's way out of their league," Currie stressed to the others. "They don't have a clue of what they're dealing with. They think this is about *crime*. It's not about crime. It's a way of life, a code that Satanists live by. The DA will never see it. And because they can't see it, they can't stop it."

When Currie first pressed the topic of Satanism, nobody wanted to consider it. "People were actually concerned that I had totally lost my sanity," Currie said. "Even my wife stopped talking to me." For several months, Currie said, he was alone, isolated in his opinions, a pariah within the parents group.

"So," Currie said, "it took a long time until I was able to meet Jackie McGauley, and she decided to talk to me, to listen to me."

Currie said that once he and Jackie met, they began spending most of their time together. Jackie became his closest ally.

"We used to sit on the floor," he said, "and we would talk about what we thought we had, the evidence we'd come up with. We would talk for hours."

Currie and Jackie believed they were on the forefront of something massive, that they were about to break the case wide open. Convinced that the occult stretched well beyond Southern California, to communities all over the nation, they wanted to alert the broader society about what was happening in Manhattan Beach.

Their first step was to work with a national news journal.

For several weeks, Currie, Jackie, and a few others had collaborated with producers from ABC News's *20/20* on a segment called "The Best Kept Secret," an exposé of "sexual abuse at an elite preschool in California."

The segment aired at 10:00 p.m. on Thursday, June 14, headlined as a "clear warning" for those who had "a child in a nursery school."

Tom Jarriel, a highly respected senior correspondent, presented the story. Jarriel had gained national recognition in 1968 for his coverage of the civil rights movement as the only network reporter on the ground in Memphis covering the assassination of Dr. Martin Luther King, Jr. A recipient of several Emmys, Jarriel brought real credibility to the topic.

The segment was widely viewed, even though it competed with *Knots Landing* and *Hill Street Blues*. It opened with the familiar face of Hugh Downs, just weeks before he began co-hosting with Barbara Walters, a reunion of their years together at NBC's *Today*.

"Could it be your child?" Downs asked before warning viewers that "this particular circumstance is the most wrenching and infuriating we've ever had to deal with on *20/20*."

Tom Jarriel appeared against a backdrop of Manhattan Beach, a community "torn apart" by a scandal that had since become the nation's "largest reported case ever of suspected child sexual abuse."

Throughout the piece, a standard twenty-minute segment, Jarriel interviewed various legal and medical professionals to validate the story, legitimizing the state's case, followed by the personal touch of testimonies from those most affected—the victims, or in this case, the parents of the victims.

Mothers and fathers appeared in the form of silhouettes, their identities masked in shadows, telling of how the owners of the McMartin Preschool had, as Jarriel put it, "turned a harmless nursery into a sexual house of horrors."

CHAPTER 18

By July 1984, Detective Jane Hoag sought to prove that the directors and operators of the Manhattan Ranch Preschool were conspirators in the McMartin child sex abuse network. Hoag theorized that these people, under the guise of "child caretakers," administered a pornography ring, using Michael Ruby as their in-house enforcer. Michael Ruby, Hoag suspected, had been hired for the sole purpose of facilitating the crimes. He kept the children in line; he punished them when they failed to obey. The directors and teachers, all adult women, acted as Ruby's cover, shrouding his crimes—a conspiracy motivated by the massive profits from a growing worldwide kiddie porn industry.

Detective Hoag just needed the evidence to prove it, to link the two preschools, and she believed she was close.

Hoag's initial focus on Manhattan Ranch had come in late January, when Judy Johnson claimed that Mitchell had been taken there—the place he called "The Zoo"—and Judy's statements had been supported by an alleged McMartin victim four months later.

In May, Hoag had interviewed Betsy Warren, the alleged McMartin victim, who'd identified Manhattan Ranch in a photo, saying that Ray had "killed animals" there.

By July, Betsy's mother, Cynthia, had more information. Cynthia had been taking Betsy to therapy, where the child began remembering many details of her abuse. Cynthia called Hoag at the station.

"She was taken to Hansen's Studio. It's in Hermosa Beach," Cynthia said. "Betsy just told me *that's* where they took her. She went there with Ashley and Laura." Both girls were schoolmates of her daughter at American Martyrs Parochial, both alleged McMartin victims.

Detective Hoag drove to the Tree section homes of nine-year-old Ashley Welsh and five-year-old Laura Lieberman. Hoag showed each girl a photo of Manhattan Ranch, and both remembered the facility as a place they'd been taken, swapped between the two preschools.

Days later, Detective Patty Picker had a follow-up interview with Ashley Welsh.

"Ray and Betty took us there," Ashley said. "There were other adults there, too, men and women. They said that our parents knew what was going on, but that we should keep our mouths shut. They took off our clothes and touched us. They made us play the Naked Movie Star game. We would dance around, five or ten of us at a time, and Virginia took pictures.

"Miss Peggy told me she had special powers," Ashley said. "She said she was a witch. She said she could see if I told my mom. And if I did, she would make me die."

Ashley told Detective Picker that Ray took the kids to Manhattan Ranch because he had "a male friend there."

Detective Picker then called the Lieberman home to speak with five-year-old Laura, who'd been removed from McMartin in late September 1983, after the police letter had made the investigation public. Laura was one of the complaining witnesses in the McMartin case but, up until that day, had never spoken of Manhattan Ranch.

"Ray took us in his van," Laura said. "He took us to Manhattan Ranch. We would go pick up those kids and bring them back to McMartin. Ray molested them, and then drove them back."

* * * * *

Many of the Manhattan Ranch parents had heard something about Linda Jacobson's complaint against Michael Ruby, but most had ignored it. The backstory, her grudge against the school, had played out in front of everyone months before, so she lacked credibility. But when rumors of a "child-swapping ring" shot through the community—when it was said that McMartin victims had specifically named Manhattan Ranch—some wondered.

One mother, Carla Jamison, spoke to her five-year-old daughter, Emma, the first Manhattan Ranch preschooler to lend credence to Linda and Jimmy Jacobson's accusations.

At 3:00 p.m. on Tuesday, July 10, Detective Patty Picker spoke by phone with Carla Jamison.

"I really think Emma was sexually molested," Carla told Picker.

Carla said that a week earlier she'd asked Emma if she'd ever played any "undressing games at school." Emma said that she "could not tell" because she would "get spanked." Three days later, Carla again asked Emma if she "ever took her clothes off aside from the times she undressed for ballet class," and again, Emma said she'd been "instructed not to tell her mom or dad about it." [12]

"I got suspicious," Carla said, "so I talked it over with a co-worker who said that I should take her to see a professional to make sure nothing bad happened to her at the school."

Carla took Emma to the South Bay Center for Counseling for a therapy session with Dr. Cheryl Kent, the therapist who'd taken the initial disclosures by Jimmy Jacobson and who'd been giving post-traumatic therapy to dozens of alleged McMartin victims.[13]

Picker placed a call to Dr. Kent.

"Emma said that teachers touched the children in sexual ways," Dr. Kent said. "She said that the teachers took nude photos of her. She named several teachers—Jill, Nina, Mary, Kathy, and *Mr. Mike*.

"Emma told me that her mother would get mad if she knew, and that if she told anyone she would be put in jail. She said Mr. Mike told her he would hit her if she said anything."

The next day, Carla brought Emma to the station.

"Emma," Detective Picker said, "can you tell me what happened at the school?"

But Emma shook her head. She would not speak.

"What's wrong, Emma?"

---

[12] The investigation in respect to Emma Jamison is documented in the MBPD police report, DR-84093, administered by Detectives Jane Hoag and Patty Picker. Throughout the entirety of the report, neither Hoag nor Picker ever noted that they asked Carla Jamison what compelled her to ask her daughter Emma if she'd "ever played any undressing games at the school."

[13] According to the police report, Detective Picker did not ask Carla Jamison how she came to know of the South Bay Center for Counseling, or if someone specifically referred her to Dr. Cheryl Kent. During Emma's therapy session, she told Dr. Kent that a girl named "Lisha" had also been abused. Lisha was the name of Jimmy Jacobson's younger sister.

Emma looked up at her mother. "I don't want to talk about it in front of Mommy," Emma said, dropping her head.

Detective Picker asked Carla to leave the room. Once she did, Emma spoke freely. "One time in the playground, Mr. Mike pulled his pants off. He grabbed my hand and made me touch his privates."

Emma made a series of disclosures—graphic descriptions of sexual acts—and how all of the other teachers had witnessed Michael Ruby molesting her.

"How often did this happen, Emma?"

"It happened almost every day."

The next morning, Emma Jamison was taken to UCLA-Harbor Medical Center and physically examined by Dr. Carol Berkowitz, a pediatrician, and one of the South Bay's leading experts in child sexual abuse. Dr. Berkowitz, an associate of Dr. Roland Summit, followed the theoretical guidelines of the "Child Sexual Abuse Accommodation Syndrome." Dr. Berkowitz determined that Emma had in fact been sexually abused.

Following the diagnosis, Detective Picker interviewed Emma a third time.

"Lots of kids took their clothes off," Emma said. "Mr. Mike put a pen and a crayon inside of me." Emma pointed to her groin.

"Did anyone see this, Emma? Any other teacher?"

"Yes," Emma said. "My new teacher, Kathy. Kathy was there. She took pictures of us with our clothes off."

Emma was referring to Kathy Lorde, a woman who'd just begun working at Manhattan Ranch a few weeks prior.

Hours later, Detective Hoag called the home of Betsy Warren, the first McMartin student that implicated Manhattan Ranch two months earlier. Betsy confirmed that she'd been molested by both men and women at the school.

"Were any pictures taken of you there?" Hoag asked.

"Yes, naked pictures," Betsy replied.

"Betsy," Hoag inquired, "did you ever see animals at the Manhattan Ranch Preschool?"

"Yes," she said, "I saw a chicken, a chicken that Ray killed."

"Did any of the teachers from Manhattan Ranch ever come to the McMartin Preschool?"

"Yes," Betsy said. "They came lots of times. I even saw them at Gooch's Market."

* * * * *

On the morning of Friday, July 20, 1984, Detectives Hoag and Picker, under the direction of Deputy District Attorney Glenn Stevens, a member of the McMartin prosecution team, prepared search warrants for three locations: Harry's Market, Mrs. Gooch's Market, and Hansen's Studio. Each business had been named by former McMartin students as places they'd been taken during a typical school day, where they'd been molested by their teachers as well as by strangers.

A team of officers and investigators convoyed from location to location, roping off the entrances, instructing patrons to stand back. Employees at each site were stunned; they had no idea what the police were looking for.

At Harry's and Gooch's, officers tore through the aisles and the stock rooms; they inspected the walk-in refrigerators and freezers, searching for anything to support the children's claims. Nothing was uncovered.

At Hansen's Studio, they confiscated cameras and equipment, taking several rolls of film and volumes of photographs—anything that could be linked to the kiddie porn network that had been alleged. Again, nothing incriminating was found.

* * * * *

The lack of discovery did not deter Detective Jane Hoag. In her experience, confirmed through her specialized training, the absence of tangible evidence did not necessarily mean that a crime did not occur. To a sexual assault investigator, when children make specific claims, they're not lying, for they aren't geared to be malicious. They aren't sophisticated enough to make false allegations of sexual abuse against innocent adults to inflict damage out of spite or amusement. If children at McMartin and Manhattan Ranch said that they were abused at their preschools and taken to other locations where strangers molested them, then they were likely being truthful even if the details of their memories were muddled.

There was, Hoag believed, a modus operandi in play, where a small but significant group of influential residents of this affluent seaside town had entered a covenant—a secret society; a lucrative enterprise—and the underpinning of the scheme was to manipulate the minds and emotions of young children who would never be believed by rational thinking adults.

But Hoag did believe them. She believed Judy, despite her increasingly bizarre claims, and she believed what each of the children had told Kee MacFarlane and the therapists at CII. Everything the children had said in their videotaped sessions had been repeated in their weekly psychotherapy with Cheryl Kent. There was simply no way that so many children could have made this up, that they could articulate such a corroborative sequence of events without there being some truth to it all.

The investigation into McMartin, started by Hoag, now eleven months old, had become a much broader inquiry. The District Attorney had given her immense power, a mandate to push forward, to prove their conspiracy theory—and push forward she did.

Following the raids of the local businesses, Detective Hoag prepared a request for several search warrants, all related to the inquiry of the staff at the Manhattan Ranch Preschool.

In the conclusive assessment of her official report, Detective Hoag stated that it was the "affiant's reasonable belief based on extensive past experience with this type of crime" that, if search warrants were issued, evidence would be uncovered that would support a felony crime. Hoag intended to search the Manhattan Ranch Preschool, and the homes and vehicles of all directors and employees of the preschool, as well as the home of Michael Ruby's parents.

Hoag, according to her report, suggested that "animal/fowl blood and semen" may be found at the Manhattan Ranch Preschool. She also stated that she'd consulted with Los Angeles County Sheriff's Department serologist Barbara Johnson, an eight-and-a-half-year veteran of the department, who'd related to Hoag that "blood and semen are detectible for six years," and referenced an FBI investigation that had detected a bloodstain that was forty-six years old.

Hoag, according to her report, believed that Lois Jansen, the school's director, had knowledge, to some degree, of the sexual and physical abuse cited in the report. Hoag referenced the four former McMartin students—Betsy Warren, Ashley Welsh, Becky Wendt, and Laura Lieberman—as having made specific statements that they'd been taken to Manhattan Ranch and molested during the time that Lois Jansen was in charge. Hoag emphasized Betsy Warren's disclosure that children were "photographed naked" and that Ray Buckey had "killed a chicken" in their presence.

Detective Hoag further stated that DPSS Inspector Richard Furikawa, after re-opening the Manhattan Ranch case in response to the Jacobson complaint of "sexual abuse," had returned to the school on June 8, 1984, and discovered "the school records to be in substandard condition." Furikawa had issued a formal warning to the school to have the records updated. He also cited the school for "improper supervision," observing that Michael Ruby was alone, "out of the visual contact of the other teachers," and was responsible for twenty-three students at one time. Hoag stated that she believed this was "ample time and opportunity for the suspect [Michael Ruby] to physically and/or sexually abuse children."

*****

The summer of 1984 had been a rough time for Michael Ruby, both at work and at home. The situation with Jimmy Jacobson rattled him more than he cared to admit. The man from the DPSS, Richard Furikawa, had come back to the school in early June to question him, which left Michael a bit unnerved.

"Did you smash snails in front of the kids, Mike?" Furikawa asked.

Michael shrugged. "Yeah, I guess I did, a couple of times."

"You know you shouldn't have done that, right?"

"Yeah, I know," Michael admitted. "I talked to my mom about it and she was disappointed in me. I didn't mean to scare 'em, but I'll never do it again."

Furikawa nodded, a stoic acceptance of Michael's contrition. "You know that some serious accusations have been made against you."

"I know," Michael replied, thinking that Furikawa was referring to the complaint of physical abuse, not knowing that he was being observed as a possible child molester. "But I would never do those things to a child, I swear. The only time I ever got rough with Jimmy was when he jumped on my back, and I had to wrestle him off. But I never hurt him, and he always seemed like he was having fun."

Inspector Furikawa left that day seemingly satisfied, as if all questions had been answered. Six weeks passed, and Michael hadn't heard anything. He thought it was over.

More bothersome to Michael was his situation at home. His relationship with his parents was in decline. Michael had been skipping church, far more than his father deemed acceptable. The Rubys worried that Michael was backsliding, what with the beer drinking, the punk music, his new look, and quite possibly experimenting with sex.

Michael had a girlfriend, a freshman-turning-sophomore, a pretty girl named Nicole. They'd met at church, and she was the first girl Michael had been serious with.

Prior to that summer, Michael planned to wait for marriage to have sex, a moral his folks had ingrained in him over the years. Still, every generation has its temptations, and the 1980s were especially challenging for a young man clinging to his virtues—the images of excess and exploration—all the things that make strict, church-going parents uptight.

Six months earlier, Paramount Pictures had released *Footloose*, a film about high school students in rural Oklahoma suppressed by the church's "no-dancing law"—the stereotypical coming-of-age story in a changing society. Glenn Ruby, to his credit, was hardly a Southern California version of the fanatical Reverend Shaw Moore, but Michael's life mirrored that storyline, the conflict between pop culture and the underpinnings of religious fundamentalism in America.

Michael, the "church kid," just wanted to be like the others—the surfers, the punks, the preps—and to live the full experience of Manhattan Beach. His parents, or at least their traditional beliefs, cramped his style.

Such was the case with the Rubys' annual summer vacation.

Each July, as part of their calling to get away from the fast-lane of Los Angeles County, the Rubys packed their station-wagon for a road trip. In the summer of 1984, Michael chose not to go—the first time he'd done so. His parents were upset—hurt, actually. They could see Michael slipping away. He knew how important this trip was to them, what it meant to their family as a whole, yet he didn't feel the need to be a part of it, as if he no longer cared. The child they'd raised, the boy who'd once walked with the Holy Spirit, had lost his moral compass.

Michael, however, just wanted to stay back and hang with his bros. He wanted to spend time with Nicole, to go to parties and drink beer, to surf when the sets were nice, and not be stuck in a station wagon in the thick of summer.

On top of that, Michael had a job. If he stayed, he could surf at the break of dawn, sleep through lunch, and head to Manhattan Ranch for a few hours before hitting beach parties at night. His older brother, Glenn, Jr., had skipped the Rubys summer excursion the year before, and he too was again staying home. If it was okay for Glenn, Jr., why wasn't it okay for Michael?

Michael's decision caused a bigger rift with his father than he'd expected. It ended with a fiery argument that resulted in Michael moving out.

A month earlier, on June 25, Michael had turned seventeen, California's legal threshold for a teenager to live on their own. Michael decided to exercise his rights, moving into the home of Edel Thomas, a family friend. The Thomas's sixteen-year-old grandson, Scott Stillings, was a life-long buddy of Michael's. They resided at 1500 Faymont in Manhattan Beach, just a mile-and-a-half from the Ruby home on Curtis Avenue, and less than half a mile from the Manhattan Ranch Preschool.

On the day the Rubys left for their vacation, Michael stopped by to wish them well. He hugged his parents and his sisters. His mother cried, while his father showed little emotion.

"I love you," Michael said, welling up as he embraced his mother.

"I love you, too," Evelyn said, pulling back and looking him in the eyes. "We will always love you and we will always be with you." She hugged him again.

Michael's father patted him on the back. "Be careful. And stay out of trouble," he said with a grin.

That scene reassured Michael, reminding him that everything would work itself out. This was just an obstacle, one of God's challenges that he would one day look back upon as a blessing, the day his parents allowed him to become a man. The Rubys knew that Michael needed to experience life and love and failure and fear, the same journey that awaits every teenager. As difficult as it was to look back at their boy, waving to him through their rearview window, the Rubys realized that whatever hardships he endured would help him to become the man they'd raised him to be.

*****

On Monday, July 23, just before 5:00 p.m., Detective Patty Picker placed a call to the Manhattan Ranch Preschool. Picker, a tall attractive former cheerleader at Lawndale High School, changed her voice, pretending to be a teenage girl. Picker was hoping to speak with Michael Ruby, so she was pleased when he answered.

"Manhattan Ranch," Michael said, figuring it was one of the afternoon parents.

"Hi, can I speak with Michael Ruby?"

Michael didn't recognize her voice, but he was flattered that a woman had called him.

"This is Michael. Who is this?"

"Hey, Michael," Picker said. "This is Patty. Do you remember me?"

"No," he replied, confused but intrigued.

"Yeah, we met at a party a few weeks ago."

Michael's memory couldn't keep up with his imagination. This was the first time a mystery girl called him at work. They spoke for a moment, small talk, and Patty drove the conversation in the direction of "where he lived."

"I moved out of my parents' house a few weeks ago," Michael said, proud to say that he was living the bachelor's life. "I'm staying over on Faymont."

"What's the address," Patty said. "Maybe I'll swing by."

"1500 Faymont," Michael said. "Definitely come by."

Patty asked for his phone number, which he gave to her. Michael ended the conversation trying to act cool. "You should cruise by the house. We can share a couple cold ones."

Michael hung up, feeling good, not realizing he'd just been played by a detective.

For the past weeks, Michael had been getting to work at 10:00 a.m., as the other teachers were staggering their vacations. That day, after a seven-hour shift, he wanted to bust out. The conversation with Patty had kept him there longer than he'd planned. He wanted to get home, grab his board, and head out for a late-afternoon set.

Just before 5:30 p.m., he stepped out of the preschool's entrance and hopped onto his moped. A small girl and her mother were walking out behind him. As he rode away, the girl called out, "Goodnight, Mr. Mike!" He waved back to her.

Michael headed westbound on 10th Street and turned right onto Harkness Street, riding north toward Manhattan Beach Boulevard.

Down the street, parked in an unmarked police car, sat Detective Jane Hoag. She watched Michael, charting his path. She slowly pulled out and followed him from a distance.

CHAPTER
19

Early the next morning, on Tuesday, July 24, Chuck Elliott arrived at the Torrance Municipal Court Building. He was an hour early for his scheduled hearing, where he faced a charge of domestic abuse against his former girlfriend, Jackie McGauley.

Three weeks prior, on Sunday, July 1, Chuck and Jackie had taken their kids to Knott's Berry Farm to see a relatively new attraction called Camp Snoopy. It had ended with their children nearly being placed in protective custody following an incident at a traffic light—a violent episode where Chuck punched Jackie in the head several times after she'd spat in his face. Later that night, after Chuck punched her again—his reaction to her throwing a shoe at him—Chuck called the police, worried that Jackie would use her .22 caliber pistol against him. The gun was removed from the home. A few days later, Jackie, fearing for her physical well-being, obtained a restraining order against Chuck and the police intervened. Chuck was escorted away from the apartment, prohibited from returning.

Chuck hadn't seen Jackie since that night, but as he stood in the lobby of the Torrance Courts building, he looked around for her, hoping they could talk beforehand. He wanted to reconcile, to avoid playing out their dispute in public. He kept looking but didn't see her.

When it was time for their case to be heard, Jackie failed to appear. The judge dropped all charges against Chuck.

According to Jackie, she'd mistakenly written the hearing on her calendar for July 26, not the 24th, explaining that she'd been under a "great deal of stress."

* * * * *

The next afternoon, Wednesday, July 25, a band of officers huddled on the sidewalk of Manhattan Avenue, a residential street in Hermosa Beach, not far from the shoreline. They stood in front of the home at 1348, ready to storm inside. Then they rushed up the walkway that led to the door.

Kathy Lorde, an instructor at the Manhattan Ranch Preschool, stood at the threshold between her kitchen and living room. She held the phone against her ear, speaking with a friend. Their conversation was interrupted by an abrupt, loud banging.

"Hold on a second," Kathy said to her friend, placing the phone to her chest. The sound came from the front of the house. The entrance door was open, but the screen door was locked. Someone was trying to rattle it open.

Kathy, thirty-seven, average height, thin, with brown hair and green eyes, had a seventeen-year-old-son Douglas, who, like Michael Ruby, was a few weeks away from entering his senior year at Mira Costa High. Kathy knew it couldn't be Douglas or one of his friends; they would never act this way. As the noise increased—the violent sound of someone trying to enter—it came to her, and the fear set in.

For the past few weeks, as rumors of what was alleged to have happened at the Manhattan Ranch Preschool ran rampant, Kathy received several threatening phone calls from an anonymous caller, a particular young male's voice.

"When school starts," the voice had said into her message recorder, "we're gonna blow up your house."

Kathy went to the Hermosa Beach Police Department and asked that they put a tracer on her phone, but they refused. They said it was probably just a teenage prank. After she "threw a tantrum," the police allowed her to file a report.

That same day, after she'd returned from the station, there were three more messages by the same caller. It seemed to Kathy that whenever she left home, for work or to run errands, the messages, the threats, were left on her machine. It was if she was being watched, or stalked.

The forceful pounding grew louder, too loud to ignore. It sounded like the screen door was about to come unhinged. Kathy heard muffled voices yelling from the porch, but couldn't make out the words. She set down the phone and hurried toward the front door, where several police stood on the porch. They yelled intensely as she approached.

"We have a search warrant," the lead officer hollered.

"I'm coming," she yelled as she stepped closer. But before she could get there, the door swung open.

Three officers barged in. A short stack of papers were thrown at her feet—the warrant documents. The lead officer grabbed her and forced her up against the wall. Two other officers walked past her toward the back of the house.

"You can't do that," she yelled as they stepped into the bedrooms. "You have to let me read this first."

"We can do anything we want," said the officer holding her. "We have a warrant."

Kathy Lorde had been in the workplace for several years, never a non-working housewife like many of the women in the beach cities. Kathy wasn't the type to see herself as a victim, even in a situation like this.

"Get your hands off me," Kathy told the officer. He released his grip and stepped back. He, too, began searching the house, rummaging through drawers and cabinets. Kathy hurried back to the kitchen and grabbed the phone. Her friend was still on the line, listening.

Walking up the outside steps and through the opened doorway was Manhattan Beach Police Sergeant Jim Noble, the man in charge. According to Kathy, Noble had a reputation for having "a tremendous temper," that even people who lived in Hermosa Beach knew the Manhattan Beach sergeant as an intimidating man with a tendency to use filthy language.

Kathy spoke into the receiver, giving her friend the play-by-play. "I gotta go," Kathy said. "I need to call my husband and my lawyer."

At first, Kathy said that Sergeant Noble "didn't address her in any particular way," but he turned to one of the officers and said, "Get her off the phone. It's irritating the hell out of me."

Kathy knew her rights. At least she thought she did.

"I'm calling my attorney," she said.

Sergeant Noble was not pleased, but he didn't stop her. Moments later, Kathy's son Douglas walked up the outside steps and into the foyer.

Douglas had witnessed the entire raid from the base of the sidewalk. He'd seen the police approach the steps, and he'd listened to them as they rushed the door. They were angry, fired up to get inside. Douglas was frightened for his mother. He knew she was a fighter, a proud woman who wouldn't stand back silently while these men tore through her home. He knew she would be vocal if she felt mistreated.

Douglas, however, also knew what he'd seen and heard from Sergeant Jim Noble just moments before, and his mother had no idea what she was up against. Douglas heard the ire in Noble's voice, a vicious tone that invited anyone, any suspect of this inquiry, to challenge his authority.

Douglas stepped into the house, and he realized his foresight was correct. His mother was already getting into it with the sergeant.

"I'll arrest you for having that open beer can on the table," Noble warned her.

"You can't do that."

"Watch me," Noble replied. "I'll have you in that squad car so fast it'll make your head spin."

Kathy saw Douglas walk in, and she went to him. They hugged. Douglas pulled her to the side and spoke quietly.

"Mom, listen to me," he said. "You have to be quiet. Please, don't say anything."

Kathy started to pull back as if she were going to openly express a piece of her mind, to show her son that what these men were doing wasn't right, that she was innocent, and that she wouldn't stand for this. But he pulled her in tightly. He didn't need her to tell him what he already knew.

"Mom," Douglas said, "this man is not okay. He's crazy. I'm telling you, I've listened to what he's been saying, and he's disturbed. He'll take you away if you give him the chance. *Don't* give him the chance."

Douglas had made his point, and he'd made it well. Kathy sat back and bit her tongue, allowing the police to do their job. Kathy grabbed the search warrant, sifting through it. It took her nearly forty-five minutes to digest it all; it read like a creepy novel, the graphic descriptions of alleged sexual abuse.

As Kathy read further into the report, she discovered that the basis of the search warrant was related to allegations that occurred on the grounds of Manhattan Ranch, all of which had taken place well before she worked there.

Kathy's employment at Manhattan Ranch had started three weeks earlier, on July 2, nearly two months after the first allegations against Michael Ruby were made. She'd only worked there a total of sixteen days. Kathy was astonished that the police were so misinformed about her brief history with the school, and she confronted Sergeant Noble about it.

"Are you here about the preschool?" Kathy asked Noble. "Because if you are, so you know, I just started at Manhattan Ranch a few weeks ago."

"We're not here about Manhattan Ranch, ma'am," Noble said.

"Well, that's not what it says in this warrant," Kathy replied, holding up the document. Sergeant Noble did not comment. "Then why are you here?" Kathy probed.

"We're here because of McMartin," Noble answered.

"But I didn't work at Manhattan Ranch when McMartin was open," Kathy replied. "How could I possibly be involved with McMartin?"

"Take my word for it," Noble said. "We're here because of McMartin."

Kathy couldn't believe that her home was being turned upside down based on a search warrant that, according to the officer running the operation, was misstated—that the true intent of the raid contradicted what had been authorized.

But just as troubling, Kathy realized as she continued to read over the warrant, was that she wasn't the only one experiencing this bogus search and seizure. The police were simultaneously raiding the homes of her fellow staffers at Manhattan Ranch, including forensic searches of their vehicles.

Kathy looked out the window, down to the street where her 1966 Ford sedan was parked. The police were already tearing it apart, removing the seats and opening the side panels.

The search of Kathy Lorde's property lasted three hours.

When it was all said and done, nothing was found to support the claim that she was a co-conspirator in an underground child pornography network.

PART IV
Forsaken

CHAPTER 20

Wednesday, July 25, 1984

As police conducted raids throughout the South Bay—including the Curtis Avenue home of Glenn and Evelyn Ruby—Michael sat in the office at Manhattan Ranch, eyes on the clock. Unsure what he would do that night, he figured something was going on. Michael had gotten comfortable with his new lifestyle, enjoying the freedom of being out on his own.

Still, as Michael had found out, freedom can be lonely, especially for one not used to such solitude. Life at the Edel Thomas home was fine, a nice family setting, but they were not his family. Despite their kindness and the comfort they'd provided, their hospitality was no substitute for love. The warm spirit of the Ruby home had a place in Michael's heart. He loved and respected his parents for who they were, the same love and respect they had shown by giving him his space. Michael missed them more than they knew, and he looked forward to seeing them upon their return.

When the hand struck 5:30 p.m., Michael walked out the entrance, hopped onto his moped, and rode off. Unknown to Michael, sitting in an unmarked police car, detectives Jane Hoag and John McKewen conducted surveillance, "awaiting the departure of Suspect Michael Ruby." They made a positive identification the moment he came out of the building: "Caucasian male, five-foot-six, brown hair, wearing gray shorts, yellow thongs, a striped green-and-white jacket with a white-and-blue T-shirt."

As usual, Michael headed westbound on 10th Street toward Harkness Street. He reached the intersection and turned right. Detective Hoag radioed Michael's direction of travel, and before Michael could reach 11th Street, a police car shot through the upcoming intersection, sped toward him, and screeched to a swinging stop, blocking his path.

Michael braked and looked around, wondering if he'd ridden into the middle of an ongoing crime scene. Two officers stepped out of the squad car and approached him.

"Michael Ruby?" the first officer asked.

"Yeah…I'm Michael Ruby."

"Michael Ruby, you're under arrest."

"What?"

"Place your hands behind your back."

Michael did as the officers commanded. Handcuffs were applied and ratcheted tightly.

"You have the right to remain silent…" and it went on from there.

The officers placed Michael in the back of the squad car, mounted the moped to a rack on the bumper, and transported him to the Manhattan Beach Police Department. With his hands cuffed behind his back, Michael was led inside, booked, and taken into an interrogation room where he waited.

The room consisted of four concrete walls with a two-way mirror on the wall opposite the door. Michael sat in one of two folding chairs placed on opposite sides of a small table. The cuffs had been removed, and his hands trembled as he tried to rub out the soreness in his wrists. He stared at the table, teary-eyed and confused.

He assumed that the Jacobsons had filed a complaint against him. *But it's not true. No one could possibly believe this is true.*

At 5:45 p.m., Detective John McKewen entered the room and approached Michael. He verified that Michael had been advised of his Miranda rights. He asked Michael if he wished to give up his right to speak with an attorney, or to have an attorney before or during the interrogation.

"Yes," Michael replied. He wanted to talk, to straighten it out.

Detective McKewen explained that certain charges had been made against him; that a young girl, Emma Jamison, had claimed that Michael had taken nude photographs of her while at the preschool.

Michael was stunned. "That's not true," he declared, shaking his head. "I never took *any* pictures of *any* kids."

"Well," McKewen replied, "She said you molested her."

"I never molested any child…never, ever."

Detective McKewen looked Michael over, sizing him up. He stood and walked out.

Michael, confounded, thought it through. He hardly knew Emma Jamison. Outside of Jimmy Jacobson, he didn't know of any other child who'd complained of anything.

Several minutes later, McKewen returned, accompanied by Detective Jane Hoag. She sat in the chair across from Michael.

Detective Hoag looked him in the eyes, a judgmental glare, the way a parent looks at a child while anticipating a lie. Michael shifted in his seat.

"Do you know Raymond Buckey?" Hoag asked.

"Raymond Buckey? No, I've never met the man."

"Do you know any of the teachers who worked at the McMartin Preschool?"

"No, no way," he said. "I don't know any of those people."

Hoag asked Michael about his parents and his current living situation. He explained how his folks were on vacation and that he'd been living with his friend, Scott Stillings.

Detective McKewen asked, "Do you have a girlfriend?

"Yes," Michael replied. "Nicole...Nicole Dent."

"Can you describe her?"

"She's pretty, real cute," Michael said. "She's short, very petite."

"She's petite?"

"Yes."

"How old is she?"

"She's fifteen."

In the police report, Detective Hoag noted that Michael's girlfriend had a "very small build."

The interview continued for hours, and once it grew monotonous, they threw him a curve.

"Have you ever met any of the teachers who worked at the McMartin Preschool?"

"No. I told you that earlier. I've never met any of them."

Detective Hoag asked if he'd ever left the school grounds during working hours. Michael said that he "occasionally went to Manhattan Beach Hardware" for certain supplies, such as "light bulbs, keys, glue, duct tape, paint, and a ladder."

By 7:00 p.m., the interrogation hit a wall. Michael wouldn't break. Detective Hoag played her cards.

"Tell me about the snail, Mike," she said out of the blue.

"The snail?"

"Yes, Mike, the snail."

"Well, one time I smashed a snail in front of the kids and kicked it into the bushes," he said. "One of the kids ran and told Mrs. Jansen, and she told me that I shouldn't've done that."

"But you smashed it?"

"Yes."

Detective Hoag redirected her focus back to Jimmy Jacobson. "Can you think of any reason why this boy would make an accusation against you of a sexual nature?" she asked.

"No," Michael said, shaking his head. "I don't believe that he did."

"Oh, so you think his mother just made this up because she couldn't pay her bill?"

"Yes, I do."

"Really?"

Michael thought about what he'd said. "No...I don't know. I just know that I did *not* abuse Jimmy in any way, and if he said I did, then I don't know why."

"Did you ever expose yourself to a child, Mike?"

"No."

"Did you ever take Jimmy into the bathroom?"

"No."

"Did any child at the school ever touch your private parts?"

"No. No. Never!"

"Jimmy said you put your mouth on his penis, Mike. Did that happen?

"This is crazy," Michael shouted. He pushed back into his chair. "I don't want to talk anymore. I can't believe this."

Michael's eyes welled, and he became withdrawn. Hoag asked him if he knew the present whereabouts of his parents.

"I don't know," he said. "Last I heard, they were in Texas seeing my grandmother."

Detective Hoag told Michael that she would stop the interview since he'd said he didn't want to talk anymore. "Let me know if you change your mind," Hoag said as she stood. Michael looked up and said, "Okay, scratch that. I'll talk. I want to talk. I'm sorry for how I reacted. I'm sorry."

Hoag sat down and McKewen stood behind her.

Michael spoke slowly. "These accusations are completely false," he said, and began to weep. He wanted to talk openly, to be truthful, but he couldn't catch his breath. His mind raced with images of his afternoons at the preschool, and he couldn't fit any of his past experiences with these accusations. *What are they talking about?*

"Did anything *close* to this happen?" McKewen asked.

"No," Michael replied, shaking his head.

"Do you know this girl named Emma that we mentioned earlier?" Hoag inquired.

"I think she's the black girl, but I hardly know her," he said, and gave an account from a month earlier when the child's father had come to pick her up. She'd left her jacket in the classroom, so Michael took her back to get it. When they got to the room, there was no one else there, just Michael and Emma. He said they were in the room "maybe three minutes" looking for the jacket. They found a jacket that had an "E" on it, but when they got back to her father, he said it wasn't Emma's. Michael put the jacket back in the teacher's room.

"I hadn't met her before that," Michael said, "and I never had any contact with her since. She wasn't one of my kids."

"Is there any reason she would've accused you of sexually abusing her?"

"No...no way."

"Well, she said you made her perform oral sex on you," Hoag revealed. "That's what she said about *you*."

"There's no way," Michael declared. "There's never enough time for that. I'm never even alone with the kids."

Hoag sat back for a moment. She looked over to McKewen, then back to Michael. She leaned in and spoke softly.

"This little girl...Emma...she just had a medical exam, and a doctor confirmed that she has an *abnormal anus*."

"Don't tell me that," Michael cried. "Don't say that. I'm a virgin. I've never had sex, not even with my girlfriend, I swear. I'm a Christian." He lurched over and whimpered.

The detectives gave him a moment. Once he gathered himself, they asked him about his "bedroom at home," if he shared a room or if he had his own room. He said that he shared a room with his brother, Glenn, Jr., and everything on the right side of the room was Glenn's.

Detective McKewen stepped up to the table holding a bag. He dumped the contents onto the table—items confiscated during the raid of Michael's parents' home, which the police identified as "nude and sexually explicit magazines."

"These were found on *your* side of the room, Mike," McKewen told him. "How do you explain that?"

"I've never read those. They aren't mine, I swear."

Michael admitted that he'd "seen a *Playboy*" in the past and that he'd seen his brother reading those types of magazines, but not him.

Hoag noted in her report that "Arrestee Ruby has repeatedly been told that he didn't have to talk to the police and that he could have an attorney" if he desired.

"No," Michael said time and again, "I want to talk...to get this straightened out."

At 9:20 p.m., the interview concluded. Detectives Hoag and McKewen left the interview room. Michael remained alone for another hour. Periodically, he cried like a scared little boy, powerless against the accusations. He'd seen the look in Detective Hoag's eyes and knew she didn't believe him.

Around 11:00 p.m., an officer entered the room. "You have a phone call. Come on."

Michael jumped to his feet and followed the officer down the corridor to a desk with a blinking phone.

It was Margaret Moore, a close family friend.

"Mike, it's me, Margaret. Are you okay? Are you all right, honey?"

"I'm okay," he replied, choking up, trying to hide his tearful face from the officer standing next to him. "I don't understand. I don't know why they're saying I did these things."

Margaret told him that the police had ransacked his parents' home. They'd broken the back window to get in. Greg Moore, her son, and Mike's brother had come home to find the house turned upside down. The search warrant had been placed on the dining room table.

"I didn't do it," Michael insisted. "You have to believe me."

"I know you didn't, Mike," she said, "and we're doing everything possible to get a hold of your parents. You just stay strong, okay?"

They spoke until the officer signaled that his time was up.

Michael was taken to the back of the department and placed in a small holding cell. A guard came in and took his shoes, socks, and wallet; he was given a pair of paper slippers and a small blanket, no bigger than a beach towel. The concrete walls were ice cold.

After a few minutes, an officer brought Michael a melted cheese sandwich, but he was too nauseated to eat it. He had moments of calmness, then spontaneous bouts of crying. He wondered if he was being punished in some way for his recent behavior, if his backsliding had finally caught up with him, the karma that follows life's bad choices.

In the solitude of his holding cell, having not spoken to God in six months, Michael got on his hands and knees, tears running down his face, and he prayed. *God, help me...please, Lord, help me. Forgive me for the life I've been living...for all of my sins and transgressions...please, Lord, forgive me...please deliver me from this place.*

As midnight neared, Michael lay down on the concrete floor with the small blanket wrapped over his shoulders. He closed his eyes and fell asleep.

* * * * *

Shortly after 3:00 a.m., the cell door was flung open by a guard. "Okay, get up! Get up. You're leaving," the guard said.

Oh, God, thank you. Thank you, Lord. Michael thought his prayers had been answered. Margaret Moore must've worked a miracle, because there was no way his parents had made it back that quickly.

Two Manhattan Beach police officers entered, one taller than the other.

"Put your hands behind your back," the taller officer said.

"Why?" Michael asked. "Where am I going?"

"Put your hands behind your back," the officer yelled. The other officer turned Michael around and forced his hands behind his back. He put the cuffs on Michael's wrists. Michael felt a sharp pain and asked if they would loosen them. The officers ignored him.

As much as the carbon steel embedded in his wrists wrenched, the letdown of knowing he wasn't going home hurt even more. When he'd fallen asleep on the floor of his cell, all was calm. It was his only method of escape, elevating him above the madness. Once he'd awoken, the nightmare continued.

The officers led Michael out of the building and into the back of their squad car. As the car pulled out, Michael spoke nicely. "Hey...these cuffs really hurt...ya think you can loosen them up a bit?"

The taller officer drove while the other sat in the passenger seat. The taller officer snapped back, "Kid, for the things you did, they're gonna lock you up forever. This is *big time*. You have no idea."

"I didn't do it," Michael replied. "I swear to God, I'm not a molester. I have a girlfriend...seriously."

The officer in the passenger seat looked back at him, shaking his head slowly. "Let me tell you somethin', *dude*. You are so *fucked*! Child molesters last about two seconds in jail."

"Is that where I'm going? Am I going to jail?"

The two officers looked at each other and laughed. The taller officer looked at Michael through the rearview mirror.

"You don't even wanna know where you're going," he said. The other officer kept shaking his head in disgust.

Michael's face turned white, his eyes welled. "I swear to God, I didn't do this stuff—none of it. I'm innocent. I swear."

The taller officer took a somber tone. "Are you really innocent? Really?"

"Yes," Michael spoke. "I swear."

The taller officer was quiet for a moment, then said, "Well, that's unfortunate, because you're still gonna take it in the ass!"

Both officers laughed again. Michael fell back in his seat.

After twenty minutes, Michael again tried to warm up to them, hoping they would give him some details. He looked at the computer screen mounted below the dash.

"Hey," Michael said, leaning up to the metal gate, "do you guys have everything on me in that computer?"

"Sure do," the tall officer answered.

"Are my speeding tickets on there?"

"Let me see what the computer comes up with," the other officer said as he punched the keyboard. Michael looked into the screen, expecting his personal information to be displayed.

The officer pressed a button, and "Dickhead" appeared.

He looked back at Michael with a smirk. "See, even the computer knows about you."

The officers laughed louder than the time before.

Michael slumped back in the seat and gazed out the window. They headed east on Interstate 10.

CHAPTER 21

On the western end of Downey, tucked conspicuously behind the Los Amigos Country Club, is Los Padrinos Juvenile Hall, the equivalent of county jail to the youths of Los Angeles. Kids stay anywhere from two hours to two months, sometimes a year, depending on the nature of their alleged crimes. The facility holds up to six hundred children, some as young as eight years old. They hold first-time offenders, some with multiple priors—carjackers, armed robbers, sex offenders, as well as less violent druggies and vandals.

To some, Los Padrinos is a refuge from the chaos of the neighborhoods they were born into, sanctuary from the poverty and degradation that awaited their return. Inmates called it "LP," and it wasn't so bad for those with nowhere else to go. The average stay was about twenty-one days, a sort of way station before re-entering society or taking the next step into the hardened journey of the State Department of Corrections' Division of Juvenile Justice.

For Michael Ruby, the journey had just begun.

The two officers escorted Michael through the front entrance and into a waiting room. They removed his handcuffs and ordered him to sit down on a bench next to two other inmates. The officers left.

For the first time, the harsh reality of Michael's incarceration set in. A guard came through a security door and led him and the others down a corridor and into a latrine. He ordered them to undress and take showers. He tossed them each a set of beige trousers, a white T-shirt, underwear, a pair of socks, and black tennis shoes with white stripes.

The guard picked up Michael's clothes. "You won't need these anymore."

After they showered, the guard led them down a corridor. One of the other inmates asked a question. The guard, a well-built black man, stopped, turned around, and got in the kid's face.

"Shut the fuck up," the guard said, eyeballing the kid up and down. "You don't talk to me. You don't ask me shit. Got it?"

The kid, a heavy-set Latino, younger than Michael, nodded and looked to the ground.

The guard led them to a room with a long table. Three trays of food were placed in a row.

"Sit down and eat," the guard ordered, "and don't say a fuckin' word."

Michael sat, taking the tray on the right. The tray had four sections—a square biscuit, orange wedge, beef soaked in gravy, and a small carton of milk. Too upset to eat, Michael slid the tray to the heavy-set Latino. The kid dug in.

In prison, it's well understood that child molesters are the lowest form of life; the accused are presumed guilty and are at high risk of being beaten or killed. With that in mind, precautions are taken to protect high-profile inmates, those like Michael Ruby whose potential link to the McMartin case made him an asset to the DA's office. Michael had to be protected—yet there was still time to see if he would break.

Michael was taken to a unit called "the Box"—a concrete compartment reserved for violent criminals and sex offenders. Situated one on top of the other, they looked like cages in an animal laboratory, with just enough space to fit a medium-sized body—LP's version of solitary confinement.

As the guard opened the Box, Michael stopped and looked inside—nothing more than a cement cube. He ducked his head to step in, turning his face from the fume of chemicals used to mask the stench of defecation.

The guard nudged him in, making sure his legs were clear. Michael crouched over and looked back at the guard who held the door open. Bright light streamed over the man's shoulders. The guard wore no expression, no sympathy for the teenager accused of raping a little girl.

The door slammed shut.

* * * * *

About ten hours later, at 2:50 p.m. on Thursday, July 26, Detective Jane

Hoag conducted an interview with Lisha Jacobson, the five-year-old sister of Jimmy.

According to Hoag's report, Lisha "denied sexual abuse," but something in the girl's responses to Hoag's questions "caused [Hoag] to strongly suspect" that abuse had occurred.

"Is Mr. Mike nice, Lisha?" Hoag inquired.

"Mr. Mike is a criminal," Lisha replied. "I'm glad he's in jail because he did bad things. He's bad. He made me throw up."

Lisha went on to describe how Mr. Mike had performed sexual acts on children, but she denied that he'd abused her.

"Did you tell Cheryl [Dr. Kent] the truth about Mr. Mike?" Hoag asked.

"Yes," Lisha said. "Mr. Mike did a bad thing."

Hoag asked Lisha a series of questions about specific sexual acts, but Lisha continued to say "nothing happened to me," and she denied that Michael had molested her in any way.

"I'm afraid to talk about Mr. Mike," Lisa explained. "He took Jimmy away from the school."

The interview dragged on. Lisha went back and forth, one minute describing a sexual act performed by Michael Ruby, using the anatomically correct dolls that Hoag placed before her, and the next minute describing perfectly normal behavior by Michael and the other teachers. Hoag noted that Lisha became "uncomfortable" as the dolls were undressed, and she eventually became so "anxious and evasive in answering questions" that Hoag concluded the session at 4:30 p.m. The interview lasted an hour-and-a-half.

While Hoag interviewed Lisha Jacobson, Detective Patty Picker took a call from Karl Dolan, the father of a former Manhattan Ranch student.

"I'm not sure if my daughter was molested," Dolan said, "but back in April, when she attended the preschool, she started acting peculiar."

"How do you mean?"

"Well, the teachers told us she was doing poorly…acting spacey. So we took her to an eye doctor in Torrance, and he said she was fine, but that she lacked self-confidence.

"Not long after, she started getting headaches and acting up, really misbehaving, and then she started wetting the bed. One night, she walked into the kitchen and peed on the floor right in front of me and her mother.

"Before she started going to Manhattan Ranch, she was a splendid artist," Dolan said, "but once there, she just started scribbling nonsense; she really digressed. So we took her out of the school."

"How is she now?" Picker asked.

"She's great, a complete change of attitude," Dolan said.

"I appreciate the information," Picker said, "This is very helpful."

"So you know," Dolan said, "my wife and I just had dinner with a group of Manhattan Ranch parents, and we're all amazed that each of our kids have had the same symptoms."

Dolan provided the names of three other parents for Detective Picker to speak with.

* * * * *

After several hours in the Box, Michael fell asleep. When he came to, he had no way to gauge the time. He felt warm, very warm. His body was drenched with sweat.

Michael lay on his back and lifted his legs at an angle to stretch out, the only way to fully extend. He kept his body against the cool concrete with his knees bent and his hands in prayer position between his face and the floor.

Michael thought of his parents. He thought of God. He drifted in and out of consciousness and, eventually, emotionally fatigued, he fell into a deep sleep.

Michael woke, shivering. The concrete surface had chilled his body. The sweat that had drenched his T-shirt had turned to a cold, damp cloth stuck to his torso. He rocked back and forth, trying to warm himself. It did no good. His arms and legs cramped as he squirmed atop the smooth, cool surface. Minutes turned into hours. He went in and out of consciousness.

Sometime later, Michael sat up, feeling hopeful when he heard the distant sound of the door in the corridor open and the footsteps of someone approaching his cell. The lock turned and the door opened. Light flushed in, a piercing brightness. Michael covered his face with his forearm.

"Get up. Let's go," the voice said. It took a few seconds for Michael's eyes to adjust, and when they did, he realized it was a different guard—the night guard.

The guard escorted Michael to the nearest latrine, then led him to a separate room and told him to wait. Michael was prepared to go back to his concrete cell, but the guard said, "Let's go," and stepped toward the security door that separated solitary from the rest of the facility. He looked back at Michael and said, "Come on! You got a visitor."

Michael, elated, figured his parents had arrived. But when he got to the visitor's hall, he saw his youth pastor, John Woods, sitting at a table with a sympathetic look. Michael gave him a long, loving hug. Michael cried in his arms.

"I didn't do these things, John," Michael said. "I swear."

"I believe you, Mike," Pastor John said. "You don't have to explain yourself to me."

"What about my parents?"

"They're on their way back, but I don't know how long it'll be. Just hang in there."

Pastor John said it had taken many hours to get in to see him since John didn't have parental consent.

Within minutes, the guard stepped over. "Okay, finish up."

Michael and John held hands and said a prayer before Michael went back to the Box.

This time, before the guard shut the door, Michael asked, "How long will I be in here? I think my parents are on their way."

The guard shrugged. The door closed. Michael, again, curled up and wept.

* * * * *

Detective Hoag located a phone number where she could reach Michael's parents. They had crossed the border of California by way of Arizona and were headed to the city of Highland, a small community in the southwest corner of San Bernardino County. Each year, upon their return, the Ruby family passed through Highland to visit Glenn's sister, Lillian. They arrived at dusk.

The moment they pulled up, Lillian rushed out of the house and asked if they had spoken to their boys.

"Yes," Glenn said, "just a couple of nights ago. Why?"

"Michael's in jail," Lillian said. "They left a number for you to call. You need to call now."

Lillian handed Glenn a piece of paper that had a phone number written below the name "Det. Jane Hoag." Lillian had just spoken with their friend, Margaret Moore, who'd said that their house had been ransacked by the police. "They had a search warrant," Lillian said. "They're accusing Michael of child molesting."

When Glenn Ruby got through to Hoag, the detective said, "Mr. Ruby, I wanted to inform you that your son's been charged with felony child molestation."

"Yes, I've heard about your charges," Glenn replied, "and I think this is all totally absurd. You didn't need to arrest him. The state's known about these crazy accusations for months, and there's no proof of anything."

"I understand you're upset," Hoag replied. "But you can see your son as soon as you make arrangements with the detention center. He's at Los Padrinos Juvenile Hall in Downey."

"Well, I think this is all a big lie," Glenn said. "My son's being framed, and you know it."

Glenn hung up and retrieved his roadmap to chart the fastest route to Downey, 66 miles away.

* * * * *

Two hours later, Glenn and Evelyn Ruby sat in the visitor's hall at Los Padrinos, anxious for their son to appear. They had left their daughters in the waiting area outside of the secured section, trusting that fifteen-year-old Linda could watch over nine-year-old Lisa.

Evelyn, even though she was aware of the charges, couldn't grasp what was happening. She tried to convince herself that it was nothing serious, that he was only being held because he was a minor.

Glenn knew better, that the police had a plan. The whole circus represented something much bigger. Back in May, when the allegations at Manhattan Ranch surfaced, Glenn worried where things were headed, and he wanted Michael to quit. Michael, however, wasn't in the habit of listening to his father, and they'd ended up here, at Los Padrinos. Glenn took no solace in being right.

A door buzzed and opened. A guard walked in with Michael at his side. Michael looked in his parents' direction, but he just stopped and stared. His eyes squinted, shifting from side to side, a confused and distrusting look.

Evelyn's face flushed and she broke into tears, holding on to Glenn. "They've turned him into a zombie. He can't even smile."

As Michael stepped closer, his face lit up, realizing they'd finally arrived.

The guard stepped away. Michael rushed into their embrace. He trembled, refusing to let go.

"I don't know what's happening," Michael cried. "I don't know why they're saying these things,"

Michael pulled back and wiped his face. "When can I go home? Get me out of here, please," he pleaded. "When can I go?"

The Rubys had no answer; they could only prescribe faith. They hugged and kissed him the entire visit, and they prayed together for nearly an hour. Michael kept saying how scared he was, and he emphasized to his father how important God had become in his life. He begged his father for forgiveness, and he speculated that God may be punishing him for all of his backsliding.

"God is *not* punishing you," Glenn reasoned. "*People* are punishing you, and they're misguided. God loves you. And God will stand by you through this. He will be with you every step of the way. And *we* will be with you every step of the way."

Moments later, the guard stepped in.

"Visiting hour's over," he said. "You got two minutes."

They stood for a final group hug and a good cry before Michael was led away.

* * * * *

The next morning, Michael was given breakfast—biscuits and gravy, two orange wedges, and milk. He hadn't eaten since the morning of the day before. He scarfed the biscuits and gravy; he chugged the milk.

Michael went through a brief orientation with a counselor, a forty-year-old Latino man.

"Don't you feel awful for doing all this shit to these little kids?" the counselor asked him. "What kind of a person are you?"

"I didn't do it," Michael said, all passion gone from his denial.

But the counselor didn't care. His job was to make sure Michael understood how things worked at LP. Once he got his message across, the counselor looked up at the guard. "Take him to his cell."

Michael dreaded the thought of going back to the Box. But this time the guard led him to a standard cell, a ten-foot by ten-foot space with a high ceiling—a luxury suite in comparison to what he'd just lived through. He had a cot and a toilet; he could stand up and stretch at will. Michael said a prayer, thanking God for this blessing.

For the most part, as his first days in prison went by, Michael was kept isolated from the general population. His label of *child molester* remained a secret.

One evening, however, while sitting in the TV room, a counselor walked by with an inmate at his side. The man saw Michael on the couch and, knowing of the charges against him, yelled across the room, "They're gonna hang you by the balls for what you did, son."

Michael turned away, demoralized, fearing that it was only a matter of time until the word spread.

But he wouldn't be at LP for long.

On his eleventh day, in the early morning, Michael went through the normal routine, standing in formation with his unit. A guard approached. "Get your stuff together. You're leaving."

Michael, euphoric, thought he was going home. But they didn't take him out front. Instead, they walked him to the back of the facility where a line of inmates stood next to a white bus. The guard chained Michael's ankles to the last guy in line. The inmates stepped into the bus, the first man walking to the back.

Once on the bus, Michael turned to the guy next to him, a black kid who looked to be sixteen or seventeen.

"Hey, where we goin'?" Michael asked, truly confused.

The kid looked at him strangely. "We goin' to Eastlake."

"Eastlake" was another name for Central Juvenile Hall, located at 1605 Eastlake Avenue in downtown Los Angeles. Unlike LP, it wasn't a temporary holding tank. Those transferred to Eastlake were staying for a while.

CHAPTER
22

On the morning of Thursday, August 23, Chuck Elliott's column in the *Daily Breeze* was headlined, "It's hard to breathe easy when your child has to be monitored." The article was short but serious, an essay on children who suffer from apnea due to heart irregularities. It described how their parents were required to learn CPR and other means of resuscitation in the event of life-threatening episodes.

For Chuck, the piece was rather prophetic considering that he, too, would soon have trouble breathing easy.

In the early afternoon, Chuck pulled up to his father's house in Hermosa Beach. He turned off the ignition, stepped out, and noticed two men parked in an old Plymouth with tinted windows. *Wow, real inconspicuous.* He'd just spotted the most obvious undercover cops in the South Bay. Chuck got back into his car and drove away.

Since being kicked out of Jackie's apartment, prior to the hearing date, Jackie had complained that Chuck owed her money, that he'd short-paid his rent. Through their once joint attorney, Francis Martin, Chuck argued that their mutual debts had offset the amount, so he owed her nothing. According to Chuck, Jackie grew hysterical on the phone, telling Martin she would "destroy Chuck."

For some time, Chuck had worried that Jackie would get back at him by going after his ex-wife, Robin; that she would make a speculative statement implicating Robin's preschool, the Parkway Preschool, as part of the on-going investigation into McMartin. As unstable as Chuck believed Jackie to be, there was no doubt that her small group of Believers had the attention of the police and the district attorney. If one of them said, "My child said they were taken to the Parkway Preschool in Redondo Beach," the cops would be there the next day with a warrant.

Chuck called a friend for advice, a captain in the Torrance Police Department. The officer recommended an attorney, C. Ramsey Randolph. Chuck went directly to Randolph's office.

"I'm not sure why," Chuck said to Randolph, "but the police are tailing me. Can you find out why? Will you represent me?"

Ramsey agreed to take Chuck on as a client, but he needed to know more about this woman, Jackie McGauley. Chuck gave him a summation of their relationship—from the joke contest to the laundromat rendezvous to the rushed cohabitation to the violent episode at Camp Snoopy to the .22 caliber pistol she'd pulled out of her closet.

Ramsey called the Hermosa Beach Police Department. A male officer came on the line, and he asked Ramsey to confirm that his client was Chuck Elliott.

"Do you know where he is?" the officer asked.

"Yes," Ramsey replied. "He's sitting right here in my office."

"Well, we have a warrant for his arrest, so keep him there. We'll be there in a few minutes."

"What's the charge?"

"Child molestation."

"Who's the alleged victim?"

"I can't give you the child's name over the phone," the officer said, "but I can tell you that it's the daughter of his ex-girlfriend, Jackie McGauley."

Randolph looked at Chuck who sat dumbfounded, unable to piece it all together. He'd only heard "victim." *Victim of what?*

"All right," Randolph said to the officer. "We'll be here."

Randolph hung up and shook his head.

"What's goin' on?" Chuck asked.

"Jackie's accusing you of molesting her daughter."

"What? No fuckin' way."

"Yes, she is," Randolph said. "The cops are on their way. They have a warrant for your arrest."

Randolph told Chuck to "say nothing" until he could get a copy of the police report to determine what evidence they had.

"They're going to book you, stick you in a cell, and you'll be out as soon as we can post bail," Randolph said. "They won't bother questioning you, because I won't allow it."

Within minutes, two officers arrived to Ramsey's office and arrested Chuck. He was handcuffed and read his rights.

According to Chuck, as if he'd not been humiliated enough, the police took an "unnecessary detour" on their way to the department—a drive by Jackie's apartment. Jackie and Julie stood on the curb, looking on as the squad car passed. Chuck slumped in the backseat.

The officers escorted Chuck into the station. He was booked and placed in a cell—a "hot box," he called it. The late-August weather had been unseasonably leaden. The cell had no windows, no air circulation. Chuck sat in a corner, beads of sweat dripping from his forehead, contemplating how he'd ended up in this place.

In a matter of hours, Chuck's father managed to come up with the five thousand dollars he needed for bail. Chuck was released.

Lieutenant Michael Lavin of the Hermosa Beach Police Department had been assigned to the case. Lt. Lavin said that a crime report had been filed on August 9, two weeks earlier, but he wouldn't disclose its origin. "As far as we know," Lavin stated, "this is totally isolated from the McMartin case."

According to the report, "a doctor" had informed the police of Julie's sexual abuse after her "examination at CII" where the child's mother had taken her before filing the complaint.

From Jackie's perspective, she "became suspicious that her daughter was molested," as the child had "shown symptoms" that were similar to those she'd displayed while attending McMartin. Since leaving McMartin and entering the child into therapy, those symptoms had "cleared up." But recently, during the time she'd lived with Chuck, the symptoms had come back. So she took her daughter to CII to be examined by the same doctor who'd previously examined her. After diagnosing the child "abused" a second time, CII's pediatrician contacted the police and informed them that the child had named Chuck Elliott as the culprit.

As his release paperwork was finalized, Chuck met with Randolph. "There's a media pack out there," Randolph warned Chuck. "Do you want to go out the back door?"

"Hell no," Chuck said. "If I do that, I'll look guilty. I'm going out there and telling them *exactly* what this is."

Randolph liked the strategy. At this point, why run from it? Chuck's story was going to be on the front page anyway; he may as well get out in front of it.

Chuck walked out of the Hermosa Beach Police Department with his head held high. He stood on the steps and answered every question, most from reporters he'd known for years. He denied that he'd ever molested Jackie's children, and he volunteered to submit to a lie detector test.

"I never did anything to those children," Chuck declared. "In fact, I cared for those kids."

Chuck made a point of giving Jackie's name, address, and phone number to the press and instructed them to speak with her.

"If you think I'm crazy," Chuck said aloud, "wait until you meet her."

While Chuck was holding court on the steps of the jail house, Jackie futilely tried to reach him at his home. After leaving several messages, she telephoned Chuck's estranged wife, Robin. Jackie wanted to make a deal. Robin, with a fellow employee listening, was shocked to hear that Jackie would drop the molestation charges against Chuck if he agreed to pay her the money he owed her. Since Jackie had already tried to have Robin charged with telephone harassment, Robin refused to be part of her blackmail. Robin couldn't fathom how Jackie could use her daughter as a pawn to destroy a man's life—all for a few hundred dollars.

When Chuck finished with the press, knowing that search warrants had been issued for his office at the *Daily Breeze*, he and Randolph led the police to his desk, cooperating with their search. Bypassing the *Breeze's* security system, and before Chuck's editors could verify the warrant was legitimate, they searched his files.

Unbeknownst to Chuck, at that very moment, Lieutenant Michael Lavin initiated a search of Chuck's apartment, his car, and his father's home.

The next morning, Friday, August 24, the story hit the front page. The *Daily Breeze's* headline read, "Breeze Columnist Arrested on Molestation Charge"; the *Los Angeles Times* had a page-one headline: "Columnist Seized in Child Molesting Case." And although the articles identified the unnamed three-year-old girl as an "alleged victim in the McMartin Preschool case," Lt. Lavin reiterated that, as far as the police knew, this case "was totally isolated" from McMartin.

The news articles didn't identify Jackie McGauley by name, the standard journalistic ethic to protect the alleged child victim—but "the mother" was quoted as saying, "I think I've been in shock, a combination of shock and being mad and taken advantage of." Jackie said that "she was not out to get anyone," but that she didn't want to "get gotten, and so far, I've been gotten twice," a reference to her daughter having previously been abused at McMartin. She also alleged that Chuck had "sexually abused her twenty-two-month-old son."

In the articles, Chuck didn't mince words. He accused the mother of carrying out "an unjustified vendetta" against him. He described her as a "very troubled Hermosa Beach woman," that she was a "McMartin Preschool parent" whose three-year-old daughter would be further victimized by her mother's "false and malicious" actions. He explained that this was "the third in a series of ever-more-serious charges this poor, disturbed woman has made against me in recent weeks as her hysteria has increased."

But the police stood by their case. Lt. Lavin announced that there was "evidence linking Chuck Elliott to the crime." Lavin declined to state what that evidence was, but said that police had seized "pornographic material and a roll of undeveloped film," and that his team was "investigating the possibility" that Chuck Elliott had also molested the girl's twenty-two-month-old brother, that "the woman's daughter and son have been examined by a physician," and that "both were found to have suffered physical trauma." Test results were pending.

The next morning, Saturday, August 25, Chuck Elliott's daily column was suspended. Bert Winrow, publisher of the *Daily Breeze*, stated that "it was in the best interest to suspend it indefinitely." Winrow said that Chuck Elliott would take a "one-week vacation" and return for "unspecified duties" on September 4, following the Labor Day break.

An article in the Saturday edition of the *Los Angeles Times* reported of Chuck's suspension. In it, Chuck said he was afraid that "the McMartin hysteria was precipitating a witch-hunt." Chuck voiced his disappointment in having lost his column, his "life-line to the people of the South Bay."

The article also noted that Chuck and his soon-to-be-ex-wife co-owned the Parkway Preschool in Redondo Beach.

* * * * *

The August heat had little effect on Eastlake, with its well-kept interior and central air, a far cry from the sweltering stench of Los Padrinos. Still, for Michael Ruby, it was prison.

Michael resided in "Unit M," a bungalow design with tinted windows and bright colors. One of just four white kids in his unit, Michael naturally gravitated toward the other three, each of them keeping a low profile, careful not to cross the clearly drawn lines. Blacks hung with blacks, Hispanics with Hispanics. Everyone else was "white"—plain and simple.

That culture shock awakened Michael. Raised in Manhattan Beach, he rarely interacted with minorities, and he'd never associated with criminals. Michael and his friends pretended to be tough, riding the shoreline, running their mouths, but this was something else. This was a teenage penitentiary, a savage world that Michael had never envisioned.

Before long, however, through his daily trudge, Michael got to know his fellow inmates, piercing that racial barrier. Most kids were more inviting than Michael had suspected, and, the more they interacted, he found them to be not so different from himself. Each kid wanted to feel safe, to enjoy a warm meal, to have a few minutes of privacy, and, once in a while, to share a good laugh.

One black kid from Compton, a fifteen-year-old Crip named Tre, constantly teased Michael for being a "dark white boy."

"Damn, man," Tre would say. "You must be from da beach."

Tre's tone was derogatory, but Michael knew he was just ribbing. Each time Tre made a wise-crack, Michael grinned, and Tre started giving him a wry smile back.

Over the weeks, Michael became intrigued with Tre and his bros—the communal code of gang life. Michael began to express those images in his artwork, and the depth of his talent came to life. His drawings and paintings—portraits of the human condition, his condition—illustrated the anger and pain and loneliness of teenagers doing time. Michael hung his art on his cell walls, and the other inmates stopped to admire his work.

Like every prison story, Michael had a buddy, a white kid known as "Buzzkirk," a wealthy sixteen-year-old from San Fernando Valley. Buzzkirk and Michael hit it off from the start. Buzzkirk reminded Michael of Hawkeye on *M.A.S.H.*—tall, lanky, highly intelligent, an avid reader. Michael and Buzzkirk joked about starting their own "two-man white gang," giving themselves nicknames—Buzzkirk "Doc" and Michael "Pokey." That gang-life fantasy helped them pass the time, a therapeutic escape for two teenagers with uncertain futures.

Both guys faced serious charges, so they seemed to have something in common, although Michael continued to swear that he'd never molested any child, while Buzzkirk proudly admitted that he'd murdered his stepfather.

* * * * *

Michael's parents came to visit on the weekends, bringing him letters from his girlfriend and sisters, but one afternoon, mid-week, Michael got a surprise visit from Richard Cherry, the public defender assigned to his case. The last time they'd spoken, Cherry had said he was trying to get the charges thrown out due to the "complete lack of evidence."

That day, as they sat together, separated by glass, Richard Cherry delivered bad news. "Michael," Cherry said, shaking his head, "they have more kids…more little girls claiming you molested them."

"What?" Michael shouted.

"Yes, three more girls. They just added twelve more counts to the complaint."

"How is this happening?" Michael asked. "Last time you told me you were getting this dropped. Now you're telling me it's worse."

"Listen, Michael, I'm doing my best, but if they keep piling on charges, it's hard for me to get the original ones dropped."

Michael had been praying for a resolution, holding onto his faith, but his prayers were not being answered.

And it kept getting worse.

The next time Cherry visited, he told Michael that two more girls had been added. Michael broke down.

"I didn't do any of this, Mr. Cherry. I didn't do it. I didn't do it," he yelled aloud, his hands in the air. "Does anyone even care about the truth?"

Richard Cherry was not a seasoned public defender, but he knew that the truth no longer mattered. There were forces at work that wanted Michael's case to move forward—powerful people within the district attorney's office—and so, forward it went.

CHAPTER 23

In a low-lit courtroom in downtown Los Angeles, Michael Ruby stood before Judge Gaye Herrington for his competency hearing.

"This case should go before a jury," Judge Herrington concluded, ruling that Michael would be tried as an adult. "This evidence needs to be examined and analyzed. That won't happen in a juvenile court." The gavel came down.

A cry bellowed from the front pew, the despair of Evelyn Ruby imagining her son spending his life in federal prison. Evelyn had prayed for Michael to be tried as a juvenile, where guilty meant ten years with a shot at parole.

Michael was led away, his hands cuffed across his waist. He paused and looked at his folks, giving them a reassuring smile. He didn't share his mother's fear; he'd gotten just what he wanted.

At Eastlake, Michael had learned a good deal about the system. His fellow inmates had told him how things work—that the path of the juvenile courts would be rough for a seventeen-year-old accused of molesting little girls. A juvenile conviction might be a lighter sentence, but any term would devastate a kid like Michael. He would never survive as an accused pedophile.

"Bro, you can't let one person make this decision," Buzzkirk had told him. "If you let a judge make the call, you're dust. You think a judge is gonna look at those girls and set you free? No way. No chance. Get it to a jury, man. Whatever you do, whatever you have to say, get it to a jury. It's the only way."

And Buzzkirk was right. Michael's fate needed to be in the hands of twelve people, a group of adults from various backgrounds and life experiences, people who could look at the facts objectively and make an informed decision about his future. They would have to agree unanimously, all twelve of them, which meant that he only needed one reasonable person to see how ludicrous the accusations were.

From the media circus surrounding his competency hearing, Michael knew his case was big time, a bellwether for a district attorney's office looking to prove their "McMartin conspiracy." The DA would assign a hotshot prosecutor. The daily proceedings would be covered by every network and major newspaper. The public would see it every day; thus, the system—those out to destroy Michael—would be held accountable.

"I want people to see my case," Michael told his folks during a visitation at Eastlake. "I want people to know what's happening to me. This is wrong. They shouldn't be able to do this to me...or anyone. People need to know about this."

Due to the nature of the charges, Judge Herrington recommended that Michael retain more experienced counsel. Tommy Allen, a South Bay attorney and fellow parishioner at Rolling Hills Covenant Church, stepped in, replacing Richard Cherry. Because the case was so large, involving so many alleged victims, Allen requested that a second attorney be assigned. Judge Herrington agreed and offered James Hallet, a seasoned public defender. Hallet requested that Allen also be court-appointed, lifting the financial burden from the Rubys, who could never afford such fees. Judge Herrington granted Hallet's request. Bail was set at five hundred thousand dollars.

The following week, on Thursday, September 6, Michael arrived to the Torrance Municipal Court Building for his bail hearing. His attorneys would plead for leniency, as there was no way the Rubys could come up with fifty thousand in cash.

Michael was in shambles, his sixth week at Eastlake. As much as he'd tried to adjust, he wasn't immune from the subtle effects of incarceration—the monotony and the gradual loss of hope. He hadn't shaved in six or seven days, and his hair, short when he entered LP, had grown scraggly.

Handcuffed and ankle-locked, two guards walked Michael off the elevator, down a corridor, and into a small office adjacent to the courtroom. Minutes later, the bailiff walked in and approached Michael.

"Look, when you go out there, you're gonna see a lot of people you know. This is on national TV. There are cameras everywhere. So you can't be waving or saying *anything*—no gang signs, none of that shit. You got it?"

"Yes, sir."

"You gotta toe the line," the bailiff warned. "This is an official courtroom, and this is *not* a lenient judge."

Michael nodded. He appreciated the advice.

The bailiff led Michael into the courtroom, swinging the door wide so Michael had a full view of the pews—and he then understood what the bailiff was talking about. The room was filled to capacity, most of them there in support of him.

Michael panned the rows of familiar faces—Rob Pearsall, his girlfriend Nicole, Kenny Campbell, Gary Moore, his parents and sisters. He couldn't keep up with the faces, each of them smiling with love and compassion. Michael tried to hide his smile, but there was nowhere to turn. He grinned from ear to ear, mouthing "thank you" and "I love you" to all.

The hearing itself was uneventful. Judge Benjamin Aranda III had been assigned to the case, and he agreed to reduce the bail to three hundred thousand, but it made little difference. The Rubys didn't have the cash or the equity to get him released.

That night, back at Eastlake, Michael wrote a letter to his family and supporters:

Dear Friends,

Do not give up hope.
"Rejoice in the lord always."
He never promised we'd only see sunshine;
He never said there would be no rain;
He only promised a heart full of singing . . .
At the very things that once brought pain.

I'm learning patience. We have a big and mighty God. And all things will work together for our good through Him. He's got only my best interest in mind.

What can I say? What really can I say? I'm speechless. Yesterday afternoon at my bail hearing, as I stepped into the courtroom, I was presented with a hundred loyal faces and friends. Some people I don't even know. I can only express my gratitude to my "inner-self." Nothing I could put in words would describe my feelings for you all. You won't ever know how lonely I am.

Have you ever wondered that if you disappeared, or went away on vacation, if you'd ever be missed? Well, the thought of that has crossed my mind a million times in the last six weeks I've been here. And then to see you all there yesterday...all the love I felt. How proud you made me, just the feeling that no matter what, you're all behind me.

Kenny Campbell even flying in from out of state to be there! Thanks, Kenny—I love you. And all of you taking time off work and unselfishly sacrificing it for me. I love you. I love you all so much. So badly I just wanted to jump out of that chair and into that crowd of security behind me, and just be with familiar faces and loving arms. And just to be able to break down and cry, and just for a moment escape into a world of hope beneath my burden.

* * * * *

Michael fell back into his daily life at Eastlake. By October, with the date of his preliminary hearing set, the media's coverage picked up. Wayne Satz, simultaneously covering the McMartin proceedings, broadcast a series of reports about "the seventeen-year-old teacher's aide at the Manhattan Ranch Preschool accused of molesting five young girls."

One night, while sitting in the TV room with some other inmates, a news bulletin flashed: "Update on the case of accused child molester, Michael Ruby." A picture of Michael appeared on the screen.

Michael froze. Up to that point, he had, for the most part, kept the truth hidden. Only Buzzkirk and few of the white kids knew of the accusations against him. It had finally caught up with him.

The room went silent. A few guys turned to face him, some in disbelief, others angered. The next day rumors circulated through the unit, and three black inmates confronted him.

"What the fuck, man?" one asked. "What's that shit about?"

Michael shook his head. "It's bullshit, man...all bullshit."

Michael explained the story, how it all went down, how none of it made any sense. To his surprise, they believed him. When he spoke with others, they seemed to believe him as well. Almost to a man, they said that the DA would do anything—bend the law, extract testimony from a known perjurer, even falsify documents—to put them away. "That's just how it is, man."

Each week brought another set of motions, and Michael was transported to and from the Torrance Courts Building. Any given weekday, the morning guard would round up Michael and the others who had to be in court.

"All right, campers. Let's go. Get up. Get up."

The inmates dressed, had a quick breakfast, and went through their basic roll call before loading onto their buses. Each time, they stopped by the Men's Central Jail to pick up the adult inmates and drop them off at the downtown courts. Since Michael was being tried as an adult, he traveled with adult convicts. Some were hardened, but most were well-behaved.

On the morning of Tuesday, October 9, Michael sat on the bus, pressed tightly against the window, watching the traffic along East Cesar E. Chavez Avenue. This day, once he got to Torrance, he would enter his plea. Allen and Hallet had already told him the prosecution would be offering a plea deal, which would guarantee Michael a reduced sentence—with, of course, one catch: He would have to admit he was guilty. He would go to prison as an admitted child molester, and when he got out, whenever that was, he would be a registered sex offender.

The bus turned left on North Vignes Street, the road to Men's Central. Once through the gates, the bus drove to the back loading area where a line of inmates waited, chained together. They boarded in a straight line. The spot next to Michael was open so the first man took it as the others filed in behind him. The man was black, thin, balding, about thirty-five years old, with a thick beard. He looked Michael over, confused.

"What the fuck you doin' here, boy?"

Michael paused a moment then turned away. "I got framed," Michael said, the answer his buddies in Unit M told him to *always* give.

"Yeah, you did," the man said, chuckling. "Yeah, you did."

The next line of inmates came out of the building, a group of ten. One extremely large black man stood in the middle. He was a mammoth, a beast, all muscle, about six-foot-six, close to three hundred pounds. As he stepped inside, all the guys on the bus started laughing. The large man looked up at them and grinned. They laughed even louder.

The guard stepped inside the bus and yelled, "You all better keep it down. We ain't doin' this shit today." The guard stepped out and went back inside the building.

Michael, confused, turned to the man next to him. "Who's that?" Michael whispered, motioning toward the large black man.

"That's Donkey Kong, man."

Once the guard was out of sight, Donkey Kong reached inside his shirt and pulled out a Sucrets box. Inside were some match-books and roaches. He casually put a roach to his lips and lit it, then passed it to the prisoner on his right. It moved around the bus, quietly with the exception of the rattling cuffs and chains. When it got to Michael, he just smiled and shook his head. The bus filled with smoke and reeked of herb. When the guard stepped back toward the bus, all the inmates jumped around, hands cuffed together, fanning the air.

The guard smelled it and rushed inside, knowing who to blame. "Goddamnit, Kong! Wha'd I say?"

Donkey Kong remained straight-faced while the others fell about laughing. Even the guard had trouble hiding his grin.

That episode stuck with Michael, as silly as it seemed. It taught him that life, his life, wasn't so different than the lives of the men with whom he was imprisoned. It showed him that, despite the decision he was about to make—determining the course of his future—he would always be able to smile, to laugh, something no one could ever deny him. It helped him to forget how dire things were, and it gave him courage on a day he needed it most.

* * * * *

When Michael reached the Torrance Municipal Courts Building, the media huddled outside the entrance. Dozens of parent activists were being interviewed. Some held homemade signs, demanding justice.

The sight of it sent a chill through Michael, seeing so many people out for blood, random people from the community who wanted Michael to spend the rest of his life in jail.

Not long after, inside the courtroom, as the plea hearing was set to begin, Judge Aranda stood and walked back to chambers. Moments later, Lisa Hart, the lead prosecutor, followed.

Tommy Allen turned to Michael, his expression serious and his tone imminent. "Michael," Allen said, grabbing his shoulder, "I think you should consider a plea deal."

"Seriously?" Michael replied, stunned. "You want me to say I did it?! I thought you wanted to defend me. I thought you believed me."

"I *do* believe you, Mike, and I'll defend you like you're my own son. But you have to at least consider it. You need to listen to what the judge has to say, to know your options. But in the end, it's your call. This is *your* decision."

Michael didn't like it, but he knew Allen was right. No one could force him to take a deal. As long as he stood before the judge and pleaded "not guilty," he would get his day in court. He agreed to meet with the judge.

Michael and his lawyers entered the judge's chambers. Judge Aranda sat at his desk, a dark-haired man, mid-forties, with glasses and an intimidating glare. Deputy DA Lisa Hart sat in a chair not far from the court reporter. She never looked Michael in the eyes. A security guard stood at the door.

Michael sat in front of the judge, with Allen and Hallet on each side. On the wall behind the judge's desk were a collage of pictures, many of him and his wife's eleven children—seven biological and four adopted. Michael looked over the photos and the innocent glee in his young children's eyes. *This guy's gonna hang me.*

Out in the courtroom, Evelyn Ruby sat bewildered as to why the proceeding had halted and her son had been escorted away.

While she waited, *Eyewitness News* reporter Wayne Satz approached her. He wore a cynical smile. "It looks like it's going to be a rough day."

"What does that mean?" Evelyn asked, offended by his tone.

"Well," Satz said, leaning in, "everyone knows what Michael's gonna do."

"What are you talking about?"

Satz stood back. "Trust me, by noon today, you'll be told that it's all over." Satz smiled and stepped away.

In chambers, Judge Aranda broke it down for Michael.

"Michael," Judge Aranda said, "you've been charged with thirty-two counts of child molestation, which, if convicted, means anywhere from fifty years to two hundred-fifty years...basically life imprisonment."

Michael said nothing. He ran the numbers in his head. The best case scenario had him getting out in time to celebrate his seventieth birthday.

Michael looked at Allen and Hallet for support, but they gestured for him to keep listening.

"If you're guilty," Judge Aranda continued, "you should take the plea bargain, because you don't want to do life. It's ludicrous to do life if you don't have to."

Michael shook his head in disbelief.

"So you know, Michael," Aranda said, "I've personally sentenced five child molesters to state prison and not one of them is alive today. Life in prison for convicted child molesters is very short."

Judge Aranda's words gave Michael little hope.

"Let's face it, Michael, you have a fifty-percent chance of being found innocent. You have many rights and privileges under the Constitution. So, if you *are* guilty, you have the right to accept a plea. That's your right. And if you take that deal, the maximum we can keep you at the California Youth Authority is until you're twenty-five years old. So you would be looking at about seven years, and there's always a chance you'll get out earlier. All you have to do is plead guilty to one count for one child, and it's all over."

It all sounds so simple. Seven years in a youth facility or life in state prison?

"No one wants to see these girls come into court and testify," Aranda said. "So you can save us all a lot of time and trouble by doing this deal. That is, *if* you're guilty."

Judge Aranda emphasized the "if" so boldly that it raised Michael's brow.

"But Michael," Aranda said with conviction, "if you're *not* guilty, if you didn't commit these crimes, then you *cannot* accept a plea bargain. You can't lie to the court and say you committed a crime if you didn't. If you're innocent, Michael, a trial's your only recourse."

Michael sat for a moment, taking it all in, realizing the stakes. Michael thought about his family and friends; he thought about his covenant with God, his oath to tell the truth. And that's when it came to him.

"Sir, based on what you've just said," Michael concluded, "I can't accept the plea deal. I can't, because I'm innocent."

Judge Aranda nodded, respecting the young man's choice.

"I would rather spend the rest of my life in prison than to say that I did these awful things to those kids," Michael said. "I would have to live with that lie...to be labeled a child molester for the rest of my life. I can't do that. I won't do that."

Michael felt righteous about his decision, like a martyr standing by his principles. But once they got out in the hall, Allen and Hallet questioned his decision.

"Whether you did it or not, we're going to represent you," Hallet said. "But if we're going to get you off, we need to know the truth. You have to tell us *everything*."

Allen and Hallet were trying to relate to Michael "as a friend," wanting him to "tell them the truth and they wouldn't disclose anything to anyone." At that point, Michael didn't know whom to trust.

"What do you guys expect me to say?" Michael said loudly, his voice carrying down the hall. "I'm innocent. I'm one hundred percent innocent, and I thought that's what you believed. Am I wrong?"

Allen and Hallet stepped back, knowing they'd crossed a line with their client.

Moments later, Steve Grubbs, another one of Michael's youth pastors, approached them, and he asked to speak privately with Michael. The two lawyers and the security guard stepped a few feet away.

"Just tell me what you did," Steve prodded Michael. "Don't worry about it. We all do things in life that we regret, and people will forgive you, no matter what."

Michael's face swelled, a natural sadness that led to anger. He'd just stood before a superior court judge and made the most courageous decision of his life, yet someone who he thought had his back seemed to believe he was guilty.

And it wasn't just Steve Grubbs. While Steve was trying to coax Michael into a plea, Allen and Hallet were working on Evelyn, hoping she could persuade Michael to change his mind.

Evelyn had already worried that, because of the stigma of the McMartin case, Michael would never get an impartial jury.

"The tide's against him," Allen told Evelyn. "His chance of an acquittal is slim. Everyone in the community wants to *believe the children*."

Evelyn could see what Allen and Hallet were doing. They'd come to her instead of Glenn, thinking she would be so devastated by the thought of Michael spending his life in prison that she'd beg him to accept the plea bargain. Evelyn knew their hearts were in the right place, but they didn't understand her relationship with her son, that she would never ask him to lie.

"I can't make that decision for him," Evelyn told them. "I've always told Michael that if he did *anything*, if he touched one child, no matter how small it may've been, that he needs to confess, and once he did, we would deal with it. But he's always said that he was innocent...completely innocent. And I believe him."

Evelyn looked both attorneys in the eyes, letting her words sink in. "So, if he's willing to fight, to risk *everything* to defend his honor, then I expect the two of you to fight for him. And if you can't do that, then you should step aside."

Tommy Allen and James Hallet chose to stay.

That moment reinvigorated Michael's defense. His lawyers discovered that, in Michael's mind, his life had no value if he had to wear the label of *child molester*—a Scarlet Letter "P" for pedophile. They could see that his steadfast refusal to admit guilt was one that only a truly innocent man would take.

* * * * *

Just after daybreak on Friday, October 12, Michael awoke to the din of a guard's baton rattling across the bars of his cell.

"Get up, kid! Time to go," the guard said, looking around the cell. "Get your shit together. You're goin' home."

"What?" Michael said, jumping from his cot.

"You're going *home*. You made bail."

Unbeknownst to Michael, an anonymous parishioner at Rolling Hills Covenant Church had come up with ten thousand dollars to meet his bail requirement. Michael hit the ceiling. He grabbed a handful of sentimental items, including his favorite artwork, but left everything else behind, handing it out to the other inmates.

The guard escorted Michael to a receiving area where he waited for his release papers. The long wait made him anxious, almost paranoid. *This is too good to be true. Someone's gonna walk in and tell me there's been a misunderstanding.*

After three hours in that room, however, an administrator came in with a clear plastic bag that contained the clothes Michael had worn the day of his arrest—the T-shirt, the windbreaker, the Bermuda shorts, and thongs. Michael would leave the way he came.

Michael's parents and sisters waited on the steps outside of Eastlake, praying, thanking the Lord for this glorious gift, the charity of the nameless parishioner. Evelyn said that during Michael's incarceration, the Rolling Hills Covenant Church had run a musical, *Joseph*, based on the biblical story from Genesis 39 where Joseph is falsely accused of molesting Potiphar's wife. Joseph was thrown in prison for something he didn't do. While Michael was in jail, members of the congregation called him "Joseph," drawing comparisons to the verses from Genesis.

Two guards escorted Michael out, and he ran into the loving arms of his family. They spent a few minutes exchanging hugs and kisses, but Michael didn't want to linger around.

"Let's get out of here before they change their minds," Michael told his father.

Forty-five minutes later, the Rubys pulled into their driveway, greeted by a large "Welcome Home, Michael" sign strung across the garage door. Inside, Michael's bedroom had been newly painted and re-carpeted.

"We wanted you to have a fresh start," Evelyn said, her eyes tearing up.

Michael, too, began to cry as he draped his arms around her, so relieved to be home.

Evelyn had promised to take Michael into downtown Manhattan Beach for a much needed haircut. As they drove along Highland Avenue, passing the quaint shops, Evelyn tried to talk to Michael about his feelings, about his state-of-mind after the past three months, but he didn't want to discuss it.

When she came to a stop sign, he undid his safety belt and opened the car door. "Sorry, Mom," he said. "But I gotta get outta here."

Michael jumped out and ran down the incline to the strand. He kept running until he hit the water, and then turned right, heading north toward El Porto.

The rush of the ocean water and the cool coastal breeze was pure ecstasy. The sand squished between his toes, reminding him of his life as a surfer. He ambled along the beach, speaking to God. Still confused about God's plan, he thanked the Lord for his freedom and accepted that his plight was God's will.

As the sun set over the Pacific horizon, Michael wandered the streets. Out of nowhere, he heard a voice, the faint call of his friend, Brad Lawson. "Broooooo!" Brad tackled Michael and pushed him against a wall. "Everybody's looking for you, bro. Let's go."

They walked to the Cookie Post, where Brad's brother, Gregor, Michael's long-time friend and fellow artist, waited out front. Gregor hugged Michael, lifting him off the ground. They went inside, sat down, and talked about old times, memories that seemed so long ago.

Within minutes, Michael's sister Linda and his girlfriend Nicole came through the door. Nicole rushed up and grabbed Michael around the waist. He held her tightly, kissing her face, not wanting to let go.

When he finally did, they sat, holding hands, enjoying the reunion they'd dreamt of.

As the evening went on, however, as Michael looked around at the smiling faces and the warm camaraderie, he couldn't shake his sense of imprisonment, aware that a dark cloud continued to hover, one that would not drift away any time soon.

Unlike his friends, Michael's freedom was transient, a reprieve not to be confused with victory.

PART V
Crucible

CHAPTER 24

That autumn, the fall semester of 1984, the students of Mira Costa High School found themselves living through the title year of their assigned reading—George Orwell's *Nineteen Eighty-Four*. It compelled them to see how Orwell had imagined the world would someday be, so unlike the way it was.

As far as they could tell, the year 1984, with its renaissance of fashion and new-wave music, was colorfully optimistic, not the dreary totalitarian state that Orwell had depicted. It was, instead, the "Age of Reagan," when dynamic social change and expanding wealth brought abundant possibilities, the opposite of Orwell's Ministry of Plenty, with its centralized regulation and rationing.

With that in mind, as they finished the novel, most considered it nothing more than a legendary work of fiction. Great author, great book, but it bore no resemblance to the 1984 they lived in. Or so it seemed.

Upon closer look, however, there was a sort of *newspeak* that had taken hold of Manhattan Beach that year, when phrases such as "Believe the Children" and "Children Don't Lie" ruled the day—definitive statements that went unchallenged.

In his masterpiece, Orwell coined the term *bellyfeel* as the "blind, enthusiastic acceptance of an idea," the misguided passion of those who bought into the dogma of the power structure.

Similarly, in Manhattan Beach, when evidence of a vast conspiracy couldn't be found, the powerful—the enthusiastically blind—determined that the crimes must have been broader and more sinister than ever suspected, since, of course, 2 + 2 = 5.

To prove their theory, they unleashed a "Child Sex Abuse Task Force"—a new-age *Thought Police*—to descend upon the community, an inquisition in search of a crime, the prelude to a modern-day witch-hunt.

In retrospect, it appears, Manhattan Beach in 1984 was not so different from the 1984 that Orwell had conceived. For the McMartin Seven, Michael Ruby, Chuck Elliott, and all other suspects of these contemporary *thoughtcrimes*, they seemed to be living an Orwellian nightmare, and they didn't even know it.

* * * * *

On the last day of October, Manhattan Beach children slipped into their costumes and went off to school, noticeably excited. Geared up for their classroom parties, schoolyard parades, and of course, an evening of trick-or-treating, it was their typical morning prep for this artificial holiday.

For many parents, however, this Halloween had a real-life feel, a sense of terror that was not so fictional. On this night, believing they were in the clutches of a satanic cult, some feared that true evil was hidden behind the masks. Their once benevolent community had taken on a new identity. Strangers, they suspected, were living among them.

That morning, huddled around a lifeguard station beneath the Manhattan Beach Pier, a large group of law enforcement officers banded—the newly established Child Sexual Abuse Task Force. Sheriff Sherman Block had created this elite force of sixteen detectives, three sergeants, and one lieutenant. Task Force Chief Robert Campbell stood before reporters, with the beautiful beach and rolling tide as the backdrop, announcing that this "specialized team" had been enlisted to investigate allegations by preschoolers across the South Bay and identify "uncharged" suspects.

"We are here to uncover the conspiratorial link between various schools and a clandestine ring of pedophiles," Chief Campbell stated. He admitted that the allegations were bizarre—the claims that the ring was in some way connected to the occult—but with hundreds of children having already implicated eight teachers (the McMartin Seven and Michael Ruby), there was no reason to believe that the conspiracy ended there.

Detective Jane Hoag, in her capacity as the lead local investigator, led the group. The other twenty-one members had been chosen for their unique experience in dealing with domestic crimes, particularly those against children. The officers were divided into three investigative units, each assigned to one or two preschools; each was given a cadre of backup detectives to assist them in interviews, surveillance, and the serving of warrants.

There was, of course, some concern that the units had been given too broad of a power, that they'd been provided with lists of former preschool teachers to interrogate, to search their homes, and to confiscate their personal belongings. The process, some argued, would create the image that everyone accused was guilty. If one's home was merely searched, or if one was taken away by the police for questioning, it could leave a mark of disgrace that may never fade.

"Innocent people could very well be caught up in the far-reaching investigation," said Task Force Lieutenant Richard Willey. But that didn't slow down the effort. In fact, it seemed to accelerate it.

In Hermosa Beach, outside of the jurisdiction of the Task Force, a small group of parents—those whose children had attended the Children's Path Preschool—began questioning their kids. A number of former McMartin students had, at one time or another, attended the Children's Path, and seven months after the McMartin indictments, current and former Children's Path students had begun to talk. Their parents contacted the local police, who'd passed the names on to the Task Force.

Within days, the Hermosa Beach Police Department announced it was investigating a "potentially very large" molestation case connected to the Children's Path Preschool, appealing to the public to come forth with "any information possible."

Some parents took a direct approach.

Tacked to a cork-board inside of a local grocery store and stapled to telephone poles along Pier Avenue, crudely manufactured "WANTED" posters were on display. The homespun signs had photographs of ten current and former Children's Path teachers, those identified as the "WANTED" child molesters.

Word spread fast. The Children's Path had two locations, one in Hermosa Beach, the other in Manhattan Beach, not far from McMartin. Many of these parents—Children's Path and McMartin—knew each other. McMartin parents relayed their children's stories to the Children's Path parents, and those parents soon determined that their children may have been victimized as part of the "kiddie porn/occult conspiracy."

Some Children's Path parents rushed their children to local therapy centers, hoping to extract more information, others went to the source.

"You bitch. You're gonna die, bitch," the voice of an angry man came over the receiver.

"Who is this?" Jan Schoen, owner of the Children's Path, replied. "Who are you?"

The caller was silent.

"Don't you call back here again," Schoen said.

The caller laughed menacingly, a low, heavy growl of amusement, knowing the fear he'd instilled. "Shut the school down, bitch. That's your last warning." The caller hung up.

Jan Schoen had received several calls that day, mostly from her staff, whose pictures were plastered all over Hermosa Beach. The teachers were terrified. Some of them had also received threatening phone calls. Each of them feared for their safety.

The threatening calls continued through the night. The next morning, Jan Schoen voluntarily shut down the Children's Path Preschool.

* * * * *

A crowd of two hundred gathered outside of the Los Angeles Press Club as the newly formed Parents Against Child Abuse (PACA) prepared for its first news conference. Amongst them, standing in the middle, Jackie McGauley held a cardboard sign that read: *Believe the Children*. The group was led by its president, Bob Currie.

"We're offering ten thousand dollars to anyone who can produce a photograph that leads to a conviction," Currie proclaimed. "And we'll even extend that offer to the defendants themselves."

Standing next to Currie was John Cioffi, a Hermosa Beach city councilman and the group's official spokesperson. Cioffi stepped to the lectern.

"This reward is being posted to help seal the case," Cioffi declared. "We know the photographs are out there, and we know for a fact that these children were abused."

The Cioffis, John and his wife, Mary Mae, were close friends of the Curries, as both families were active in the community. Earlier that year, Currie had considered running against Cioffi for their district's council seat, but chose instead to dedicate himself to the activist movement—his ambition to uproot the occult.

Currie had a high regard for John and Mary Mae, but he felt they were a bit sheltered and naïve. "Nice people" who simply "saw the world differently" than he did. "They just don't see crime," Currie said. "They just don't see how bad it can get."

When the rumors of "satanic ritual abuse" surfaced, Currie and John Cioffi would have breakfast together. Currie would talk about the information he'd come up with—how, as part of the satanic ceremony, the kids were forced to drink a mixture of blood and urine. "At first, John would take a few bites and leave," Currie said. "After a while, he got used to it."

John's wife, Mary Mae, a recognized McMartin activist, had appeared on several local news segments and regularly given statements to the press as the case developed. In the beginning, Mary Mae was a hardline skeptic, refusing to even question her children about the McMartin Preschool. Yet over time, she considered the possibility that both her children might have been abused.

Under pressure by friends whose children had already disclosed abuse, Mary Mae took her kids to CII to be interviewed and physically examined, and like the others, she discovered that both of her children were victims.

Mary Mae's nine-year-old son, Jerry, had attended McMartin in 1977–78, three years before Ray's tenure, while her daughter, Lana, had attended from September 1982 to June 1983, but she didn't have Ray as a teacher.

Then, years after they'd left the preschool, both of the Cioffi children told wild stories of what they'd experienced.

The case of the Cioffis was most compelling to the investigators because Lana had also attended the Children's Path Preschool in 1982, the year prior to her enrollment at McMartin, and with Children's Path under investigation, the Cioffis believed she'd been abused at both preschools.

Furthermore, in fall 1983, after leaving McMartin, Lana began attending the preschool at St. Cross Episcopal Church. Although no child had publically identified St. Cross as part of the conspiracy, rumors were circulating within Hermosa Beach that children had been "taken to a local church" and forced to take part in rituals. There simply were not that many churches to choose from—a church close enough to McMartin, where children could be transported to and from the site without their absence being noticed.

St. Cross Episcopal Church fit the bill. Located on the 1800 block of Monterey Boulevard in Hermosa Beach, St. Cross was exactly two miles from McMartin, a seven-minute drive of back streets and optional routes, with little chance of traffic congestion or accidents. Just a quarter-mile from the Children's Path Preschool, near the intersection of Monterey and Pier Avenue, St. Cross had become a location of interest.

* * * * *

In between St. Cross Episcopal Church and the Children's Path Preschool, within a modern two-story Spanish-style dwelling at 1509 Monterey Boulevard, sat Bob Currie, the homeowner, a man on a mission.

For more than a year, Currie had watched the McMartin case play out as a true-crime story. From the day he received the police letter to his awakening that the occult had overrun his community, Currie had turned his home into the headquarters for his private investigation. Lately, he'd been meeting with members of the sheriff's Task Force, sharing his findings with those who had the authority to act upon them.

Currie's home was centrally located to most of the sites connected to the case—2.3 miles from the McMartin Preschool, 2.4 miles from American Martyrs Church, 2.4 miles from the Manhattan Ranch Preschool, 2.8 miles from Judy Johnson's Vista Drive home, 1.8 miles from the Manhattan Beach Community Church, 1.7 miles from the Manhattan Beach Pier where the sheriff's Task Force assembled each morning, and only a half mile from the Children's Path Preschool. Whenever Currie left his home, he was minutes from the action, as if his property at 1509 Monterey was the hub of all things McMartin.

From Currie's perspective, the latest revelations against Children's Path meant that the conspiracy had been operating within a stone's throw of his home. With the whispers of the "rituals in the church" growing louder, Currie set his sights on St. Cross, the most likely target. It was an institution that, to Currie, had long associated itself with the "types of people" who were susceptible to occult indoctrination.

Established around 1900, at a time when Hermosa Beach had no other Protestant church, the founders of St. Cross purchased the lot at the southwest corner of 14th Street and Manhattan Beach Avenue, erecting a modest structure for its small parish. By the end of World War II, as the entire South Bay developed, the wealth of the Episcopal community expanded and a new, resplendent structure was built. The church thrived. Its Friday night Lenten dinners attracted people from all over the beach cities, and on Sundays, its magnificent pipe organ and resounding choir became the envy of the diocese.

Above all, though, the St. Cross parish community had been lauded for its dedication to outreach programs—none more inspiring than the 1736 Family Crisis Center. Located at 1736 Monterey Boulevard, opposite the St. Cross sanctuary, Project 1736 was available to "anyone who needed help," the only refuge of its type in the South Bay. A true secular charity, the 1736 House took in runaways, battered women, and victims of rape and domestic violence. Its 24-hour hotline ensured that no one was left without shelter and care.

Yet over the years, despite St. Cross's goodwill, some within the neighborhood were displeased with its presence, concerned that it had a negative impact on the block's property value by attracting elements of impoverishment and indecency. A handful of locals had expressed their disapproval to the church, and Bob Currie had been most vociferous.

According to Kathy Lorde, the former Manhattan Ranch teacher whose home had been raided in late July, it was no secret that Currie was "extremely mad about the 1736 property."

Kathy Lorde's home on Manhattan Avenue was near Currie's residence; only Bayview Drive, more of an alley than a street, separated the backsides of their lots. As Kathy put it, since there was rarely a shortage of gossip in a small town, and with Bob Currie not known for being discreet, the power struggle over Monterey Boulevard's real estate had been a public topic for some time.

"He didn't want the church to invest any more money into 1736," Kathy said. "He complained that it was bringing down the value of his properties." Kathy even heard that Currie had been in "a few squabbles" with Reverend Jack Eales, the minister at St. Cross, and that Currie had tried to pressure the church into selling him the 1736 property. The church denied Currie's offer; in fact, they continued to acquire even more property on Monterey, making their long-term vision of philanthropy even more apparent.

"Currie was irate," Kathy said, and word got around that he'd "threatened to take action," whatever that meant.

CHAPTER 25

On Thursday, November 29, with Michael Ruby's preliminary hearing in full swing, the broadcast media packed into the courtroom at the Torrance Municipal Building. Michael, tired of playing it safe, and against the advice of his attorneys, sat in the corridor with a reporter from the *Los Angeles Times*.

Each day, Michael had watched the crusade of parent activists proclaim that they "believed the children" and condemned him as a vile child predator before a shred of evidence had been presented. They were driving the narrative.

Michael decided it was time to fight back, to get his story out—to at least let the community hear his voice.

Inside the courtroom, Jimmy Jacobson testified, alleging that Michael molested him in the school's "bathroom," as well as two "Manhattan Beach public parks," a "manhole," and a location he described as a "pink haunted house." According to Jimmy, it all occurred during school hours, which meant that Michael could not have operated alone.

Nevertheless, Michael was the only defendant charged.

The next morning the *Times* article hit the stands, headlined: "Victim of 'Witch-Hunt,' Accused Molester Says."

The article showed a side of Michael the public hadn't seen—a "former football player," a senior at Mira Costa High, whose life centered on his "Volkswagen, surfboard and girlfriend." Michael said that despite the charges against him, "it was fun working with the kids," that they were "great kids." He only took the job, he said, to earn money to "fix up his car."

When asked about the McMartin Preschool, about the allegations that he'd been part of their pornography ring, Michael denied any knowledge of the McMartin-Buckey family, stating emphatically, "I never even knew the name 'Buckey' until the day of my arrest."

"It's a witch-hunt," Michael declared. "After this McMartin thing, people are being pulled in right and left." Michael speculated that the charges against him were the product of a "single child's fantasies," which ended up "mushrooming into a wave of accusations" after parents and police continued questioning other children.

The article pointed out the conflicting positions of the Department of Social Services, how the DSS had suspended the license of Manhattan Ranch in August because of a "child-swapping" ring with McMartin, but later admitted there was "no evidence linking" the two cases.

The article concluded with Michael—the teenager faced with "fifty years in prison"—vowing to "stay strong," that the support of his family and friends and church, and, most of all, "God," which he described as his "main backbone," would carry him through.

* * * * *

Four days later

In the early morning of December 3, an urgent tip came to the sheriff's Task Force—an allegation that five children who'd recently attended the Learning Game Preschool in Manhattan Beach had disclosed sexual abuse on the school grounds. Three of them, all former McMartin students, said they were "brought from the McMartin Preschool to be molested."

The Learning Game preschool was on Eighth Street, a block from McMartin, a two-minute walk. Lieutenant Doyle Davidson confirmed that "medical evidence supported the children's claims."

The Task Force, with warrants in hand, prepared to search the premises of Learning Game, as well as the private residences of seven individuals associated with the preschool. Standing outside of the school, Deputy David Hogan briefed a group of investigators.

"There are twenty-two kids in there right now, you got it?" Hogan instructed the team. "You need to move fast, but stay poised. I don't want these kids to be frightened."

The officers rushed into the facility, handing the warrant to Helen Stearns, the school's owner-director. They began their search. Children, some as young as two years old, sat in wonderment as the officers scoured the rooms, opening closets and cupboards, rifling through desks. The walls, covered in Christmas décor, were systematically stripped down. Stacks of papers and partially filled boxes were confiscated.

When the raid ended, the officers stepped out, emotionless, leaving the rooms in shambles, like the aftermath of an earthquake. Nothing incriminating was uncovered. No arrests were made.

The following morning, as Helen Stearns and her staff picked up the pieces, she told the press that the accusations were completely unfounded. "We never had any visitors from any other preschools," Stearns said. She denied any connection to the alleged child-swapping scheme with the McMartin Preschool. She confirmed that some of her students had once attended McMartin, but there was never a time when the two schools had their students "co-mingle."

Stearns complained that the authorities wouldn't tell her which of her teachers had been accused. "This leaves a taint of suspicion on this school and our staff," Stearns said. "This could wipe out a lifetime of investments and ruin reputations."

Stearns, an educator, had been dedicated to teaching children the ethics of right and wrong. "You can forget your civic classes about justice," Stearns said.

Eight days later, at a press conference, the Department of Social Services announced that the Learning Game's license would be suspended pending a hearing. DPSS lawyer Lawrence Bolton clarified that, although the state had made "no connection" to the alleged crimes committed at McMartin, a three-year-old Learning Game student had "allegedly been sexually abused on numerous occasions."

"The Learning Game's operators either knew what was happening or they should've known," Bolton said, "and therefore they failed to take any action to safeguard this child and other children under their care."

The DPSS did not identify a suspect.

In response, Helen Stearns issued a formal statement, declaring, "We are innocent of any wrongdoing. We will be vindicated." She thanked the many families who'd stood by the school through the controversy.

"Once the facts are known," Stearns declared, "we *will* be exonerated."

Nonetheless, following the Christmas break, the Learning Game Preschool remained closed—and it never reopened.

* * * * *

By the beginning of 1985, Judy Johnson had become a pariah in the eyes of many McMartin parents. Although not openly ostracized, Judy was being conveniently ignored. Never a member of Manhattan Beach's social elite, the fact that she was the mother who "broke the case" didn't seem to mean much, not anymore.

Judy, fractured, lonely, and depressed, spent her evenings in the silent darkness of her tiny kitchen, counting the days until her divorce would be final. Her closest friend, her most loyal companion, was the booze in her hand, that glass of Bacardi with a splash of Coke over a bed of ice.

For nearly a year, Judy had drifted farther into solitude. She fell back into the shadows, trying to deal with her struggles as a rational adult. But her problems were more severe than anyone knew. Judy's psyche, askew and misguided, spoke to her, quietly, a faint murmur that warned of the dark specter that surrounded her.

With nowhere to run, Judy stayed put—and she drank.

More often than not, with the boys in bed, Judy stayed up late, seated at her low-lit kitchen table, sipping her cocktail as she wrote down her scattered memories. What once seemed harmless—a few drinks to relax the mind—had become an addiction.

Through the summer and fall of 1984, as Judy's drinking steadily increased, no one had noticed the effects. But by January 1985, Judy could no longer disguise it.

One winter night, according to Bob Currie, Judy showed up at a parents' meeting openly intoxicated. She stumbled into the bathroom and threw up. Before she caused a scene, Currie escorted her out of the building and drove her home.

"She was really out of it," Currie said. "She was going through a lot, and some people, noticing she wasn't all there, really didn't want anything to do with her."

At that time, Noreen Noel, a social worker for the Department of Children's Social Services (DCSS), had been assigned to "the Johnson case," and she'd been keeping a watchful eye on Judy. For several months, Judy had failed to comply with the California Education Code regarding Mark's "poor attendance." He had missed more than forty-five days of school in the fall semester. Judy and Mark had met with the School Attendance Review Board (SARB), which gave Judy a set of ground rules—mainly that Mark would have to attend school on a regular basis. The board provided a list of special programs suited for students with such illnesses, but Mark didn't qualify for the home teacher program. If Judy continued to ignore their recommendations, her case would be referred to another government agency, such as the Probation Department or the Juvenile Court.

In addition, SARB did not assign Noreen Noel to Judy Johnson by chance. Noel was chosen because she'd already formed a relationship with Judy, and the board hoped that Noel would be able to talk some sense into her.

Several months earlier, in the fall 1984, Noel was approached by Dr. Roland Summit—a man Noel considered a mentor—who'd asked her to "reach out" to Judy, to stay close to her.

Dr. Summit, Noel said, "had attended a parents' meeting" where one of the mothers expressed her deep concern for Judy. Dr. Summit, who had conducted a "therapy session" with Judy in February 1984, had watched her emotional and psychological decline ever since.

Noel went to a parents' meeting and introduced herself to Judy, and they began a friendly dialogue, though Judy remained suspicious of the state worker.

"I tried to establish some kind of rapport with her," Noel said. "I told her to call me any time if she wanted to talk. A few weeks later I got a call from a different mother who said she was very worried about Judy, that Judy was falling out of touch, even more so than before."

The problem, Noel suspected, was that Judy had begun to drink heavily, every night. "Judy did a good job of masking it whenever we met in person," Noel said. "But if she failed to show up somewhere, it usually meant that she was drunk." Judy's sporadic behavior kept Noel on alert. The booze had caused Judy to completely transform—more so than the standard alcoholic—resulting in a dramatic change of persona where her core identity fragmented. Not a split personality, per se, but a dim version of herself, a side of herself that she kept hidden away.

"When Judy drank," Noel said, "she became extremely mean and hurtful…far more paranoid and defiant."

Judy's most charged outbursts involved her conflicts with Brad.

"I would get calls from Brad," Noel said, "that Judy had done something really radical…like she'd gone to his house and scratched on his door…bizarre stuff. Brad said she was drunk, and that she was driving the van with Mitchell in it."

Noel told Brad that, if Judy was driving under the influence with the kids in the car, he had a responsibility to report it to the police. But, Noel explained to him, she couldn't do anything about it, for she had no authority, not if the information came to her secondhand.

"But Brad didn't want to get involved," Noel said.

To Brad, Judy was a nuisance, a headache, but as soon as he took formal action, such as calling the cops, it would become his problem. And the last time he got heavy-handed with her, he found himself the target of a child sexual abuse investigation.

For Noel, as much as the volatile side of Judy's drinking made her unpredictable, the flip side—the calm, cool and sober Judy—left Noel just as apprehensive. It was as if Judy were playing a peculiar game of charades, forcing her social worker to decipher between which character Judy pretended to be on any given day.

* * * * *

With the New Year 1985, citing an atmosphere of violence, Jan Schoen, director of the Children's Path preschool, publically announced that the school would remain closed.

"I have elected not to reopen," Schoen declared in a press release, "because I have received a number of anonymous threats of personal injury and property damage." Schoen noted that there had been "several incidents of vandalism" during the preschool's temporary closure.

Apparently, during a recent parents' meeting at the Manhattan Beach Community Church, physical threats had been made against Jan Schoen and her staff—the individuals whose names and pictures had appeared on the WANTED signs posted throughout Hermosa Beach. The threats had been made "openly," and word had gotten back to Schoen, who then realized that she could no longer risk staying open.

Attending that particular parent's meeting was Chuck Elliot, who'd been fired from the *Daily Breeze* following Jackie McGauley's accusations. The charges had been dropped because Jackie's children were deemed too young and unreliable to testify—but the case remained open, a reminder to Chuck to not get too comfortable with his freedom.

Since his break up with Jackie, and needing a preschool for young Max, he'd enrolled the boy into the Children's Path. Chuck had attended that meeting at the Manhattan Beach Community Church as a "Children's Path parent." Chuck didn't believe that Max had been sexually abused at Children's Path, but he wanted to hear what the other parents had to say.

During the meeting, Chuck later told the press, certain parents made threats of "picketing" Children's Path and "bludgeoning its staff with baseball bats." Chuck said the comments had been voiced in the presence of Sheriff's Task Force leader Lt. Richard Willey. "Willey did nothing to discourage the real and violent loose talk," Chuck claimed.

In response, Lt. Willey said that he hadn't heard any threats of violence and that he "did not condone violence"—but he admitted that many of the parents were very angry. "I heard a lot of frustration," Lt. Willey stated. "I heard a lot of anger. But the vast majority of parents have conducted themselves very well."

Chuck disagreed, saying that the reactions of the parents were far more unlawful than Lt. Willey led on, and that what he'd seen was further evidence of a "witch-hunt atmosphere" that had taken hold of the South Bay.

Chuck made reference to the *Daily Breeze* article which reported that "rabbit ears" had been recovered during the task force's investigation of a suspect's home. It was being offered as evidence of a "satanic cult," even though the suspect of the search claimed that the rabbit ears were a "souvenir from a hunting trip."

"I imagine all of Hermosa Beach must've gotten rid of their lucky rabbit's foot and their Halloween costumes," Chuck quipped.

But for Chuck, even though his best method of self-therapy was finding comfort through humor, his current situation was no joking matter. In essence, his life had been destroyed.

On that volatile evening in question, with nowhere to go, with no personal column to write, Chuck found himself lurking in the background of a parents' meeting, taking notes, just thankful that the vengeful crowd wasn't targeting him.

03-5-82

I was at Mrs. Gooches when I noticed Honda keys were missing from my key chain, both ignition & lock.

▓▓▓▓ I yelled I was over spending — I asked him directly in front of Mark if we had any savings. He said "no, we hadn't been able to save a cent in 3 years."

He again didn't take a shower. He claimed he exercised today & continues to lie about the circumstances.

Judy Johnson's personal notes describing the volatile atmosphere within her home prior to the enrollment of her 2½-year-old son at the McMartin Preschool. (*Continued next page.*)

04-6-82
eve:
████████ claims he took keys this morning because he locked his in his car. He tried to replace them without me knowing. Claims he doesn't know what happen to other keys. Even time he would degrade me I swear I would minince it back. He became so angry he almost hit me instead he bashed a stain steel bowl from Dori. I told him unless he gave me "retainer $," I couldn't afford a lawyer.

8am — MAY 29 1983
████ seems to have thrown 2 pairs of shoes away — ████ comed over — 2 hrs late to pick up ████ who was just going to sleep for a nap. Says he wants to file immediately — if we are married 14 yrs he has to pay alimony for life of wife —
most lawyers don't understand how I feel — also developed a new thing called discounting — claims repairs will be 250 a month — which is split — even tho ½ this property is his & Land locked takes care of his property — "whoever said this world was fair"

called me slut & free loader — won't see kids until I work — If I work he wants adjustment in his payments even tho I must pay sitter fees — O gack — has threaten to take pass. + V.N. fix his name fraud —

The McMartin Preschool—Circa 1983

Checks written by Judy Johnson to Virginia McMartin Preschool for her youngest son's 14 total days of attendance.

```
                                    1944
REPORTING OFFICER                                    DR.NO. 83-04288
JAG, DET. J. #159
CONTINUATION OF:

    [X] CRIME REPORT                    [ ] INCIDENT REPORT
    [ ] ARREST/BOOKING REPORT            [ ] SUPPLEMENTAL REPORT
```

On 8-12-83 at 1200 hrs. R/O was contacted via phone by R/P Judy Johnson. R/P Judy Johnson advised R/O that she just learned from her son, ████████, that he had been molested by a male employee, Ray, of the Virginia McMartin Pre-School in Manhattan Beach. R/P Judy Johnson told R/O that Ray is the grandson of the owner, Virginia McMartin, and the only male employee at said pre-school. R/P Johnson further related that based upon information received from the victim it appeared he had been sodomized by the suspect. R/P Judy Johnson states the victim came home yesterday from the pre-school and she noted that his anal area was very red which it had not been prior to his going to said school the same day. R/P Johnson also informed R/O that on several prior occasions she has noted redness and irritation to the victim's anal area after having been at the pre-school which was not present at any time prior to attending the school on each occasion. R/P Johnson recalls having observed blood on the victim's anus on one occasion after returning home from the pre-school when she was preparing her son for a bath. R/O informed R/P Judy Johnson that a thorough medical examination by a specialist experienced in treating sexually abused children was essential and should be done immediately. R/O requested that R/P Judy Johnson respond to the station that afternoon with the victim so an investigation could be initiated. R/P Judy Johnson related to R/O that she had already made some preliminary arrangements to have the victim examined by Dr. Scott McGeary in the emergency room at Kaiser Hospital, Harbor City. ████████ requested that R/P ████████████████ to having the victim examined instead at Harbor General Hospital in the pediatric emergency department but she was unwilling to have her son treated at said facility.

On 8-12-83 at 1615 hrs. R/P Judy Johnson responded to the station and contacted R/O. R/P Judy Johnson told R/O that the victim began attending the pre-school about three months ago and has attended on Tuesday and Thursday mostly between 9 AM and Noon though there have been occasions when he stayed until 3 and 4 PM. R/P Johnson believes the victim has stayed beyond the noon hour at the pre-school on four or five occasions.

Copy of the original Manhattan Beach police report by Judy Johnson against Ray Buckey on August 12 1983.

Virginia McMartin (left), founder of the McMartin Preschool—one of Manhattan Beach's most decorated citizens. Detective Jane Hoag (right) initiated the investigation into Ray Buckey and the McMartin Preschool, and spearheaded the twenty-two member Sheriff's Task Force that later shut down seven local preschools.

Kee MacFarlane (left), the therapist at CII who determined that hundreds of former McMartin preschoolers had been concealing dark secrets of sexual abuse.

Wayne Satz (right), the award-winning KABC-TV *Eyewitness News* investigative reporter, broke the story on February 2, 1984.

> Pete is a flight engineer for United. He is planning to sell his business (Nautilus) very soon. A friend of mine had lunch with Verna Stubb Luckman (Scurti's Studio) who said Pete fired her to make the books look good.
>
> The red circled people in this ad are all similar to Michael. The 3 women are witches. The man poked him.
>
> Peggy, Babs, & Betty all dressed up as witches too.
>
> ~~The person who buried~~ there were no holes ~~in the coffin~~ ████ is Miss Betty
>
> Babs went with him on a train with an older girl where he was hurt by men in suits. Ray waved good bye. The train moved fast. It had lights. Ray took him back to school. Poss. San Diego Big Brothers.
>
> Peggy gave ████ an enema before he was taken away. (from the Martin Sch.)
>
> Stapples were put in ████ ears, nipples, & tongue.
>
> Babs put scissors in his eyes. She hit them a lot. She chopped up animals and said she would come in the night and take him away. She pushed his stomach and threw him against a wall. He has extreme fear regarding Babs. ~~something awful would come in the window~~
>
> Ray made small babies cry.
>
> ████ was hurt by a lion. An elephant played with the lion. squirted H₂O. Then the lion didn't move. Michael was on his back. Ray lit him ~~pull the lion's tail~~. The lion roared ~~but didn't move~~. Betty was there, and other people. One lady took ~~pictures~~.

Judy Johnson's handwritten letter to Detective Jane Hoag dated February 16, 1984—later identified as the "smoking gun"—just weeks before her grand jury testimony where, according to eye witnesses, Judy appeared "lucid" and mentally sound.

March 23, 1984: The indictment of the "McMartin Seven." Left to right: Virginia McMartin seated (bottom left), Babette Spitler (third from left); Betty Raidor (fourth from left; face partially covered); Peggy Ann Buckey (fifth from left); Danny Davis (at podium); Peggy Buckey (to the right of Davis); Ray Buckey (far right). Maryanne Jackson is not shown in this picture.

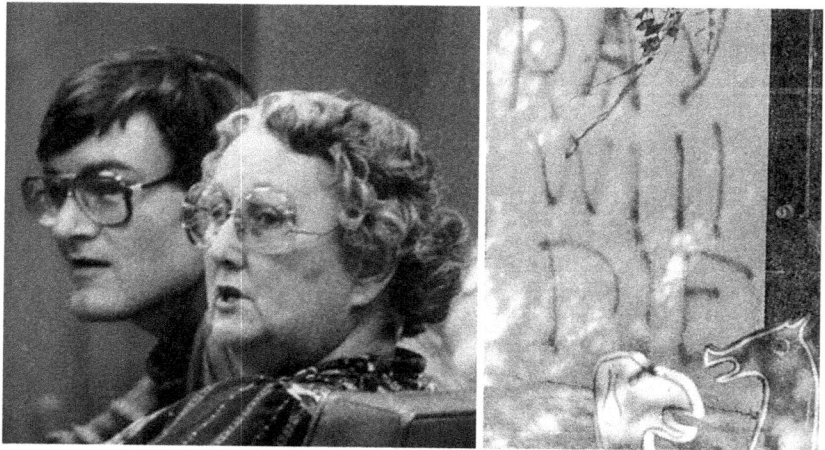

In January 1984 after numerous threats the McMartin Preschool closes its doors after 27 years of business.

November 16, 1984: Announcement by "Parents Against Child Abuse" (PACA) at the Los Angeles Press Club. PACA's Spokesperson, Hermosa Beach City Councilman, John Cioffi (at the lectern); Cioffi's wife, Mary Mae, stands in the background (fourth from left) with Jackie McGauley (sixth from left).

Bob Currie, the vocal parent activist, seen here on Geraldo Rivera's prime time special, "Exposing Satan's Underground."

October 1984—Michael Ruby and family after his release from Eastlake Juvenile Detention Center.

(Left) Michael returns home. (Right) Michael surfs El Porto.

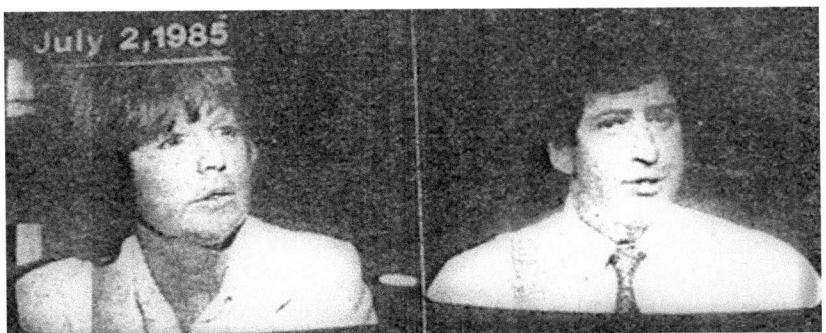

In July of 1985, ten weeks after her release from UC Irvine's Psychiatric Hospital, Judy Johnson (left) agreed to an interview with KABC-TV reporter Wayne Satz (right).

```
UNIVERSITY CALIFORNIA IRVINE MEDICAL CENTER
MENTAL HEALTH, BUILDING TWO PASS

 Judith Johnson            2 East
 Name of patient           Ward
 has been granted permission to have ground
 privilege

 Unaccompanied  ✓

 Accompanied by friend or relative_____

  4/16/85         S. Pituck  M.D.
  Date            Physician
```

Judy Johnson's VW Van in which she traveled the countryside and later lived in when she left Manhattan Beach for Washington to be closer to her children.

6-4-86

Dear Mom and Dad,
   Sorry I haven't called more often but have been out of funds and busy trying to make ends meet! Did try to call Mother's Day and one day after church with Steve.
   Certainly appreciate all your help. Seems a shame ▓▓▓▓▓ is so disruptive. He & Marie certainly make enough to live on and then some. Perhaps, they need a good dose of Christian love!
   Nevertheless, everything has really gotten worse. I know how super you've been through all this and I can't stop thanking you enough. I believe you can use me as a tax write off. I have no reportable income. My only funds have been from you. That should be a sizable amount if I remember right.
   The worst will be the next 3 months as the job market is overwhelmed with summer teenagers. I need re-training and join a union to make anything really livable. I can survive on $300⁰⁰ a month but it requires a lot of budgeting. If you can help for the next 3 months, hopefully I will be nearly independent. If the courts decide to keep the children in their custody I am considering moving to Forest City. Hope to talk to you soon to get your ideas.
   My major concern is car repairs now. I have managed to stay afloat since

Judy's Notes to parents in which she describes her struggles while living near her brother in Bellevue, Washington. (*Continued next page.*)

[2]

~~Bernard~~ cut funds Dec. 1st. Perhaps, I fought it out too long. I think I need some sunshine to cheer things up.

To top it off I have had to deal with a legal system, which is very mundane. So much for our taxes?! ya —

Hope all is well. Look forward to seeing you soon, I hope.

If you decide you can help me it would be a real gift of love. Steve's address is still currant for me.

A lot of love,

Judy

P.S. If you happen to see ~~Richard~~ give him a lot of hugs from me. ~~Bernard~~ won't even let me talk to him.

They Must Be Monsters

Clement Edmund Renaud, pleaded "no contest" in 1986 for sexually abusing children on the grounds of American Martyrs Parochial School in 1982.

> Judy —
> I have come over many times in the last week and called your name and knocked. I know you are in there and I'm very sorry that you won't answer me. Please don't shut us all out again. What if Mark get's sicker and we can't reach you? Would you want to do that to him? Mark had his Chemotherapy last Mon & Tues. and he did fine. He is home from school for a few days and then he's going back to school. Maybe you could call him during the daytime. I'm sure he would love it. Judy please take care of yourself and remember we are here if you need help.
>
> Gayle

The letter written to Judy by her neighbor and best friend, Gayle Shaffer, dated Monday, December 15, 1986, where Gayle pleaded with Judy not to "shut us all out."

Ray Buckey spent five years in County jail without bail before being released on a three million dollar bond in April 1989.

CHAPTER
26

On Tuesday, February 12, 1985, ten-year-old Billy Sampson, a third-grader at American Martyrs Parochial, concluded his ninth day of testimony at the McMartin preliminary hearing, a proceeding that had hit its eighth month and had no end in sight. Eight of Billy's nine days on the stand had been cross-examination.

Little Billy had grown tired of his daily trip to the Criminal Courts Building in downtown Los Angeles. The excitement had worn off. The courtroom wasn't as packed as it had been the first week. The media contingency had dwindled down to the local print and broadcast reporters assigned to the case.

From the stand, Billy looked out at the crowd of familiar faces—his mother, Terri, Bob and Angela Currie, and all the others who had shown up in his support. Having them there gave Billy confidence as the defense bore down.

Seated behind the long wooden table separating him from his accuser, Ray Buckey remained stone-faced, shaking his head in disbelief. As Billy spoke, providing graphic details of his alleged abuse, Ray dropped his head to look at the yellow legal pad on which he wrote his thoughts, where he focused on the factual inconsistencies of Billy's testimony:

Never saw Billy before in my life before I saw him on the CII video tape...honestly, that I can remember.

I went to the open house each year at the school, mostly because I had to and the remaining reason was to eat the cookies. Billy could

> *have seen me then, but I wouldn't have stuck out like a sore thumb because the school was packed with older brothers and fathers...*
>
> *Terri Stafford, the mother, I knew by name and sight because she stopped by the school occasionally when I was there...and I think as a carpool mother.*
>
> *She was very involved in the woman's group in Manhattan Beach...American Martyrs family...*

As Billy continued to describe a fantastical story of a far away trip, an account that seemed impossible based on the time frames and the fact that it had to have occurred without anyone in town noticing, Ray was astounded that the prosecution considered Billy a credible witness.

> *Billy is the case's premiere pathological liar. Smart enough not to be cornered in a lie or admit an obvious lie...he just lied his way out again...probably the child with the most testimony and growth of his stories.*
>
> *Reason for lying? This child looks like he wouldn't be accepted by his peers—red hair, freckles and fat. What I see is a child getting more attention than he could ever imagine and love (pity, attention; negative in a way) from his family. An inadvertent free rein and reinforcement from his parents to make up a flat out lie on the stand...*
>
> *I don't think he'll testify at the trial because his stories are too easily chopped down to their pure essence, stories beyond possibility...*
>
> *I was not at the school around '79 when he attended.*

Ray was correct. Billy Sampson had last attended the McMartin Preschool five years earlier, in 1978-79, three years before Ray began his employment. Nevertheless, Billy alleged that Ray had snuck in and out of the campus in the years prior, when Ray was a non-working drifter in his early-twenties, and that Ray had taken part in the group sex with the other female defendants.

On this Tuesday afternoon, however, Billy's testimony grew even more bizarre. In response to rapid-fire questions from the defense, Billy provided a graphic and detailed account of being "taken to a church" where adults wore "masks and black robes" and "danced and moaned" while Ray Buckey "went to the altar" and killed rabbits, turtles, and birds, threatening to kill the children's parents if they told.

"On a trip to a farm," Billy testified, "Ray chopped a pony to death with a long knife."

Billy explained that, in an effort to locate the church where the rituals took place, he and his mother had "went searching for it," driving around the beach cities, and during their search, they actually found it.

"St. Cross," Billy said. "I was taken to the St. Cross church."

When asked to verify if he was referring to the "St. Cross Episcopal Church in Hermosa Beach," Billy replied, "Yes."

Of all the families whose children had attended the McMartin Preschool in the five years prior to the scandal, the Sampsons would have been the least likely to believe that their child had been abused. Billy and his older brother Jeremy both had attended McMartin, but neither had ever shown physical or emotional signs of abuse.

Teresa Sampson, Billy's mother—"Terri" to all who knew her, and a "Sandpiper" along with Angela Currie and the others—was an educated and intelligent woman who'd always kept a close eye out for her children. A registered nurse at Hawthorne Hospital since 1964, she became a stay-at-home-mom during her boys' preschool years, putting her nursing career on hiatus.

The Sampsons, an American Martyrs family—parishioners whose children attended Martyrs Parochial—lived just minutes from both the church and the McMartin Preschool, and Terri was one of the handful of mothers who'd developed a close bond with Virginia and Peggy.

Like the others, in the beginning, Terri didn't believe any of it. In fact, she testified it wasn't until Saturday, January 28, 1984—four-and-a-half months after the investigation became public—that Terri first became aware of the seriousness of the case, the day Bob and Angela Currie showed up to her home.

The Sampsons and the Curries had been "very close friends" for fifteen years. They were fellow parishioners, and their kids were classmates at Martyrs Parochial. If not for the Curries, Terri said, her family would have never gotten involved.

On that Saturday, the Curries, having just been to CII the day before, came to the Sampson home to break the news. The Curries said that if such things had happened to their children, it was likely to have also happened to the Sampson boys, since the kids were in the same preschool classrooms at the same time.

For two days following that encounter, Terri struggled with the idea of having her boys interviewed, but she eventually gave in. Terri placed a call to CII, but the lines were busy. Minutes later she tried again, but still couldn't get through.

Determined to get the interviews scheduled, Terri jumped into her car and drove to downtown Los Angeles to do it in person. Due to the high volume of potential victims, the Sampsons were given the date of February 22, three weeks later.

In the days leading up to the Sampson interviews, the community was in an uproar, with a massive amount of media exposure. Night after night, Wayne Satz captured the attention of all of Los Angeles, as the alleged crimes committed at the "preschool in Manhattan Beach" gave every parent pause. The story was, in every sense, the talk of the town.

Still, Terri Sampson claimed that during those twenty-four days—January 30 to February 22—she didn't hear "anything about the McMartin Preschool," nor did she believe that her son Billy discussed it with any of his classmates at American Martyrs, some of whom had already disclosed that they'd been abused.

On the morning of Wednesday, February 22, 1984, after finishing breakfast, Terri told Jeremy and Billy to get ready, that they had an appointment to attend.

"Some people want to talk about what happened at the nursery school," Terri said.

Jeremy went to his room, got dressed, and came back out. But Billy took a long time getting ready, longer than normal.

"Go check on your brother, would ya," Terri told Jeremy.

A few minutes passed, and the boys hadn't come out. Terri went to see what was holding them up, and she heard Billy's voice projecting down the hallway.

"If they ask me any questions about that school," Billy screamed at Jeremy, "it's gonna be 'No. No. No!' "

When Terri got to the room, Billy was throwing a tantrum.

"I don't wanna go! I already told you nothing happened to me."

For several minutes, Billy pounded on his dresser and cried hysterically.

But Terri persisted, and eventually she convinced Billy to go. By the end of the day, after being interviewed by Sandi Krebs, the same therapist who'd interviewed the Currie children, and after his physical examination by Dr. Astrid Heger, Billy was determined to have been sexually abused. His medical examination revealed evidence of rectal scarring that was "consistent with a history of sexual abuse." Billy was said to be one of the "worst cases of trauma diagnosed in the case."

Billy was added to the list of alleged victims, one of the "older children" who could articulate what had happened to him in 1979, more than five years earlier.

Sitting on the witness stand, almost one year since he first told therapists about his abuse at the McMartin Preschool, his accusations against the St. Cross Episcopal Church ignited a firestorm of suspicion. Word of St. Cross made its way to the coast well before it hit the news.

Bob Currie, having just witnessed the first official allegation of satanic ritual abuse, contacted parents of St. Cross children. "You better get your kids the hell outta there," Currie warned.

Most parents found it too difficult to imagine, that this type of wickedness could exist, and that it could have happened right under their noses. Some challenged Currie's line of thinking.

"Don't say I didn't warn you," Currie told the naysayers. "If something happens to your kid, it's on *you*."

Not only did Billy say he had witnessed strangers in black robes, with "some wearing devil masks," he also said they "danced around in a circle" in the "candle-lit church."

"As the ritual ended," Billy testified, "Ray sacrificed a rabbit on the altar, and he made me drink its blood."

Days later, with warrants in hand, the Task Force entered St. Cross Episcopal, scouring the altar for remnants of blood and other forensic evidence to support Billy's claims.

St. Cross, a spectacular place of worship, a magnificent sanctuary with concrete arches and dark-brown trusses against a beige backdrop, was so typical of the colorful images the Episcopal Church had put forth. Its massive, high-rising stained-glass window stood above the crucifix, spreading a soft blue light upon the altar—the last place anyone would think a satanic cult would molest children.

The investigators uncovered no evidence.

In the aftermath of Billy's disclosures and the subsequent raids, the *New York Times* stated that the picture being painted by prosecutors and their witnesses was "so horrifying" that it seemed like a "Gothic catalogue of evil."

* * * * *

Noreen Noel, following up on the letters the DCSS had mailed to Judy Johnson on March 4 and March 11—a last-ditch attempt at urging Judy to comply and send Mark to school—stepped onto the porch on Vista Drive. Noel knocked and waited. Mitchell came to the door.

"Is your mom here?" Noel asked.

"She's out back," said the four-and-a-half-year-old.

Noel followed Mitchell through the living room and toward the back, where a small patio was connected to the alley. Noel stepped outside and saw Judy lying in a lounge chair, basking in the sun, in a mellow mood as she read her Bible.

Noel, knowing the unabridged backstory, found it too tranquil to believe.

"Thank you so much for coming," Judy said. "This is just *wonderful* to have you here. It is so nice of you to come by and see us."

Noel said Judy started talking about "spirituality" and quoting the Bible, "overflowing" with kindness and gratitude. Judy kept repeating that they were having "no problems, no problems at all," and that "Mark didn't need to go to school." Noel didn't buy it.

Before leaving, Noreen spoke with Mark. He liked her for the most part, but remained suspicious of anyone critical of his mother, particularly the professionals who seemed to know what was "good for the family." Mark was, in every way, the man of the house, his mother's protector, the role his father had left unfulfilled.

Yet, like it or not, the issue of Mark missing school was not going away, at least as far as the DCSS was concerned. Noel needed Mark to cooperate, but she knew he preferred being home where he could look after the mother who'd always looked after him.

By spring 1985, Mark's cancer had been out of remission for several months, and he'd just started another round of chemo. He was deteriorating rapidly, more so than the time before. His face had swelled grotesquely. It embarrassed him. He hated being a spectacle, those awkward moments when his classmates turned their heads at the mere sight of him.

"What are you trying to do?" Mark asked Noel, suspecting she needed a reason to take him and Mitchell away from Judy. "Are you trying to hurt my mother?"

"No, Mark," Noel replied. "Your mother's a wonderful person, when she doesn't drink. But when she does, she's not well."

Mark couldn't argue with her. He knew his mother had many

personalities, and the one he liked most was the sober woman sitting on her lounge chair with a Bible in her hand.

Still, Mark didn't have a better option. If his mother lost custody, which seemed likelier by the day, he and Mitchell would go to their father, and Mark's relationship with Brad was in a very bad place.

The previous July, with Brad under tremendous stress after being accused of molesting Mitchell, Mark lashed out at his father, blaming him for abandoning the family.

According to Gayle Schaeffer, while on the stand in the Johnsons' dependency hearing, Mark "told Brad off" using hateful language that only a child who felt mistreated and neglected would use. It said a lot about their family life, and it made Brad look less than stellar in the eyes of the jurist. "Brad wouldn't speak to Mark after that day," Gayle said.

Brad, however, despite his flaws, believed he was acting in the children's best interest.

On a day in mid-March, in the heart of the Lenten season, Brad wrote a letter to Judy telling her that her decisions were "not good for Mark," and he warned of her "isolation." He asked her to consider him a "dear friend," and he pleaded with Judy to "trust someone." He warned her that the bank was foreclosing and the homeowner's insurance had been cancelled because she hadn't made the payments.

Despite the dire situation, Brad tried to give Judy hope. He ended his letter by proclaiming:

Easter is a good time for renewal.
Christ Has Risen.
Judy Has Risen!

Brad, however, in his own detached state, miscalculated how intense Judy's religious convictions had become. Judy had taken her faith to a new level, no longer interpreting the scriptures philosophically, but literally.

In the dead of the night, while her boys lay asleep, Judy sat alone, her Bible opened. She spread a cloth across her table, an Egyptian-blue fabric.

Judy stitched feverishly, sewing an image to its center, making a banner that she would hang outside her door. The flag, a crude piece of art, represented the divinity of the Passover season. Once hoisted, the flag would protect her, keeping at bay the evil that surrounded her home.

CHAPTER
27

"The Dig," as it came to be called, was a Bob Currie production. On that day, Saturday, March 16, 1985, Currie decided he would "find the bones," even though the Los Angeles District Attorney had warned against it. The DA wasn't particularly fond of Currie and his band of parent activists.

Currie and his group had repeatedly asked the DA to dig up the McMartin grounds, ever since children had said that carcasses of slaughtered animals were buried there. Time and again, the DA refused.

After two kids testified at the preliminary hearing that turtles had been killed—stabbed and ripped from their shells—Currie took action. He called Arnold Goldstein, the owner of the lot, who granted access. Currie rented a backhoe and they went in.

Currie claimed to have "spoken and listened to a number of children," so he "felt pretty confident" that he "knew where to look." From there, he directed the backhoe operator.

With the dig underway, Keith Hearn, a private investigator for the McMartin defense, drove by the lot and saw a crowd gathered. He slowed down and watched the backhoe drop its bucket into the dirt. He hurried home, changed his clothes, put his dog on a leash, and went back to the site as if he was out for a stroll.

When Hearn arrived, he noticed the crowd had grown, and that it seemed more like a party than a search for critical evidence. Parents were laughing while kids ram amok. Someone spotted him—a parent who recognized him from his days at the courtroom—and went to tell the others. Within minutes, a gathering of angry parents surrounded him.

"Get the hell outta here!" one father yelled, stepping up and holding the blade of his shovel at eye level.

Hearn said nothing, standing his ground.

Another man got in Hearn's face. "You better get movin'. You might just get an ass kickin'."

Hearn smelled alcohol on their breaths and clothes.

Then Currie rushed up, getting nose-to-nose with Hearn. "I know who you are. You better get the fuck outta here. Now!" Then Currie bumped Hearn with his chest.

"I'm not going anywhere," Hearn said. "I have just as much right to be here as any of you."

Currie looked him over, then shook his head and stepped away. "Come on," Currie said to the crowd. "Let's get to work."

Hearn stuck around for another thirty minutes, but walked away once he knew they were wasting their time.

Around 3:00 p.m., after digging for seven hours, Bob Currie reached the same conclusion. He looked around at the crowd of parents, and he saw defeat in their eyes. Some of them, exhausted, were sitting in the shade. Currie called it a day, whistling to the backhoe operator.

"Shut her down," Currie hollered. "That's it. We're done."

As Currie walked toward the others, dejected, he felt a tug on his pants. He turned and saw little Ricky Morrow, an alleged victim, a child he knew well.

"Bob," Ricky said, "you didn't find the bones?"

"No, Ricky, I didn't," Currie replied. "I'm sorry, but I don't know where they are."

"I'll tell you where they are."

"Where?"

Ricky pointed toward the northeast corner of the lot. "Right over there, between the pine tree and the building."

Currie and two others went over with shovels. They dug aggressively, about two feet deep, then they heard the first clank—the sound of the blade striking a solid object.

"We got something," Currie yelled, as mothers and fathers surrounded the hole.

Currie reached into the loose dirt and wiped off the item. He raised it over his head—a small piece of a shattered turtle shell.

"Here it is," Currie proclaimed. "Evidence."

The parents cheered. As Currie put it, "We all quit digging and began to celebrate."

The next morning, a *Los Angeles Times* headline read, "Parents Dig for Bones!" The article reported that the "first physical evidence to support the children's claim of animal torture" at the McMartin Preschool had been uncovered, that "fragments of tortoise shells and an animal bone were excavated" from the vacant lot adjacent to the preschool.

The DA dispatched specialists from the Sheriff's Crime Lab to take over the parents' investigation. A deputy, accompanied by four forensic experts, went to work. Before long, they unearthed more shell fragments and animal bones.

As the specialists worked, parents stood nearby and gave statements to the press.

"For a month we've been getting the runaround from the police and the district attorney," one father declared. "Now, they're finally taking an interest."

Another father pointed to an avocado tree in the lot.

"My son told me he witnessed animal sacrifices and devil worship, that it happened right over there. My son said *that* is where 'the devil lives.'"

Despite the elation of the parents, Deputy DA Roger Gunson, the head of the Child Abuse Division, downplayed the findings. "When they called and told us what they'd done," Gunson explained, "we had to come out here in the middle of the night to secure this area instead of coming in with the experts we would've liked."

The experts Roger Gunson referred to were brought in a few weeks later. "SRS," a team consisting of ten specialists—excavators, surveyors, and a geologist—searched for "evidence of underground structures or animal remains," the first forensic study of whether the theory of "underground transport tunnels" had any basis.

In their analysis of the "northeast corner" of the lot where the animal remains were uncovered, they found the soil to be "darker," with a mix of different colors, which "sometimes" indicates that the soil had been disturbed. They also identified "duff," defined as "decaying plant material mixed with soil, usually found around trees or bushes."

In respect to the animal remains, the specialists determined the tortoise shells didn't reveal anything that showed "pre-death trauma," that they were "consistent with an arrival of death by natural causes rather than a tortured animal." They found "no flesh" on the turtle shells, and the shells looked to have been underground for twenty years or longer. They determined that one tortoise had been "placed into the pit and buried," concluding that it could have been placed there by "parties other than those under criminal investigation."

The SRS technicians found no evidence that underground tunnels had been constructed and filled in.

* * * * *

Six days later

A cool morning, about 7:30 a.m., as a thin fog lifted and a heavy dew set, David Robinson, a thirty-four-year-old black man, an electronics technician at TRW in El Segundo, warmed his car and wiped his windows clear, ready for work. David's apartment sat directly across the street from the McMartin Preschool.

Less than a mile west, the sheriff's Task Force assembled at the lifeguard shack beneath the pier, ready for its next set of raids—the four locations that had just been implicated. The officers started their vehicles and headed east over the incline, slowing to a stop in front of the apartment complex where David and Patricia Robinson lived. The officers exited their vehicles and surrounded the perimeter.

As David opened the driver's side door, about to step in, he heard noises, the sound of running boots. He looked up, startled to find the entire complex filled with police. Two officers ran toward him and drew their guns.

"Are you David Robinson?" a plain-clothed officer yelled. "Are you David Robinson?"

David put his hands out before him.

"Get your hands up," the officer ordered, pointing his gun. "I asked you if you're David Robinson. Are you David Robinson?"

"Yes, sir," he replied. "I'm David Robinson."

Two officers braced David against his car, while the others ran up the stairs to his apartment. Inside, David's wife, Patricia, and their newborn daughter, Jessica, just three weeks old, slept.

Half awake, Patricia enjoyed the peacefulness of the morning light, knowing that any minute her daughter's cry would prompt the day. A resounding thud came from the front room. Patricia sat upright. It continued rapidly, a banging and rattling as if someone was breaking down the door.

Jessica woke and cried, a high-pitched squeal that voiced her displeasure with being rousted so abruptly.

Patricia, terrified, lifted Jessica from her crib, held her tightly against her chest, and rushed to the living room. The door burst open. Officers filed into the apartment, each of them wearing windbreakers to cover their bullet-proof vests. The lead investigator moved toward Patricia, waving the search warrant.

"You need to sit down, ma'am," he ordered, reaching out to her. "You need to give us the baby."

"Why?" Patricia cried aloud. "No. Why?"

"We're taking this child into protective custody," the officer responded.

"What? Why?" Patricia asked, shaking her head.

"You've been deemed an unfit parent."

"Unfit?"

"There's an accusation that you may have molested this child, ma'am," he said, placing his hands gently on Jessica. "You need to let go of the baby, ma'am. You need to do it now."

Patricia wept as the officer pulled Jessica from her clutches.

"Please don't," Patricia begged. "She's hungry. She needs to eat. Please just let me feed her." Patricia stood and walked toward the officer.

The officer turned away, shielding her from Jessica. "Step back. Do it now."

They argued for nearly a minute while baby Jessica screamed for her breakfast. Finally, the officer couldn't take it anymore.

"All right, sit down!" He handed Patricia the baby. Patricia rocked Jessica slowly, calming her. Patricia looked up at the officer, an unspoken request for privacy. The officer grabbed a blanket from the sofa and draped it over them.

Once fed, Jessica fell asleep against her mother's bosom. Patricia pulled the blanket back, and the officer lifted Jessica and placed her into a car seat. He strapped her in and carried her away.

"Can I please change her diaper?" Patricia yelled. But the officer left the apartment with Jessica. Patricia fell back on the sofa, devastated.

At the same apartment complex, members of the task force raided the unit of Malcolm and Gretchen Campbell. Gretchen was Patricia Robinson's sister.

Police pounded on the Campbells' door. Gretchen thought it might be Patricia and the baby coming over for a cup of coffee—but it didn't make sense, the angry sound of a fist, over and over.

"Malcolm!" Gretchen called out, "Can you see who that is?"

Malcolm, not pleased, had already made his move toward the front door. He swung it open, and a gun was in his face.

"We have a search warrant!" the lead officer said, handing Malcolm his authorization. "Stay out of the way."

A female detective began questioning Gretchen.

"Do you believe in Satan?" the detective asked.

"What are you talking about?"

"Do you practice Satanism?"

"No, I do not," Gretchen replied.

Simultaneously, one mile east, at 1833 3rd Street, Patricia's and Gretchen's mother, Mary Lou Briesler, waited for her children to arrive. Mary Lou, fifty-seven, had run a home babysitting service for the past nine years.

A fist pounded repeatedly on Mary Lou's door, a violent sound. "This is the police. Open up. This is the police. We have a search warrant."

Mary Lou froze, unsure. Her fourteen-year-old daughter, Penny, a freshman at Mira Costa High, came from her bedroom.

"Mom, what's going on?" Penny asked. "Who's that?"

"Go into your room," Mary Lou told her. "Close your door and don't say a word."

Mary Lou opened the front door. A team of officers rushed past her, dropping their warrant at her feet.

"What's going on?" Mary Lou said.

"Stand back," the lead officer yelled, directing her to the couch. "Sit down and stay out of the way."

Mary Lou did as he instructed.

A few blocks away, at 1327 Gates Avenue, Mary Lou's sister, Fran Gammer, ran her own baby-sitting service. Fran often took her kids over to Mary Lou's house to let the children play together. For years, Fran had coordinated with the McMartin Preschool to provide after-school childcare for parents who worked past 4:00 p.m. Several of Fran's kids were former McMartin students, and the police considered Fran's business to be the "unofficial-official babysitting service" for McMartin families.

Like her sister, Fran had been startled by the pounding on her door and the mad rush of investigators who took control of her home. Fran, too, stood to the side while officers tore through each room, pulling out drawers and dumping the contents onto the floor.

At both locations, investigators dug up the backyards looking for animal bones.

The raids of the four homes had been initiated by five children, all former McMartin students. Each child had accused the Breislers, or members of their extended family, of rape, sodomy, oral copulation, and pornography. Two of the children had started going to the Briesler home after McMartin shutdown in January 1984. They alleged that Mary Lou Briesler "drank blood from goblets, lit candles, and danced in a red devil outfit," and that animals had been slaughtered and "buried in her backyard." One child claimed to have witnessed "family members sexually abusing Penny."

While officers dug up the Brieslers' backyard, a female detective approached Penny. "Get dressed," the officer said, "you're going with me."

Penny ran to her mother, weeping. They embraced.

"I don't wanna go. Please don't let them take me," Penny cried. "Please, Mom, don't let them take me."

Mary Lou pulled back and looked Penny in the eyes, doing her best to calm her. "You go, Penny. You do as they say," Mary Lou said, kissing her cheek. "Everything will be okay, I promise."

The officer led Penny out of the house and placed her in the back of an unmarked vehicle, then drove away.

At the Robinsons' apartment, the police used a card table to run inventory of the items confiscated, creating a checklist. Patricia viewed it as "Gestapo" tactics, the way they ripped Jessica's mattress from her crib, dumped open all of their shelves, and took eight boxes of their personal belongings. They even took all of Jessica's newborn photos, images the Robinsons had only enjoyed for twenty-one days.

The officers were fascinated by anything scary. They collected Halloween makeup, a camera, videotapes of *The Thing* and *The Dead Zone*, and a tiny rubber skeleton from the garage.

About an hour after Jessica had been taken into protective custody, apologetic officials returned with her.

"We're sorry," said the man in charge. "We received false information that your daughter was over a year old, not three weeks." He handed Patricia the baby and left.

The police spent seven hours at the Robinsons' apartment but came up with nothing. As the last investigator left, with the Robinsons' home in shambles, he handed David the business card of a Manhattan Beach Police detective.

"She's the one to sue," the deputy snickered.

The card was that of Detective Jane Hoag.

Nearby, at the Manhattan Beach Police Department, Penny Briesler went through an interview.

"Your entire family's being accused of child molestation," an officer told Penny. "Is there anything you want to tell us? You don't have to be afraid anymore. It's all over."

But Penny said nothing. Over several hours of questioning, Penny told the police repeatedly that they were making a big mistake.

Once left alone, Penny scribbled a note to her parents:

I love you. We did nothing wrong. Somebody is lying.

Penny was taken to UCLA-Harbor Medical Center, where she underwent a physical examination to determine if she'd been sexually abused. Nothing conclusive could be determined.

As the night grew long, they brought Penny a McDonald's Happy Meal, then transported her to MacLaren's Children's Center in El Monte. She would not be allowed to have any contact with her parents.

Weeks later, sitting in the darkened kitchen of a foster home, Penny grabbed a butcher knife and slashed her wrists. *If I can't live with my parents, then life's not worth living.*

The cuts, fortunately, were not deep enough to be fatal, although she may have never fully healed.

CHAPTER
28

The morning of Friday, April 5—Good Friday to the faithful—Judy Johnson's brother, Steve Knutson, enjoyed breakfast at his home in Bellevue, Washington. The phone rang. His wife Debbie answered. She listened. She looked concerned. Debbie placed her hand over the receiver. "Steve, its Noreen Noel. There's something wrong with Judy."

Steve rushed to the phone. "Noreen, what's going on?"

"Judy's locked herself in her house," Noel told him. "She's totally recluse. She won't speak to anyone, not me, not Gayle. We have no way of checking on the kids." Noel paused. "This is a new low, Steve. You need to get down here."

"I'll get the next flight out of Seattle," Steve said. "Meet me at Gayle's." Steve hung up, called his father, Pastor Knutson, who agreed to meet Steve there.

Hours later, the four of them—Steve, Gayle, Noreen, and Pastor Knutson—stood in Gayle's living room.

"How did it get to this?" Steve asked Noel. "The last time I spoke with her she seemed fine."

Noel, who had witnessed Judy's transformation, explained her plight as a "classic bout between good and evil," that Judy was at war with the devil, all of it fueled by alcohol. The more she drank, the more intense she became.

"When Judy's sober," Noel said, "she talks of God. But when she's drunk, she speaks of the devil."

"Judy doesn't *admire* the devil," Pastor Knutson replied. "She's a good Christian."

"No, no, it's not that," Noel clarified. "She's not espousing Satan—she fears him. She thinks that a demon's entered her life, that it's living in her home."

Noel went to the window. She pointed toward Judy's porch, to the banner on display. "Judy made that flag," Noel said. "When it goes up, she's in bad shape. And when it comes down, she's okay." Noel turned back to the others. "She's never told me what it represents."

Pastor Knutson had some idea.

The hand-made flag, he suspected, was Judy's attempt to ward off "evil spirits"—a three-foot-wide by two-foot-high banner with the Paschal Lamb laid over a field of blue—a crude variation of the traditional Christian portrait where the young sheep hoists a staff over its shoulder. Judy's flag embodied the Paschal Lamb from the Book of Revelation, "slain but standing," spilling its blood of redemption. Yet she added an artistic twist: the gory image of the staff piercing the lamb's body as blood dripped from its chest.

For Noel, though, more concerning than the flag was that Judy had been suffering from a severe ulcer.

"Judy's been really dehydrated lately," Noel said. "She saw an internist at Kaiser, and they treated her for a gastro-intestinal condition. But she won't stop drinking, which compounds the problem."

Noel told them that, on several occasions, Judy had vomited blood. "I haven't seen it firsthand, but she's talked about it," Noel said. "And when I tell her to lay off the alcohol, she gets angry and dismissive."

Steve had heard enough. He would confront Judy, letting her know that he and her father had come to help. Once Judy looked him in his eyes, Steve figured she would snap out of it.

Steve walked out the Schaeffers' back door and hurried to the back of Judy's house. He opened the wooden gate, where a tiny backyard separated the house from the one-car garage where he found Mark working on his bicycle.

"Hey, Mark," Steve greeted him. "What'cha doin'?"

Mark looked up, surprised to see his uncle unannounced. They went through a minute of small talk before Steve got direct. "Where's your mom?"

"Oh, she's in the house," Mark replied, turning the socket wrench. "But she's sick. She doesn't want to see anyone."

"I think she'll want to see her brother," Steve said, moving past Mark toward the house.

Steve stepped cautiously through the kitchen. "Judy. Judy, it's your brother." He noticed a shadow move across the living room and into the bathroom. "Judy?"

No response.

Steve panned the house. Dirty dishes were stacked in the sink, clothes were strewn through the hallway, and a pile of garbage had been pushed into the corner of the living room. "Judy," Steve yelled again, but once more, she didn't respond. Steve headed back to the garage.

"Mark, I know she's in there," Steve said. "Why isn't she answering me?"

Mark, about to respond, widened his eyes as he looked over Steve's shoulder. Steve turned around to find Judy holding a double-barreled shotgun to his face. She had rage in her eyes.

"Get off my property," Judy said. "This is Holy Land!"

Steve took a step back, his eyes focused on the gun. "Judy, are you talking to me? It's me...your brother...Steve."

"You're damn right I'm talking to you," Judy screamed. She pumped the shotgun and leaned in with the barrel.

Steve walked backward, slowly but steadily, keeping his eyes on Judy until he cleared her crosshairs. He ran to the front of the house, and seconds later, the door swung open. Judy stepped out holding the shotgun at her side.

Judy's metamorphosis stunned him. Once an avid jogger and hiker, running a 10K while pregnant, her waist and thighs had bloated, and she looked filthy, as if she hadn't bathed in a week. Steve had only known Judy as a health-conscious woman, a "very pretty girl in high school who never wore a lot of makeup or fashionable clothing." Steve said she was a naturalist with a true, organic beauty, and, most off all, she had a "pleasant spirit, a good soul."

But as she stood on her porch, holding her shotgun, glaring down upon him with her flag of the sacrificial lamb in the backdrop, Steve didn't know how to break her from the spell.

This isn't my sister. This is something out of The Exorcist.

"Judy, please," he begged her. "You can't be serious about this. Can we just talk for a minute? Will you put down the gun? Please, Judy? Please put down the gun."

"I'm not telling you again," Judy said, lifting the shotgun. "Get off my property." Judy went inside and slammed the door.

Steve heard the deadbolt slide into place, and he walked back to the Schaeffers' house.

"Should we call the police?" Pastor Knutson asked him.

"Absolutely," Steve said. "We have no choice. We can't leave the boys in there with her like that."

Steve called the Manhattan Beach Police Department, and they requested that he come to the station.

Once there, Steve met the Incident Commander, who dispatched a SWAT unit. The situation fit the profile. The suspect, Judy, armed, with potential hostages, was a threat to public safety.

A team of officers, as well as a specialist trained in hostage negotiation, examined the details of the neighborhood layout. They couldn't get in from Vista Drive through the front door; they would have to go in the back, from 31st Place, just as Steve had done. If Judy was startled, if she thought they were trying to break in, there was no telling what she may do.

From inside the Johnson home, Judy heard them lurking about the porch. The phone rang and rang, every twenty minutes it seemed. She only wanted peace, sanctuary, to be alone with her boys on this holy day, to protect them.

The SWAT team moved in, each man in place. They waited.

The afternoon grew long. Night approached—a full moon on the rise.

That Good Friday, a day when people flock to church to mourn the Passion, had not been so good for Judy. Through those afternoon hours, while her fellow Christians observed the Stations of the Cross, depicting Christ's tortuous path to Calvary, Judy sat in wait, clutching her shotgun, ready to fight.

Dusk approached. The police and the SWAT unit converged, opening the gate and entering the backyard, quietly but with purpose. They found Mark in the garage. An officer grabbed him by the arm and signaled him to be silent. The officer led Mark out and placed him in the back of a squad car. Mark's face flushed, and he yelled as the door shut. "Don't shoot her! Please don't shoot her!"

The police entered the kitchen, and Judy, standing in the hallway, spotted them. She'd left her gun in the living room, so she bolted for it, but an officer tackled her and dropped her to the floor. He held her down forcibly, pressing the side of her face against the carpet. He cuffed her hands behind her back and lifted her to her feet.

"This is a Holy Place," Judy screamed as they dragged her out of the house. "You can't do this. This is Holy Land."

They put Judy in the backseat of a squad car and the door closed her in. She dropped her head in despair.

An officer approached Steve and Pastor Knutson, who stood nearby. "She was lucky she didn't get killed," the officer said, holding up Judy's shotgun. "This isn't loaded, but we didn't know that. If she would've pointed this at us, she would've been shot, no doubt."

Gayle had stood back, allowing the Knutsons and the police to deal with it, but once she saw Mitchell escorted out and placed in the squad car with Mark, she ran over.

"Why are you taking them?" Gayle asked an officer. The officer continued toward the driver's side. "They can stay with me," Gayle yelled. "You don't need to take them away."

Gayle ran to the back of the squad car to speak with the boys. Mark held Mitchell, rocking his little brother, who screamed for his mommy.

"You'll be okay, I promise," Gayle assured them, trying not to cry, to appear hopeful. Gayle then yelled to the officer to "Please, stop the car." But he pulled away. Mark, tearful and confused, waved to Gayle through the rear window.

Gayle looked at the other squad car, where Steve and Pastor Knutson stood. Inside, slumped in the backseat, Judy sat with her head down. Gayle ran over and knocked on the window.

"Judy," she yelled. "Judy, I love you. I love you, Judy."

Judy lifted her head and glanced upward. Eyes glazed, Judy looked right through Gayle, as if they'd never met.

The police car drove away. Pastor Knutson held Steve and Gayle's hands, leading them in a prayer—a loving moment for Judy and her boys—then they returned to Gayle's house to regroup. The drama had ended, but the crisis lived on.

As the sun set upon that Good Friday, with the first shadows of the night streaming down the narrow roadway of Vista Drive, a full moon waned, illuminating the face of the Johnson home. The once vibrant dwelling had taken on a Stygian darkness, an abandoned, lifeless aura. The shades were tightly drawn, the potted plants unfed, nearing death.

Steve stepped onto Gayle's back patio, looking for a peaceful moment to gather his thoughts, but his eyes were drawn across the street. There, beneath the light of the moon, riding the wind, the flag of the Paschal Lamb disrupted his mood.

CHAPTER
29

At Kaiser Hospital in Harbor City, Judy received immediate care—sedated, examined, and strapped to a bed through the night.

Come dawn, an ambulance transferred her to the Psychiatric Clinic of the UC Irvine Medical Center, where she spent the next thirteen days undergoing a psychiatric evaluation.

Life outside of the psychiatric ward carried on without Judy. The joy of Easter Sunday and a precious memory with Mitchell escaped her, as did Mark's fifteenth birthday on April 16.

Coincidentally, during her incarceration, on Thursday, April 11, her marriage legally ended. Brad had been granted his freedom, while Judy had been confined.

A week prior to her arrest, Brad had written Judy a few letters. In them, he indicated that he had no intention of walking away from her and the boys. He promised to support her emotionally, to consult and guide her. Yet his missives revealed that he could see her coming undone.

On Saturday, March 30, six days before her Good Friday episode, Brad wrote, "We cannot change what has happened. But we can change and choose what happens in the future of our lives." Again, he pushed her to "listen to someone" she could "trust." He questioned if she believed that "everyone" was "lying and untrustworthy"? He demanded that he "be able to see the children," and he instructed her that "Mark must go to school." He told her she needed to "immediately start functioning as an adult," or else she should "enter Intensive Psychiatric Care."

On April 5, Good Friday, the day everything came to a head, he'd written her again, informing her that he'd received a "notice of foreclosure," that she owed "$709.50." He wished her a "Happy Easter!" and, just as he'd done a month earlier, ended his letter proclaiming, "JUDY HAS RISEN!"

On the morning of Thursday, April 18, 1985, the Psychiatric Clinic released Judy. She had been diagnosed an "acute paranoid schizophrenic."

* * * * *

Two days after her release, Judy noted on her calendar that "Paul & Friend" were "Here to Pray."

According to Steve, who stayed with Judy during that time, the moment she returned home she complained that her "house was filled with evil spirits."

"Judy had been in contact with our distant cousin, Paul Anderson," Steve said. "He was a pastor at a Lutheran Church in Hawthorne. Judy would discuss the devil and satanic rituals, and how this had become a popular topic around the community of Manhattan Beach."

Pastor Paul told Steve that they "did not like to do this kind of thing," but there was a person in his congregation—a man he didn't name—who could "come and do an exorcism on the house."

Steve took Judy's claims seriously, regardless of her recent diagnosis. He'd spent many sleepless nights in that house, and he too believed that something strange lay beneath the surface, something he couldn't explain.

The home, Steve recalled, had gone through a transformation similar to Judy's. "Prior to her mental illness, Judy had always cut flowers and set them out on the dining room table. She would open the windows to let the fresh air into the house. She had beautiful curtains that she would pull back, and the house always looked and smelled clean." But, he said, as she started to degenerate, so did the house.

Upon Judy's return from the psychiatric clinic, Steve said, the windows were kept closed, and she rarely opened the front door. "She constantly worried about people peeking in, so she would put clothespins on the window shades to keep them shut. There were a lot of reporters hanging outside looking for a story, which made her *very* paranoid."

Judy had old-fashioned hooks on her door, and Steve said that she added a thick steel bar, a second heavy-duty slide bolt. "The place had a *fortress effect*, a dark and gloomy feel and a musty smell that made it seem like it hadn't been lived in for years."

That first night with Judy back, Steve slept on the couch. Before he fell asleep, he sensed the negative energy, something he couldn't describe, but a bizarre sense that he was not alone.

Around 3:00 a.m., Steve got up to use the restroom. He stepped through the narrow hallway, and he felt it all around him, like an entity or a "presence" of some sort, something not visible that wanted to make itself known.

"Because of that," Steve said of the dark energy, "I knew that I owed Judy the benefit of the doubt, that maybe it needed to be given a second look.

"I'd played with the idea about doing an exorcism," Steve said, "but I really didn't know enough about it."

The next morning, Steve told Judy he would arrange it. She was pleased.

Pastor Paul Anderson had told Pastor Knutson that the Lutheran Church "doesn't recommend doing this ceremony anymore," but after a thorough discussion, and considering that Judy was family, he complied.

On the evening of the ritual, they congregated at the house—Judy, Steve, Pastor Knutson, Pastor Anderson, and Paul's friend, the exorcist. "If there's an evil spirit," Pastor Anderson said, "then let's find it."

Pastor Paul walked through the house, turning on every light—the notion being that "dark was bad." He went from room to room taking down negative artwork—including a picture of a man riding a horse beneath a threatening cloud. "This type of picture," Pastor Paul warned, "will make an evil entity feel welcome."

Once they'd gone through each room, they formed a circle in the middle of the house, which Steve described as "the highpoint," where the exorcist began his prayer against evil.

"Spirit of our God, Father, Son, and Holy Spirit," the exorcist spoke. "Most Holy Trinity, Immaculate Virgin Mary, angels, archangels, and saints of Heaven, descend upon me."

The exorcist and the others raised their hands and connected in a circle. He continued.

"Please purify this dwelling, Lord. Mold this home. Fill this place with Yourself. Banish all the forces of evil from this place. Destroy them and vanquish them."

The group maintained their circular bond, hands raised above their shoulders.

"Banish from this place all spells, witchcraft, black magic, maledictions, and the evil eye. Banish all diabolic infestations, oppressions, possessions, and all that is evil and sinful. Burn all these evils in Hell, so that they may never again touch this holy place."

He concluded the ritual by saying, "I command and bid all the powers who molest this home—by the power of God, in the name of Jesus Christ our Savior, through the intercession of the Immaculate Virgin Mary—to leave this place forever, and to be consigned into everlasting Hell, where they will be bound by Saint Michael the archangel, Saint Gabriel, Saint Raphael, our guardian angels, and crushed under the heel of the Immaculate Virgin Mary."

When the ritual ended, about forty-five minutes had passed. Steve wasn't sure what it had accomplished, but he believed it had put Judy at ease, just knowing that men of faith had entered her home and stood in the face of this evil.

* * * * *

Late in the evening on Monday, May 7, outside of the Cat Patch Topless Bar in Pico Rivera, Bob Currie sat, parked in a dark spot, a .22 caliber pistol tucked into the seat. Next to the gun, he had ten thousand dollars in cash, ready to make an exchange. His associate, Vicki Meyers, entered the club, looking for the "informant," a man who claimed to have possession of a "snuff film."

Currie and Meyers were acquainted through their mutual pursuit of the occult. Meyers, the mother of a ten-year-old boy allegedly abused at the Planter Street Preschool in Pico Rivera—another Los Angeles County molestation case spawned a year earlier—had been running her own investigation twenty-five miles east of Manhattan Beach. The Planter Street case involved eleven children from one neighborhood who'd accused four people, all of whom were arrested and charged. A four-month preliminary hearing explored claims of molestation, child pornography, infanticide, and satanic rituals. The recent discovery of bones and shells at the McMartin site had reopened the Planter Street investigation and put into the hands of the sheriff's Task Force.

Meyers stepped out of the club with the alleged informant, a shady-looking character who shifted his eyes as he approached Currie's vehicle. The man leaned down to speak to Currie through the half-opened window.

"So I hear you got a film," Currie said. "Is it true? You got somethin' that can help these kids?"

The man nodded, but before he could reply, flashing lights shined upon them and a siren blared. A police car rolled up to make a bust—what they believed to be a drug deal. They removed Currie from his car, conducted a search, found the gun and the cash, and placed him under arrest. They charged him with "illegal possession of a loaded weapon in a public place." The gun was registered to Jackie McGauley, the same gun the police had taken during her dispute with Chuck Elliott. Later that night, Jackie posted Currie's $1,000 bail.

Currie didn't know how the police became aware of his intentions that night, and they likely had no idea that he was trying to obtain a snuff film. In retrospect, it seemed that Currie and Meyers had simply picked a bad place to make the exchange—the parking lot of a topless bar. It looked like a typical drug deal in a location where drugs flowed freely.

Meyers had told Currie that the informant had "shown her samples of kiddie porn and the snuff film" the weekend before, and that she'd seen Planter Street "suspects" on the footage. Meyers claimed that she'd recently been "shot at" while investigating a nearby cemetery, so she brought Currie, the ex-Marine, to help make the transaction.

Currie's arrest set back his cause, and it drove a deeper wedge between the parents' group and the district attorney. Two weeks later, during his hearing, Currie laid everything on the line.

"When I took the stand," Currie said, "I testified that I was trying to pick up a snuff film. I think everyone in the courtroom shit themselves, because nobody expected me to say that out in the open. The prosecution asked for a recess. They called downtown, and then came back to the courtroom and said they didn't want to pursue it."

Just like "the Dig," the DA's office wanted to forget it had ever happened. With each failed attempt at uncovering evidence, the parents scored points for the defense.

But Currie didn't back down. He threatened to publicize it even further, saying that he would turn it into "a mini-McMartin," where he would create a spectacle outside of the courtroom to force the DA's hand. "I told them that I would do it like DeLorean," Currie said. "I'll do it right out on the courthouse steps"—Currie's reference to the recent trial of John Z. DeLorean on charges of cocaine trafficking, where each day, it seemed, his defense held a press conference in front of the County Courts Building in downtown Los Angeles.

Currie no longer concerned himself with what others thought of him, all the chatter around town that he'd lost his mind, for he was fighting the most righteous cause of the day—the war against Satan.

And as he looked around, examining the trend of the American media culture, Currie concluded that more and more people, people of high stature, were beginning to catch on.

*****

Nine days after Bob Currie's arrest, *20/20* aired a segment titled "The Devil Worshippers." It had been eleven months since Currie worked with *20/20* on the McMartin piece, and this time Hugh Downs and Tom Jarriel were back, dedicating the report solely to Satan worship.

Hugh Downs headlined the segment by stating that "police are skeptical" about the "worshipping of Satan" and how it correlated to crimes, but *20/20* had "reason to believe something is going on out there, and that's why we're reporting it."

The visual cut to Long Island, New York, as Tom Jarriel described how a teenager had been dragged through the woods and murdered as part of a late-night ritual, "forced to pray to Satan as he'd been repeatedly stabbed to death." In Phoenix, Arizona, strewn throughout an open field, "one hundred forty dogs had been slaughtered." Across the country, Jarriel said, "fifteen thousand animal mutilations" had taken place in "some type of bizarre ritual." Video of a site in Walnut Grove, Alabama, appeared where "pictures of the devil" had been found, as well as an abandoned building in Maine where "satanic graffiti"—pentagrams, inverted crucifixes, the evil eye, and 666—had left the mark of the devil in locations where police believed Satanists had held secret meetings.

Jarriel made reference to the "Goat's Head" as representing the devil himself, and said it was the "embodiment of evil." Several images of the Goat Man appeared on the screen, with the main focus on the "Sabbatic Goat," or Baphomet, as the pagan idol had come to be known, based on the 19th century sketch by Eliphas Levi, the famed French author of the occult. Levi's drawing—a conceptual portrait of a mutant god, a human body with a goat's head—had become the most famous of the Goat Man images. The Knights Templar had been accused of worshipping the deity, and it later became a symbol for the Church of Satan.

"Today," Jarriel emphasized, "we've found that Satan is alive and thriving." Or, he clarified, "at least plenty of people believe he is." But, Jarriel warned, his followers are "extremely secretive" and they can be found in "all walks of life."

The visual then cut to the explosive clip from the movie *Rosemary's Baby*, where Mia Farrow's character looked into the eyes of her demonized son while cult members in her living room informed her that her baby boy was the "son of Satan" as they chanted "God is dead!" Jarriel referenced a cult investigator's quote that "this movie was the best advertisement that devil worship has ever had."

Jarriel walked through a shopping center and pointed out a book store, a music store, and a home video center, and showed how accessible images of the occult had become to America's youth—that through entertainment venues they could actually "see the Devil" and "become inspired."

CHAPTER 30

July 1985

Michael Ruby, by then eighteen years old, sat in a courtroom at the Torrance Municipal Building. With his trial set to begin, he felt the intensity. The corridors buzzed in anticipation.

Back in November, following his preliminary hearing, Judge Aranda recommended Michael be provided more experienced counsel. It wasn't a knock on Tommy Allen and James Hallet, but Aranda knew a well-seasoned lawyer would be needed to put up a strong defense against the Los Angeles District Attorney's Office. Aranda offered a man some considered the "King of the Torrance Court House"—William "Bill" MacCabe.

From his first meeting with Bill MacCabe, Michael felt at ease. MacCabe, a large, elderly man with silver hair and a booming laugh, took charge. He instructed Michael on "how things were going to be," explicit in what he expected from Michael and what Michael could expect from him.

"When I worked with Tommy and Jim, it was the three of us together, like teammates," Michael said. "But when MacCabe stepped in, he took command and allowed me to relax."

While out on bail, Michael returned to Mira Costa High School, getting his life back to normal. For the most part, his fellow classmates treated him well. Still, an unspoken tension remained. Many of the students at Mira Costa, kids in their early teens, had siblings or family friends who were alleged victims at one of the implicated schools. People knew the name "Michael Ruby," and they associated it with child molestation.

"A few dudes made some stupid comments," Michael said. "But they didn't know me, so I didn't care. My true friends...the people I really cared about, never wavered."

Before long, however, high school conflicted with his preliminary hearing, so Michael took his equivalency exams and graduated ahead of his class. He spent the rest of his senior year going to and from the Torrance Courts for various motions. When not at court, he hung out and surfed.

On a Tuesday in mid-July, Michael sat through another pre-trial motion. The jury had been selected. It all started to seem so real, so inevitable. From time to time, in the back of his mind, Michael dreamed of a scenario where the state would suddenly drop the charges, admitting they had no evidence, that the whole event had been a political game.

But that, Michael knew, was a hopeless fantasy, one that likely did more harm than good. He would have to fight for his freedom, remain strong in his defense, steadfast in his innocence. There were far too many law enforcement professionals who saw their career advancement as being dependent on his conviction.

Of them, no one gave Michael more discomfort—such a lingering sense of dread—than the lead prosecutor, Lisa Hart, a woman Michael nicknamed "Hart-less."

Lisa Hart, relatively tall, thin, with long brown hair, "an attractive, sexy woman," according to Michael, commanded the courtroom, a patented moxie she used to set the tone. "She hated me with a passion," Michael said. "You could see it in her eyes every time she looked at me, like I was a horrible child molester, and she was going to make me pay. I tried not to make eye contact with her, ever. She gave me the chills."

For Lisa Hart, the case of Michael Ruby was a stepping stone, a vertical stride in her dash up the hierarchy of the Los Angeles DA's Office. With McMartin a national news story, the Manhattan Ranch trial had become a bellwether for her boss, newly elected District Attorney Ira Reiner, and his Assistant Deputy DA Gil Garcetti. They had banked on a thrust of momentum before the start of the McMartin trial.

Reiner had confidence in Lisa Hart. She'd worked for him at the city attorney's office, and she'd been promoted into the DA's office within a year. Hart had just come off the case of Arthur K. Snyder, the city councilman accused of molesting his nine-year-old daughter. In what looked like a slam-dunk conviction, Hart couldn't muster enough evidence for an indictment. Thus, with her first high-profile case ending before it started, Hart hungered for a win.

That morning, like every other, Hart entered the courtroom, slowing up enough to look Michael over with disgust, a cold stare that she held until he conceded.

Michael dropped his head. He waited a pause, then turned around to look for his parents, but instead found the pews filled with victim advocates, each giving him that same hardened glare that Hart had just expressed—their way of saying, "Guilty or not guilty, Michael Ruby, you will never be welcome in our community."

* * * * *

The Hilton Hotel
Torrance, CA

For weeks they'd met in secret, renting conference rooms, moving from place to place, not wanting anyone to catch wind of their plans. Ready to go public, believing that the time had come for their voices to be heard—their cry of a witch-hunt—they'd invited the media.

The group—Friends of McMartin Defendants—was made up of several people throughout the South Bay who'd been targeted in the Task Force's widespread investigation.

One of those targets, Claudia Krikorian, the thirty-three-year-old owner of the Peninsula Montessori Preschools in Rolling Hills and Torrance, sat at a long banquet table, reading over a document—a two-page letter the Task Force had mailed to nearly five hundred parents of former Manhattan Ranch and McMartin preschoolers. It warned that the inquiry "goes farther than those formally charged," and it asked parents to question their children to get a "clearer picture of the scope" of what had happened.

The letter, dated July 8, 1985, told the Manhattan Ranch parents to contact their "Team Leader," Sergeant Susan St. Marie, the recently married Lomita Sheriff's Deputy better known by her maiden name, Sue McGirt.

Krikorian shook her head as she read over the letter—the idea that Sergeant McGirt, who was leading the crusade against Michael Ruby, had just spent the last year trying to destroy her.

Krikorian's plight began in April 1984, in the wake of the indictments of the McMartin Seven, when a young girl at Peninsula Montessori's Rolling Hills campus claimed to have been shown "dirty pictures" by Mohsen Dornayi, a twenty-eight-year-old teacher's intern and Iranian national.

Sergeant McGirt told Krikorian she had "strong evidence" against Dornayi, when she didn't; in fact, she had no evidence whatsoever. McGirt told Krikorian "not to inform Dornayi of the allegations," that she would "be arrested" if she interfered with the investigation. And, according to Krikorian, McGirt went so far as to say, "You need to keep him working at the school. I need more victims to build a case." Krikorian, believing that McGirt had evidence, and not wanting to risk the welfare of her students, fired Dornayi, tipping him off that he'd been accused of child molestation.

Dornayi, arrested shortly thereafter—an apprehension caught on camera and plastered on the front page of the *Peninsula News*—had his four-year-old son taken into protective custody and placed in a foster home in Watts. Dornayi remained an "uncharged suspect" and faced deportation, while Claudia Krikorian, also uncharged, became embroiled in two separate administrative hearings, fighting to keep her operating licenses.

Fed up with the system, Krikorian joined up with Patti Rusth, another local preschool owner, and they rallied support to stand against what Rusth described as, "a Nazi Germany, police-style state."

Still, despite their indignation, many in the Friends group were afraid to speak out, afraid of being implicated as conspirators. "Passions are very, very high," said Marcie Braun, a neighbor of Maryanne Jackson. "If I step forward, there's a chance these suspicions will turn on me."

Walter Urban, the attorney for Betty Raidor—the 64-year-old member of the McMartin Seven—had helped to organize the group, letting them know that the law was on their side. "You people have nothing to hide," Urban told them. "There's no reason to be afraid of scrutiny by the public and the media. It's time to stand up and fight."

That night, where a large meeting room at the Hilton Hotel had filled with nearly three hundred people, the Friends of McMartin had come to tell reporters that they would be silent no more.

The next morning a full-page ad appeared in the *Daily Breeze*:

Salem Massachusetts 1692—Manhattan Beach 1985
The infamous Salem Witch Hunt of the 17th century is happening again, but this time right here in Manhattan Beach. Authorities are

acting only on the accusations of children prompted by adults. If you thought this could never happen in America, especially today, think again, it could happen to you. All it takes is for a person to point a finger.

John Jackson, a writer for the *Beach Reporter*, whose "McMartin Watch" column—a rather pro-prosecution slant—had covered the ongoing saga, criticized the Friends for overstating their complaint.

"The Salem case," Jackson wrote in response, "bears no resemblance to what is happening in the South Bay now. The differences are astounding. What impressed me first about the Salem comparison is the Friends' assumption that they and the ad's readers understand what happened in Salem nearly three centuries ago."

Jackson, a well-meaning journalist, seemed focused on the literal meaning of a "witch-hunt," not the metaphorical.

The Friends, accused of the most heinous crimes, were simply pleading with their community to recognize the injustice they'd endured. True, unlike Salem, no one would be hanged, no one "pressed to death," but, they asserted, their characters, their good names, had been assassinated in a misguided campaign.

It raised the question: Is it worse to die unjustly for being a witch, or to live with the wrongful label of "child molester"?

Arthur Miller's play *The Crucible* drove that theme. The allegorical drama about Salem, written in the era of McCarthyism, made a martyr of John Proctor, who, despite the threat of execution, preserved his name and the reputation of his family, refusing to admit that he was a witch—and he died for it.

In comparison, in 1984 and 1985, all around the South Bay, allegations from the mouths of babes stretched beyond belief—a slew of mystical claims, much like the "spectral evidence" that fueled Salem. The preschool inquisition moved from one town to the next, based not on the discovery of evidence, but the absence thereof, just as the denials of witchery in Salem meant absolute guilt. The taboos of devil worship in Manhattan Beach were akin to the witchcraft of puritanical New England. And, it seemed, both Manhattan Beach and Salem were progressive societies confronted with a diabolical crisis, where fear and superstition suppressed common sense.

The difference, of course—which John Jackson failed to recognize—is

They Must Be Monsters

that the events of 1692 had a direct impact on American society, prompting change. The metaphor "witch-hunt" supports that notion. It cries "injustice," identifying the unjust as foolish, unhinged. It mocks the very nature of western civilization, where supposedly good Christians, through their confusion and paranoia, wrongly persecuted their neighbors—in the same manner the martyr they glorified had been crucified—and, in retrospect, showed remorse. That is, in and of itself, the sober lesson of Salem.

In Manhattan Beach, to the contrary, despite what could've been learned, repentance was not in sight—only a mission to justify.

* * * * *

Days later

In a quiet neighborhood within the Trees lived a family of four—a fireman, his homemaker wife, and their two young children, an eight-year-old boy and a four-year-old girl. Like many other families in Manhattan Beach, they were normal people, good people, getting ready for another day.

At roughly 7:30 a.m. on an uncomfortably warm morning in early September, the father ended his night shift at the firehouse and headed home. His wife and kids were still in bed.

Outside of their home, holding a search warrant, stood Detective Jane Hoag, surrounded by a group of plainclothes officers, all members of the Task Force.

The mother awoke to the sound of someone pounding on the front door. She rushed to the door and opened it. As she did, Detective Hoag pushed the warrant into her face as the other officers moved in.

"We have a search warrant for the premises," Hoag told her, then stepped inside and looked around, as if she knew what she was looking for. "We're taking your children to the station for questioning."

"You can't take my kids."

"Wake your kids up and get them dressed. Do it now."

The mother woke her children and helped them dress. The kids, confused and frightened, were led to the back of an unmarked police car and driven away.

"What's going on?" the mother asked Hoag.

Hoag refused to give her any information. She just left.

The woman broke down in tears. She picked up the search warrant and began to read it. The basis of the warrant horrified her.

For the last two years, the woman had been running a home babysitting service for a handful of neighborhood families. Apparently, about a year earlier, one of the children was thought to have been molested, but it was not clear where the alleged abuse had occurred.

On that day, according to the warrant, the woman was suspected of molesting multiple children—her own two kids and the child whose parents had filed the complaint. Nothing in the warrant authorized her children to be taken from her.

Within minutes, her husband arrived to find their home ransacked. Plainclothes officers continued to rifle through their personal belongings. His wife sat on the sofa, weeping.

"They took the children," she cried. "They took them away."

For the next three hours, the police turned the house inside out looking for evidence of pornography. Nothing was found. The parents sat together on the couch, holding hands. Every few minutes they asked about their children, wanting to know when they would see them.

"I don't know," a detective replied. "They're on their way to Harbor General."

"Why?" the mother asked.

"They need to be physically examined."

Not long after, the children arrived at UCLA-Harbor General, where they had vaginal and rectal exams, checking for "trauma or scarring that would be consistent with a history of sexual abuse."

Eight hours later, as night fell, the parents waited anxiously, still in fear of what was happening to their children. The phone rang. The father answered. It was the Manhattan Beach Police Department. "You can come and get your kids," the voice said.

By the time the children arrived home, over the course of ten hours, they'd been taken away by the police, asked questions of a sexual nature, driven to a hospital where their genitalia had been examined, then taken back to the station where they waited for their parents to arrive. They were confused, unable to comprehend what had just happened—and their parents had no explanation.

In the following days, this event became an issue of public discussion. A neighbor of the family, Richard Lyman, wrote a scathing letter to the editor of the *Beach Reporter*, giving the family's rendition of what they had experienced. He accused the police, and specifically Detective Jane Hoag, of using "Gestapo-like tactics."

Days later, police officials acknowledged that "no incriminating evidence had been found," and that the physical examination of the children revealed nothing conclusive.

In defense of the Task Force, Sergeant Jim Noble argued that the raid and the medical examinations had helped the authorities get closer to the truth. "People have the misconception that our job is to prove these allegations," Noble said. "Our job is to get to the truth, and that may mean proving the allegations false."

Still, the Task Force hadn't given up its suspicion that cults of Satanists dwelled in the South Bay area. Some of its investigators cited a book published in 1972, *The Occult Explosion*, which stated that "quite a respectable bunch of devil disciples [resided] in nearby Manhattan Beach." With that in mind, Noble confirmed that "nothing has been ruled out [as motive]...straight pedophilia, pornography, Satanism—all these theories apply."

In the wake of the most recent raids, where the Task Force had stormed through more residencies, both Noble and Lieutenant Richard Willey stuck to their guns. When asked about their authority to "take a child into custody without judicial review"—a court order—they argued that it's up to the individual officer to determine if there's "reasonable cause" to suspect that a child's in harm's way.

In the case of the fireman and his wife, that discretion had been left to Detective Jane Hoag.

PART VI
God Help Us All

CHAPTER 31

Summer 1985

It had been a rough year for Sherman Block, the sixty-one-year-old sheriff of Los Angeles County. The Chicago native, a World War II veteran who'd served in Europe under General George Patton, commanded the nation's largest sheriff's department. After twenty-eight-years on the force, Block thought he'd seen it all, yet when McMartin broke, he was confounded by the thought of dispatching twenty detectives to uncover a conspiracy of pedophile Satanists. Still, he had done it.

To Block's chagrin, after eleven months, he had nothing to show for it.

Sherman Block faced re-election in June, campaigning for his second term, and there were murmurings that he'd mismanaged the department's resources. Come January, he would need to explain to the county's auditor-controller why he'd spent over one million dollars without making a single arrest, an unprecedented budget for a special task force.

Block had handpicked this elite group of child abuse experts, so once it appeared as if the unit had stumbled, the catcalls were heard all the way to the shore. The idle talk was that the Child Abuse Task Force had been "relaxing at the beach" while their fellow officers were out "fighting real crime." That critique may have started in jest, but as months passed, it became an unspoken resentment—the rancor of a department spread thin in the wake of an intense manhunt.

As the summer ended, Southern California had experienced a spree of violent crimes never before seen, a slew of horrific murders that stretched from northern Los Angeles to the lower half of Orange County. Not just murder, but a gruesome mix of homicide, torture, mutilation, and the rape of women and children. The killer had no explicit profile, no limit to the range of butchery.

In mid-March, a 34-year-old woman had been murdered during a home intrusion in Rosemead. An hour later, ten miles east in Monterey Park, a 32-year-old woman had been pulled from her car and shot to death. Three days later, an 8-year-old girl in Eagle Rock had been stabbed to death. Another week passed and the mutilated bodies of an elderly Whittier couple were found; the woman's eyes had been gouged out post-mortem.

For two months the rampage stopped, but then it picked up again. One of the surviving victims identified the slayer as "a Hispanic man with long dark hair and foul smelling."

First labeled by the press as "The Valley Intruder," the man eventually came to be known as "The Night Stalker."

The crime spree continued into the summer—the rape of a 6-year-old girl; two elderly women beaten, their throats slit; a 16-year-old girl bludgeoned with a tire iron. At one point, an entire family had been tortured: the father shot, the mother raped, and their 8-year-old boy sodomized.

Across greater Los Angeles, during an intense heat wave, people lived in terror, shutting and locking the windows they'd once left open to let in the night's cool breeze.

Sheriff Sherman Block's department had worked in conjunction with Chief Daryl Gates and the Los Angeles Police Department, forming a "Night Stalker Task Force." Headed by legendary homicide investigator Sergeant Frank Salerno, best known for his role in the search for the Hillside Strangler in the late 1970s, the police gradually closed in.

However, as much as Frank Salerno brought to the table—his experience in tracking suspects—the most frightening aspect of the murders had not been publicized: the killer's absolute devotion to Satan. During his sexual assaults, he demanded that his victims "swear to Satan." At one scene, investigators found a large pentagram drawn in lipstick on a wall.

On August 30, 1985, the serial murders came to an end when the killer's identity went public: Richard Ramirez, a twenty-five-year old high school dropout who'd been drifting around California for three years. His December 1984 auto theft arrest had produced a mug shot, and his photograph landed on the front page of every major newspaper.

Ramirez, strolling along Hubbard Street in East Los Angeles, noticed his face on display at a newsstand, and he panicked. He tried to steal a parked car but was identified by some elderly women who yelled, "El Matador"—The Killer—and a group of men captured him, beating him fiercely with a metal post before the police arrived.

By September, with Richard Ramirez locked away, Sheriff Sherman Block had time to regroup. The homicidal maniac no longer posed a threat. Yet that didn't alleviate his troubles with McMartin. Before long, as the details got out, the public would learn that the Night Stalker was a Satanist who'd invoked the name of the Devil during his slayings. Once that happened, Block suspected, the McMartin parent activists would look for a connection between Richard Ramirez and the occult activity their children had alleged. As far as Block could tell, none existed.

After six months of gathering clues, cross-referencing thousands of direct and indirect bits of information, not a shred of evidence existed to link the Night Stalker to the McMartin Preschool. Richard Ramirez, a psychopath, a drifter, had not been a trusted member of a vast conspiracy, not a true pedophile, nor a pornographer. He was, in fact, a self-proclaimed Satanist, but that seemed to be as far as it went.

Sheriff Sherman Block, despite his noble intentions, faced a disturbing paradox. After futilely expending valuable resources to uncover an underground network of cultists in the Beach Cities, an actual Satanist had been raping and murdering women and children from one end of the Southland to the next.

* * * * *

In late September, Faye Fiore, a staff writer for the *Daily Breeze,* took a call from Glenn Stevens, the deputy district attorney and co-prosecutor in the McMartin case. Stevens invited her to lunch. Fiore, like the other staff reporters, had developed camaraderie with the attorneys on both sides, and Glenn Stevens had been one of the friendliest.

Still it caught her off-guard, the idea of a private lunch. Not wanting to be compromised, Fiore called Lois Timnick, the staff writer for the *Los Angeles Times.* Fiore asked her to join them.

Over the course of their lunch meeting, Stevens made it clear the conversation was "off the record." Stevens, who'd been a staunch advocate for the alleged victims, bared his soul about his "misgivings." He had "serious problems" with how the case had been handled. He said that he believed that "at least five of the seven McMartin defendants were innocent," and that no one other than Ray and Peggy Buckey should be prosecuted.

Stevens made reference to a meeting six months earlier, March 16, 1985, where DA Ira Reiner requested a progress report on the case. Every key player in the department had attended. When the meeting concluded, Reiner, who'd come into office after the indictments, concluded that the grand jury had "over-filed and under-investigated" the case, and that "Virginia McMartin should have never been charged."

Naturally, Fiore and Timnick wanted to report the explosive news, but they had a journalistic ethic to follow. Their meeting with Glenn Stevens, for all intents and purposes, had never happened.

At some point, however, Faye Fiore had a change of heart.

On Friday, September 27, Fiore's article appeared in the *Daily Breeze*. It explained how the district attorney's office had been having second thoughts about the McMartin case for many months. She used the March 16 DA's meeting as a cover without directly naming Glenn Stevens, or even stating that a particular member of the prosecution team had been her source.

The report caused a stir in the courtroom. When questioned publically, none of the prosecutors would confirm that the March meeting had ever taken place, and each declined to comment due to the department's rules of confidentiality. Either way, the ethics of the district attorney's office came into question.

Lois Timnick, knowing she could have published her own article about the lunch meeting, didn't like the way it played out. Essentially, the *Daily Breeze* had scooped the *Los Angeles Times*.

Two weeks later, on Sunday, October 13, Lois Timnick wrote a front-page story for the *Times*, headlined "New DA Team May Take Over McMartin Case." It included a picture of Chief Deputy DA Gil Garcetti with his quote that the DA's office wasn't sure if they would "keep any of the prosecuting team [Lael Rubin, Glenn Stevens, and Christine Johnston] on for the purposes of the trial."

The article essentially named Glenn Stevens, identified as "the prosecutor insisting on anonymity," as the "Deep Throat" behind the controversy. Garcetti said that "according to our canon of ethics, if an attorney does not believe that the person he is prosecuting is guilty, that attorney is obligated to come in and ask to be removed from the case. No one has done that." Garcetti referred to the person as "he" while discussing the hypothetical attorney and Stevens was the only *he* on the team.

Throughout the article, Stevens was quoted as having made a slew of controversial comments—such as how he once believed the defendants were "animals that should be thrown to wolves," until, that is, he took the time to "study the evidence." Stevens said the prosecution had pushed the case forward "without examining the videotaped interviews of the children," that they just took the therapists' word for it. He cited the "pressure from the community," and he blamed his former boss, DA Robert Philibosian, for being caught up in the politics of re-election.

Timnick's article changed the complexity of the case, as speculation of corruption mounted. Timnick had the second-highest executive in the DA's office, Gil Garcetti, admitting that they had made a "unanimous decision" to move forward back in March, even though they agreed that "additional investigation was necessary." So, instead of pulling back, the DA chose to investigate, to press forward.

* * * * *

Locked behind the steel bars and cold walls of his high-security cell in the Men's County Jail, Ray Buckey wrote feverishly, documenting his thoughts, his disgust, with the absurdity that had ruined his life and the lives of his family. No longer scared, having grown accustomed to the quiet monotony of his incarceration, he seemed driven only by his controlled anger. The nineteen months he'd spent in that cell had taken him to the brink of hatred and back into a valley of wisdom, where he searched for insight into the madness that had shackled him.

Page after page Ray wrote, and once he grew too tired to think, he climbed onto the stationary bicycle the county had allowed him—the only way to keep him physically fit since he wasn't allowed to mix within the general population of inmates. He rode for hours each day—his teeth ground down to their roots from the stress and pressure of constantly clenching his jaw—and, after a twenty-mile ride, he stepped down and sat before his yellow legal pad, adding to his memoir.

The recent reporting—the controversy over the district attorney's misgivings—gave Ray hope, as it appeared that someone, finally, had come to his senses. Yet, he wondered as he wrote, how could it have taken so long to admit the obvious?

From the beginning—ask Jane Hoag why she pursued the Johnson mother's accusations so adamantly from a non-verbal two-year-old. How could I sodomize a two-year-old and not do more damage?

Why was the older brother who he showered with let off so easily?

Why wasn't I confronted, like the father?

Wasn't the reason for arresting me because you knew Mitchell as a two-year-old was not a reliable witness so you wanted something to tell the parents (a letter) to persuade more cooperation?

If you believe I molested Mitchell, do you also believe what his father did and the other stories his mother has said subsequently? Why not?

Why didn't you go to the school's owners for cooperation?

Calling parents...didn't you realize the fear and emotional blindness a parent would have questioning their own child?

A direct approach, but a potentially dangerous and volatile experiment that now, looking back, created uncontrollable fear.

Looking now at the Johnson mother, her sanity is in question... and being the genesis of the case, a child Hoag admitted on the stand wouldn't qualify as a witness...again, why was my guilt so easily accepted? Solely because I was a male instructor at a preschool?

Going by a child who wouldn't qualify in a conviction, and a letter sent to over 200 families—again, right after my arrest.

Why did they condemn me in that letter knowing the widespread fear it would create in a tight-knit community?

Sure the children's safety is the utmost in the reasoning process. A child is always a victim and helpless. Anything warrants their safety. But looking back, didn't the steps taken in the investigation evolve into a small-town epidemic of misguided fear?

* * * * *

By mid-October, the search for a vast McMartin conspiracy had virtually ended. Sheriff Block announced that the "Sexual Exploitation of Children Task Force" would disband on January 1, 1986. The budget had been expended, and he had no justifiable reason to spend more. The Task Force had interviewed 740 children and 400 adults. More than 100 of those children were reported as having "physical symptoms" of sexual abuse, but no details were provided.

Before announcing its plans to disband, the Task Force, the DA, and the DSS met with parents of former St. Cross Episcopal students, a final update to make them aware that the Task Force had obtained "confessions from two men" who'd "molested children at St. Cross" more than six years earlier. However, since the statute of limitations had run out, no charges could be filed.

That type of legal technicality only compounded the frustration of the parent activists who believed that a secret society of Satanic pedophiles continued to walk their streets.

"Our kids were raped and sodomized," complained Mary Mae Cioffi, convinced her children had been abused at McMartin, Children's Path, and St. Cross Episcopal. "Now we're going to have to look around the neighborhood at the people who did it."

Sheriff Sherman Block, however, despite the fact that he'd admitted defeat, made one last stand. Block agreed to an interview with Wayne Satz, where he held firm to his belief that "children had been sexually abused at all five South Bay preschools." The lack of discovery, Block said, did not exonerate anyone. The children, in his opinion, were telling the truth.

Sheriff Block's last official statement about his failed Task Force left the impression that he was content with the outcome, but one could only suspect that he remained haunted by it all. Block, a proud man, a soldier who'd long stood against the darkest elements of society, had been defeated in the worst way.

Weeks later, Sherman Block sat in a downtown courtroom observing the arraignment of The Night Stalker, Richard Ramirez.

As Ramirez stood before the court, donning his sinister grin, Block saw the embodiment of the Devil, a monster who'd raped and slaughtered dozens of people, including young children.

The proceeding concluded, but Ramirez wasn't done. He held up his left hand, revealing an inverted pentagram that he'd scrawled into his palm. "Hail Satan!" Ramirez proclaimed, staring into the lens of the news camera.

Two guards escorted Ramirez out of the courtroom, taking him to a maximum security cell, the block where the most violent and heinous criminals were kept. Ramirez was placed in the cell next to Raymond Buckey.

CHAPTER
32

October 1985

In the trial of Michael Ruby, the courtroom filled with a variety of onlookers, a mix of Michael's family and friends, news media, and of course, those who'd come to support the children.

Since the end of the preliminary hearing, the DA's case had changed considerably. The initial accuser, Jimmy Jacobson, had been dropped, as his testimony had been deemed "not credible."

The charges against Michael had been condensed to the alleged abuse of five young girls, all between five and seven years old, who were said to have been molested at the preschool between September 1983 and July 1984 at the hands of "Mr. Mike." Medical examinations showed that each girl had been forcibly raped sometime in the past.

To begin the trial, the court arranged a "field trip" for the jurors to go to the Manhattan Ranch preschool. They drove north up Pacific Coast Highway, turned right onto 10th Street, then continued on the residential side streets to the school. It allowed them to relive the experience, the ambiance of the neighborhood, giving them a first-hand view of the property's layout.

In the courtroom, Bill MacCabe brought the setting to life. He had a scaled model of the school made, like a doll house, and constructed a full-size replica of the bathroom, where so many of the crimes were said to have occurred. Those items remained in front of the jury for the entire proceeding. When a young girl testified, MacCabe asked that she step down from the stand and into the mock bathroom, taking the jury through the events.

MacCabe knew it would be a risky ploy—the idea that he would try to illustrate how absurd the charges were, how illogical the entire concept of what his client was being accused of was, simply by reenacting the moment as a way to prove that the moment itself would have been an impossible scenario.

Again: risky. The little girls were innocent, adorable, whether one believed them or not. They were there only to tell of their experiences. When they stepped into the mock bathroom, revisiting the location of their alleged abuse, there was chance it would spark a negative flashback, reminding them of that dark place.

But that never happened. Each of the five girls stepped down and entered the mock bathroom with no trepidation whatsoever. The girls, from Michael's perspective, seemed to enjoy the experience, as if they had fun being the center of attention.

Michael recalled a particular incident involving Emma Jamison, just moments after her testimony. Emma, then six years old, had given explicit testimony of the sex acts Michael had forced upon her. But she'd done so with absolutely no emotion, as if she repeated something she'd been told.

Emma came down from the stand as the judge called a recess. Michael remained seated. Emma walked past him, but stopped. She turned, looked at him closely, and spoke.

"Aren't you Mr. Mike?" Emma asked him.

Michael, unsure if he should respond, froze for a moment, but then his natural instinct reminded him to be polite. "Yes," he replied. "I'm Mr. Mike."

"I know you," Emma said with a smile. "I saw you on TV."

Lisa Hart and Emma's mother, Carla, quickly stood between them. Carla took Emma by the hand and hurried her away.

* * * * *

In Michael Ruby's defense, Bill MacCabe argued that the entire case had been fabricated—an extension of the McMartin investigation. He said the unsubstantiated claim of the Jacobson boy had spun out of control as therapists and parents contaminated the minds of these young girls. Two overzealous detectives, Jane Hoag and Patty Picker, had tried to uncover a make-believe conspiracy with the McMartin Preschool. The evidence—the undeniable proof that Michael Ruby had committed these acts—did not exist. The medical examinations, MacCabe suggested, were based on new-age techniques that lacked sufficient clinical validation.

Michael's case, MacCabe insisted, was nothing more than a proxy McMartin trial, the same charges by the same network of professionals: Detective Jane Hoag, the cop; Dr. Cheryl Kent, the therapist; Dr. Carol Berkowitz and her associates at UCLA-Harbor General; the prosecutors of the Los Angeles DA's Office—all part of a social and political movement that had presumed Michael guilty before the evidence had been collected, analyzed, and cross-examined.

The charges, MacCabe contended, were preposterous. To think that Michael could have secretly molested these girls on the preschool grounds during working hours, that it could have been done out of the sight of the other teachers, that no child had ever spoken of it, and that none of these girls had ever shown physical signs of having been forcibly raped.

Above all, MacCabe contended, there simply would have never been a case if Detective Jane Hoag had not been hell-bent to prove her theory of a "child-swapping" conspiracy. Interestingly, he argued, eighteen months after Manhattan Ranch had first been implicated, the State tried to suggest that the investigations of Manhattan Ranch and McMartin had always been independent.

During Lisa Hart's direct examination of Hoag, the detective said that she conducted her first interviews with Manhattan Ranch children in "early August 1984"—which MacCabe knew conflicted with the police report and the search warrant. Hoag had interviewed several children from May through the end of July 1984, she authored search warrants and initiated raids during that same time, and she personally conducted surveillance of Michael Ruby on the afternoon of July 25, moments before he was arrested.

During his cross examination, MacCabe challenged Hoag over her misstatement of facts. "Do you recollect an interview of Betsy Warren in May of 1984?" MacCabe asked Hoag.

Lisa Hart shot to her feet.

"Objection. Relevancy," she yelled. Hart stepped out from behind the table. "I would like to approach on this, Your Honor."

At the bench, outside of the presence of the jury, Lisa Hart argued that any information about McMartin students, like Betsy Warren, even if it had been stipulated within the search warrants as part of the Manhattan Ranch investigation, was unrelated to this case.

"It certainly *was* related to Manhattan Ranch," MacCabe rebutted. "This witness said that she made no interviews in regard to the case until

August of 1984, directly contrary to what the reports say—her own reports."

MacCabe emphasized that Hoag's police report and search warrant had suspected "alleged misconduct" at both Manhattan Ranch and McMartin, and that her inquiry had begun as far back as early May 1984, three months prior to what she'd testified to.

"Your Honor," Hart countered, "Betsy Warren was a student at the McMartin Preschool who alleged sometime in May she'd been taken to Manhattan Ranch. At that time, there was no investigation of Manhattan Ranch. That investigation wasn't initiated until a few weeks later."

Lisa Hart asserted that Betsy Warren's statement about Manhattan Ranch had been done as part of a "separate investigation." Thus, it was irrelevant to the charges against Michael Ruby.

Judge Robert T. Hight agreed. "Your line of questioning is too obscure," Hight told MacCabe. "It's going off on a tangent without a tangible tie-in."

Judge Hight didn't care to hear profound theories of "McMartin hysteria" or the notion of a "witch-hunt." He had no interest in the dynamics of how the two cases were "once connected," because they no longer were.

"I can see where she [Hoag] would consider it being a McMartin School investigation," Hight concluded. "Objection sustained."

That ruling devastated Bill MacCabe, at least in the short term. His defense of showing how an innocent teenager had been caught up in a witch-hunt would not be heard. Instead, MacCabe would have to argue that the specific charges—the lewd acts of sexual assault—were false, a far more onerous task considering the testimony of the five young girls.

* * * * *

On Friday, October 11, Michael Ruby took the witness stand for his third and final day of testimony. Bill MacCabe, through Michael's previous statements, had presented the story of the "real Michael Ruby," the seventeen-year-old kid who liked to surf and hang out with his friends. He'd always been a good kid, raised with a religious backdrop; yet, as he grew into his teens, he seemed to stray, not wanting to conform to his parents' wishes.

Michael, admittedly, had not been "the nicest guy." He'd been in a few fights, often the antagonist. His grades were below average, and he didn't seem concerned. He took the job at Manhattan Ranch to earn money to fix up his "surf car," not to save up for college. The job was all right, but he wasn't overly fond of the children. Michael definitely picked on them in subtle ways—smashing snails, rolling tires to knock them down, nudging them into water puddles—his not-so-accidental means of retribution for their disobedience.

From time to time, MacCabe showed, Michael Ruby had acted like a jerk—but he was *not* a pedophile.

That Friday promised to be a big day for both sides, when the heroic prosecutor, Lisa Hart, would get her shot at the accused molester. The courtroom filled to capacity, as every major media outlet had a seat. Wayne Satz and his crew scoured the hallways, taking statements from anyone looking to get on the evening news.

With the exception of his closing argument, MacCabe had presented his case—the facts, the evidence, or the lack thereof. His decision to have Michael testify was the final touch, a chance for the accused to be heard. MacCabe could not predict which way the jury would go. The girls said Michael did it. Doctors—specialists—had verified the girls had been abused.

But if Michael chose not to take the stand, the jury would wonder why. They would talk about it in the jury room, and they would speculate that he had something to hide. Michael had to testify, MacCabe knew it. Michael needed to look each member of the jury directly in the eyes and tell them that he'd never molested any of those girls. Seeing him speak, hearing his voice, listening to the sincerity of his tone, would force every juror to reconcile his or her decision.

Michael tightened up as Lisa Hart stepped toward him, ready to begin her cross-examination. The way she looked at him said it all, an exaggerated glare that told him how despicable she believed him to be.

Hart eased in by asking Michael a few basic questions about his role at the preschool—then she went for the jugular. Hart had a method of posing questions in the affirmative—predicated on the assumption that Michael had actually molested the girls—such as, "When you touched Emma's vagina, did she cry?" Michael responded with, "Well, ma'am, I never touched Emma's vagina, so no, she did not cry."

It went on and on in that manner. "It's true you snuck into the bathroom when the three girls were in there, isn't it?" Hart asked. "No, ma'am," Michael answered, "it isn't true." Hart asked the same type of questions in the same suggestive manner about each of the five girls. She went through each count of fondling, rape, and sodomy. With every question, Michael reiterated that it was not true, that he didn't do it.

At a certain point, after many objections from MacCabe, Judge Hight admonished Hart for using that tactic to a level of deception, where she'd tried to get Michael to admit by default that he'd molested the girls even after he'd repeatedly denied doing it.

"You asked him *if* he did it, and he said 'no,' " Judge Hight said. "And then you asked him *when* he did it."

If she had no legitimate questions, Hight instructed, it was time to move on.

Lisa Hart, thinking she had the jury convinced, didn't overplay her hand. Her cross-examination of Michael Ruby came to an end.

* * * * *

Three weeks later

On Tuesday, November 5, 1985, after sixty-six witnesses had taken the stand—doctors, therapists, subject-matter experts, parents, children, teachers, residents of the neighborhood, and so on—there was nothing left to present but the closing arguments.

Lisa Hart spoke first on behalf of the State. She walked the room, softly stepping to and from the jury, describing Michael Ruby as a "controlled, controlling young man," someone who "enjoyed his position of authority at the preschool," which he'd used to "sexually experiment" with the five young girls. Hart conceded that some of the girls' testimony was "confusing" and inconsistent.

"But remember the testimony of Dr. Gail Goodman," Hart said, referring to the University of Denver psychologist, a specialist in the eyewitness testimony of children. "Dr. Goodman verified that young children recall significant events in their lives, but are often confused when recounting the details of those events. Therefore, even if their disclosures lack sensibility, it doesn't mean they are false."

To compliment the testimony of her expert psychologist, Hart reiterated the "indisputable medical examinations" performed by Dr. Carol Berkowitz, the renowned pediatrician from UCLA-Harbor General.

"Dr. Berkowitz confirmed that each of these girls showed physical symptoms that are consistent with sexual abuse," Hart said, stopping in front of the jury for a dramatic pause. "*Somebody* molested these girls,"

Hart emphasized before turning away. She stepped toward Michael, looking down upon him. "And each of the girls said it was *Mr. Mike*."

Bill MacCabe, in his closing, went through the case detail by detail, count by count, child by child, breaking down every scenario. He argued that the medical evidence was inconclusive.

"In Dr. Berkowitz's own words," MacCabe said, "the term 'consistent with sexual abuse' is not a conclusive finding. Dr. Berkowitz also admitted that the physical symptoms the children possessed were also consistent with non-sinister causes."

In sum, MacCabe argued, the collective testimony of the girls was "so riddled with inconsistencies and contradictions" that it was impossible to determine what truly happened.

"The evidence," MacCabe said, "suggests that *nothing* happened. So if you're okay with sending this young man to prison for the rest of his life, a life sentence based on fantastical stories blended with unproven medical theories, then I can only say, 'God help us all.'"

MacCabe rested and the deliberations began.

CHAPTER

33

Wednesday, November 6, 1985

In the morning, Deputy DA Glenn Stevens prepared a confidential memorandum—his official "Analysis & Recommendations" in the case of the People v. Raymond Buckey, et al. Stevens addressed the memo to Chief Deputy DA Gil Garcetti, his superior, the man he had betrayed by leaking his doubts about the case to the press. Still, to that day, Stevens continued to deny he was the source.

Just as Stevens had told Fiore and Timnick in their private lunch, his memorandum to Garcetti affirmed that the case had been "over-filed." The State's most compelling "evidence"—the videotaped disclosures of the children—was hardly definitive; in fact, in his opinion, it could exonerate the defendants.

What should've been a simple set of charges against one man, Stevens argued, had been blown out of proportion; thus, to secure a conviction, the charges should be revised into a more cogent package—a case against a single male defendant, like the indictment of Michael Ruby.

Stevens' memorandum included a complete summary of all statements and testimonies given by four of the alleged victims, all boys, each of whom he believed should be excluded from any Superior Court pleading, as they lacked any "credible corroboration."

After an "exhaustive look at all of the evidence," Stevens wrote, he had come to the "inescapable conclusion" that it would be impossible to convict any of the seven McMartin defendants. The only reason the case against Raymond Buckey should proceed, he noted, was because "medical evidence [could] be introduced" to corroborate some of the children's claims. But even that would be "interpretive"; that is, none of the evidence—medical, physical, and circumstantial—was conclusive to any "appreciable degree."

Stevens emphasized that, at the time the complaints were filed, there was a "single count of conspiracy" that tied all seven teachers together in an "organized effort" to use children for "pornography and other illegal activities by using the McMartin Preschool as a front." It was a case filled with "complexities," he wrote, and as it grew from the initial accusation, it had "gotten away" from what Ray Buckey had actually done at the school.

"He is a child molester," Stevens determined, "nothing more." And in order to prove it, the case needed to be "brought back into proportion" and to be "narrowly tailored to acts of child molestation," removing all "other activities" and criminal plots.

In his conclusion, Stevens recommended that a "simple case against Ray Buckey"—six victims, all supported by medical evidence—"should lead any jury or court to conclude that he is guilty as charged."

For Gil Garcetti, that analysis would have been far more useful had Stevens given it to him prior to spilling his conscience to the *Daily Breeze* and the *Los Angeles Times*. Instead of developing a strategy to repackage the filing, Garcetti had been doing damage control, answering the calls of angry parents demanding to know which member of his team was the "Judas."

Reading over Stevens' memo confirmed Garcetti's suspicion—that Stevens was definitely the mole. The memo, nothing more than a smokescreen, allowed Stevens to cover his ass, to pretend he had the ethical fortitude to do things by the book, when in fact he'd already broken his covenant with the people.

* * * * *

On Friday, November 22, Michael Ruby sat in the courtroom, eyes closed, dreaming of his freedom. He envisioned himself standing on the shore, his feet in the water and the sun on his face. He took a deep breath, a wordless prayer, and he felt the Holy Spirit run through him, a warm sensation that assured him he wasn't alone.

The sound of the opening door and the entering footsteps broke his concentration. The chairs shuffled as the jury took their seats.

Michael ended his prayer. *Amen.* He opened his eyes.

The jury foreman, David Wilson, stood to address Judge Hight. Over their thirteen-day deliberation, they remained at an impasse on all eleven counts. Each day they'd been instructed to keep evaluating the evidence until they reached a consensus—but they were just too far apart.

"I take it the jury is still unable to reach a decision?" Judge Hight inquired.

"That's correct, Your Honor," Wilson replied. "Unfortunately, we're hopelessly deadlocked on all the main issues."

Wilson read the counts aloud, reading the number of votes for "Guilty," then "Not guilty." Counts one through four—5 to 7; Count five—4 to 8; Count six—2 to 10; Count seven—5 to 7; and Counts eight through eleven—6 to 6.

Judge Hight thanked the jury for their effort, recognizing how emotionally draining the case had been, and released them.

Hight looked down upon the defendant. "Michael Ruby, you're to return to court on December 6, at which time it will be determined if this case will be re-tried." The gavel came down.

For Michael, a harsh dose of reality set in. His fear of going to jail returned. He'd looked into the eyes of the jurors as the votes were read, and with each count, it became clear that several of them actually believed he'd molested those girls. At least five of the twelve jurors voted "guilty" on nine of the eleven counts. If they'd had their way, he would've been sentenced to more than 100 years in prison.

Outside the courtroom, surrounded by reporters, Lisa Hart spoke. "The district attorney's decision to retry this case will rest solely in the hands of the parents," she said. "They'll have to be willing to put their children through another trial. I think the real problem is the trauma their children will go through by testifying in court."

Bill MacCabe believed Michael Ruby should have been acquitted on all counts. "I'm disappointed the jurors were deadlocked," McCabe said. "Clearly, the children's testimony was confusing and didn't warrant a conviction. The evidence is non-existent, and it bothers me that any juror could've voted for a guilty verdict."

But several had. The panel of eight women and four men were, for the most part, split down the middle. One juror, Teresa Ley, a 51-year-old postal clerk, said it was "very difficult" to sort out what was "true and untrue" and what was "fact and fantasy." Yet despite their inconsistencies, Ley believed the girls were "basically telling the truth." She voted "guilty" on nine of the eleven counts. The problem, she said, was that some of the jurors voted "not guilty" on every count. The moment the deliberations began, she said, one juror, a man, said he believed the girls were "not telling the truth." He couldn't be swayed.

Jury foreman David Wilson remained upset by the jury's inability to reach a unanimous decision. Wilson was one of two jurors who'd voted "guilty" on all eleven counts. "I think what you come back to is: Do you believe the children or not?"

* * * * *

Two weeks later, Michael returned to court. Hours before, Lisa Hart had informed the court that the parents of the alleged victims were not willing to continue. There would be no re-trial.

Acting on a "motion to dismiss," the charges against Michael Ruby were formally dropped.

Over his shoulder, from the front pew, Michael heard his mother's joyous cry. He turned to see his father embracing her, holding her head firmly against his chest. The look in his father's eyes expressed far more than happiness. It was, instead, a look of triumph, that of a faithful man who'd been delivered.

Bill MacCabe stood, hovering over Michael. MacCabe extended his arm, and Michael came to his feet, clutching MacCabe's hand with both palms, shaking vigorously.

"It's over Michael," MacCabe said. "You're free to go."

"Thank you, Mr. MacCabe," Michael said, holding his grip, not wanting to let go. "Thank you for everything."

Bill MacCabe smiled, gracing Michael with a sincere nod of approval. It had not been a typical case for MacCabe—where the court appointed him to defend the constitutional rights of a likely criminal. This young man, MacCabe knew, had been wronged.

Bill MacCabe picked up his briefcase and walked away.

Outside, Lisa Hart stood on the courthouse steps, trying to soften the blow. "You simply can't try a case without witnesses," Hart said, dejected. "I understand the parents' position completely," she said. "I've lived with them through this ordeal."

As Hart spoke, Michael Ruby swung open the glass doors of the courthouse, and the crowd of reporters shifted his way. Michael spent several minutes weeping in the arms of his mother. He gathered himself and gave a brief statement to the media. "I'm innocent," Michael said, a proud declaration, "and I'm sorry that didn't come out at the trial."

Flanked by his parents and his two sisters—his mother's arms firmly around his waist, his sister's head rested gently upon his shoulder, his father standing behind him—Michael knew that his nightmare had ended.

Wiping his eyes, and smiling publicly for the first time in months, Michael made his farewell statement, the fitting words of any blue-blooded surfer. "I'm stoked."

* * * * *

The futility of Michael Ruby's trial carried over into the already precarious McMartin Preschool case. After an eighteen-month preliminary hearing—the longest in California history—Judge Aviva K. Bobb ordered all seven defendants to stand trial for multiple counts of sexual abuse and conspiracy.

Then, weeks later, at noon on Friday, January 17, 1986, District Attorney Ira Reiner called a press conference. With his Chief Deputy Gil Garcetti at his side, Reiner announced that he was dropping charges against five of the McMartin Seven.

The case that had begun with more than 300 counts of child molestation had been reduced to less than 100—the 79 counts against Ray Buckey and the 20 counts against his mother, Peggy. Still charged with a single count of conspiracy, they remained in jail where they'd been for nearly two years.

Gil Garcetti did his best to spin the decision.

"We've completed a very exhaustive, in-depth evaluation of the entire case," Garcetti said, "and based on all the evidence, these are the charges against the defendants that warrant prosecution in Superior Court."

A group of twenty-five McMartin parents went downtown for the announcement, unsure of what they would hear. In a private meeting, just prior to stepping out for the press conference, DA Reiner informed them that the "evidence was so slim" against the five female teachers that he had "a moral and ethical obligation not to file charges."

Following the announcement, some of the parents stayed calm, while others did not.

"I would never get involved in any vigilante-type activity," said Arvin Collins, the father of two alleged victims, "but from what I hear other parents saying, I wouldn't want to be one of those defendants walking the streets."

Collins must have been listening to Bob Currie.

"They would be better off with the trial," Currie warned. "Otherwise, I don't think they're going to live." Currie said that he wouldn't shed any tears for the "ruined" lives of the five women. In his opinion, they got what they deserved. "They've ruined the lives of a lot of parents and lots more children," Currie said. "I'm on my way home to tell my kids the truth—that the system doesn't work."

Ira Reiner couldn't explain why his office spent more than $4 million on an eighteen-month preliminary hearing just to drop the charges. "As you know," Reiner said, "we didn't file this case. This case was inherited."

Reiner, of course, was referring to his predecessor, Robert Philibosian, who'd rushed the case to a grand jury to get an indictment before their June 1984 special election.

Still, that response did not satisfy his critics, those wondering why it took so long to realize that the evidence against the five women was "so slim" that he and Garcetti had reached a "moral and ethical" dilemma.

* * * * *

Glenn Stevens, no longer a member of the district attorney's office, planned to go into private practice—but not before he maximized the opportunity he'd helped to create.

Sometime in early 1986, following his resignation, Stevens took his story to Abby Mann, an Academy Award-winning screenwriter, best known for his screenplay, *Judgment at Nuremberg*.

Stevens entered into a contract with Mann to tell his story, the story of a heroic prosecutor who bravely fights against the injustice of the very system he'd once sworn to uphold. When he realizes that innocent people are being persecuted, he exposes the truth, sacrificing his career in the process.

And there was far more to Stevens' story than what he'd leaked to the press, a sensational tale that he intended to save for himself, for his project with the famed screenwriter.

The information Stevens held onto, the words that would jump off the page, were his experiences with Judy Johnson.

CHAPTER
34

January 1986

As they traveled the coastline in her VW Bus, Judy glanced at her father and recalled their lifetime of love and spirituality, the memories of her wonder years as the clergyman's daughter. The warmth in his eyes reminded her of how pure and simple her life had once been, and how complicated and debased it had become.

They had a long drive ahead, well over twenty hours to Bellevue, Washington, a growing Seattle suburb on the east side of Lake Washington. There, at the home of Steve and Debbie Knutson, Judy would be closer to Mark and Mitchell.

It had been an unsettling time for the Knutson family, particularly Judy, as she tried to regain some normalcy in the aftermath of her psychological breakdown.

Upon her release from UCI—after being diagnosed "paranoid schizophrenic"—she'd endured an onslaught of custody hearings, doctor's visits, and bouts of sickness. She had several meetings with the Department of Child Services, part of its evaluation to determine if she was "fit" to care for her children. If not, the boys would be taken from her.

On November 20, 1985, she had her answer. The Dependency Court gave legal custody of Mark and Mitchell to their uncle and aunt, concluding that Steve and Debbie Knutson offered the stability that Judy had failed to provide. Judy would have the right to visit them, but only if supervised.

On Saturday, December 21, in accordance with that ruling, Steve took Mark and Mitchell to Seattle, the day before Mitchell's fifth birthday.

For the first time in Mitchell's life, Judy had not been with him on his special day, something that further disturbed her. According to Steve, Judy was "irritated by not being allowed to travel with the boys" and the fact that they'd been apart on Christmas morning. Instead, she'd driven alone to the desert to be with her father, where she'd waited for Steve to bring the boys down on New Year's Day for a scheduled parental visitation.

Grateful to Steve for all that he'd done, Judy remained peeved that he'd whisked the boys away so abruptly.

"Why are you working against me?" Judy asked him.

"Judy, I'm bound by a court order," Steve replied. "You understand that, right? I can be held in contempt if I don't comply."

But Judy didn't want to hear it. She didn't see herself as the problem. "Well, I'm coming up in a week or so," she told him. "I'm moving to Bellevue...to be closer to the boys."

Steve, unsure how it would work, didn't want to discourage her. He knew Judy could fall apart at any moment. He told her she would be welcomed.

On Saturday, January 4, Steve and the boys flew back to Seattle, while Judy returned to Manhattan Beach.

While there, alone in her home, Judy grew ill. On her calendar she noted that she'd been "Sick" for five days—from January 7 through 11—and she pencil-sketched a miniature image of a skull & crossbones on each of those days.

By January 13, with Judy having recovered enough to travel, Pastor Knutson arrived to Manhattan Beach to accompany her on her drive north. He didn't want her traveling alone. Since her incarceration, he'd tried to console her, to guide her, but he could only do so much. Nothing that had happened could be undone. The future, he suspected, would bring her even greater despair.

From Judy's perspective, however, her move to the Pacific Northwest brought hope of renewal. That 1,200-mile trek gave Judy and her father an opportunity to talk, to relive the past, to remember the way things had once been.

* * * * *

Sunday, November 19, 1944
Milwaukee, Wisconsin

It was a period of optimism as President Franklin D. Roosevelt instituted the Sixth War Loan Drive to raise billions in bond sales for the fighting effort. U.S. troops had made gains in the Philippines, while on the Western Front in Europe, Allied forces advanced into Germany from the Netherlands, poised to take back sections of northeastern France. Victory in the Second Great War appeared imminent.

Across the heartland, droves of war babies were born, a new generation to follow the path of the greatest one that had preceded them. One of those newborn, a baby girl named Judith Ann Knutson, came into the world by way of Milwaukee, the first-born of Pastor Myrus Knutson and his wife, Delores. They called her Judy.

By Judy's first birthday, the war had ended, and, it seemed, the world had become a better place.

Like many residents of the upper Midwest, the Knutsons descended from Swedish immigrants and were devout Lutherans. Myrus, an ordained minister, a second-generation American, had an ingrained appreciation for religious freedom. He chose his vocation at a young age. Delores, like most women of her era, was a dedicated mother and homemaker. When Judy turned five, her parents delivered her baby brother, Steve, and he became her most cherished companion.

Within a few years, Myrus received an offer to lead a Lutheran parish in Southern California, and the Knutsons relocated to Hancock Park, an upscale section of central Los Angeles built around the Wilshire Country Club. In the early 1950s, when the Knutsons arrived, the neighborhood had been built for wealth, home to the area's pioneer families who'd made their fortune from lucrative oil holdings.

Judy grew up fast, the typical preacher's daughter, adjusting to new situations. Judy had a commanding persona—blonde, blue-eyed, athletically built, with a knack for making people feel welcome, the type of girl any parent would be proud of. Judy had many friends—most wealthy—and yet she stayed grounded, content to live within the means of a preacher's salary.

Life in Hancock Park was all but a dream. The pleasant sunshine of Southern California, a far cry from the cruel winters of Wisconsin, allowed Judy and Steve to play outdoors year around, enjoying that Golden Age of American history—until the winter of 1956.

Delores's cancer diagnosis and rapid demise took something from the family that they never recaptured, the void that mortality leaves behind.

Pastor Knutson's marriage to Helen saved him—a gift from the Lord, a loving woman who stepped in to raise his children. Helen treated them as if they were her own, sacrificing her newlywed joy to bear the responsibility before her.

As selfless as Helen had been, and as much as Judy appreciated her, she never quite got over the loss of her mother.

In 1959, at the age of fifteen, Judy went through her confirmation ceremony. She wore an elegant white gown as she walked down the aisle toward the altar where her father waited. Pastor Knutson admired her beauty, how she exuded the spirit of the wife he'd so painfully lost. The congregation looked on with sympathy, a touching moment for any loving Christian.

Later that day, however, when the after-party had ended, when his good friends and neighbors had returned to their homes, Pastor Knutson heard a sound echoing down the hall—the faint weeping of his daughter.

He walked slowly toward her room, the cries more evident with each step, and he peeked through the cracked opening of the door. Judy sat on her bed, crouched over, sobbing, her hands clutching a picture of her mother, the woman whose spirit had never left. The pastor stepped in and gently sat down, placing his arms around her so she didn't have to mourn alone.

As most wounds heal with time, Judy grew to love the Los Angeles area, the only home she knew. In the summer of 1961, though, before her senior year of high school, Pastor Knutson took a position in Norway. He had to leave immediately.

Judy, although happy for her father, chose to stay in the States to finish her senior year. Her father arranged for her to move back to Minneapolis to stay with her uncle and aunt, Rob and Janet Hinderle, and her fifteen-year-old cousin, Mar.

Judy's return to the Midwest took her back to her early childhood, the way life had been before she lost her mother. Judy enjoyed getting away from Southern California, casting off the responsibilities she'd grown accustomed to, able to roam freely in a new place. Her cousin Mar became the little sister Judy never had—the two girls ran about constantly—a spell of independence Judy had longed for.

Following Judy's graduation, she and Mar took a drive around the Lake of the Isles, a popular landmark southwest of Minneapolis known for its wooded islands and wildlife refuges. Mar, who'd recently turned sixteen, had just gotten her driver's license. She wanted to command the wheel, to cruise the meandering Lake of the Isles Parkway that she'd ridden so many times from the passenger's seat.

"Come on, Judy," Mar begged. "Let me drive. Just for a while. Please."

"All right," Judy said, as she pulled over. "Just be careful. Drive slow."

Judy got out and went around to the passenger's seat as Mar scooched behind the wheel.

Parkway East wrapped around the lakefront with many sharp bends, a route meant to be driven cautiously, where sightseers enjoyed the view of Mike's and Raspberry Islands, but not the best course for a novice.

Headed north, a bit over the speed limit, Mar took the curve near Kenwood Park. To the right, parked off the side of the road, Mar noticed a group of friends. She turned to wave, taking her eyes off the road for a split second—and that was all it took. A sharp turn came upon her. By the time she slammed the brakes, the car careened off the parkway and crashed into a tree.

Mar's chest smashed into the steering wheel, while Judy flew through the windshield. Judy lay on the ground, her face covered in blood, half-conscious. She heard Mar screaming her name, but she passed out before she realized what had happened.

An ambulance rushed Judy to Fairview Hospital, where she underwent emergency surgery. Her leg had been badly fractured, but worse, she sustained an acute injury to her face. The blood that covered her forehead and cheek had come from her eyelid. It had been torn away from her left eye. The thin slice of flesh had been preserved at the crash site and delivered to the operating room.

Dr. Chris Hall, a brilliant young plastic surgeon, a friend of the Hinderles, happened to be on call that afternoon. The Hinderles pleaded with him to do what he could to preserve their niece's beauty, and he did, successfully reattaching Judy's eyelid, leaving only a blemish, but a facial scar all the same, one that reminded Judy of the accident every time she gazed into the mirror.

Judy's leg, too, would never fully heal. The force of the impact caused a compound fracture to her right tibia that left her debilitated for months.

Once notified of Judy's life-threatening accident, Pastor Knutson and Steve returned from Norway to be at her side. Pastor Knutson served as the chaplain for the U.S. Embassy in Oslo, preaching to American military personnel and businessmen, while Steve had entered his freshman year of high school. The church understood the familial crisis and encouraged Pastor Knutson to travel home, but he had to return.

Judy, viewing the wreck as an omen, a sign that her life could be taken in an instant, chose to go with her father and brother back to Norway.

Weeks later, on a glorious morning in New York Harbor, Judy, in a full-leg cast with crutches, boarded the MS Bergen Fjord. The vessel cruised from the mouth of the Hudson River, affording the Knutsons a picturesque view of the Statue of Liberty before their voyage into the Atlantic Ocean.

For Judy, again, it was as if she'd come home, so grateful to be alive, to be on that spectacular ship with her father and brother, imbibing the ambiance of the great city and its breathtaking skyline.

Getting around the ship, however, with its steep stairwells and narrow corridors, became a chore for Judy, a dangerous game when she experienced bouts of intense pain, unable to muster the strength to avoid an accident. When that moment came, Judy fell hard, reinjuring her leg.

Upon their arrival in Oslo, Pastor Knutson admitted Judy to a hospital. While there, Judy contracted a staph infection. The bacteria infected tissue clear to the bone. Due to cost restraints, Judy wasn't given anesthesia, only antibiotics. She endured the pain while the medication fought the disease.

Worse, though, was that she'd been placed in a room with a group of children, some fatally ill. "Those poor children," Judy later said, "were having operations done on them without any anesthesia or pain killers. At night, their parents would sneak in whiskey and make them drink until they became so drunk that the pain was gone."

Judy spent six months in that hospital, watching dozens of children suffer until their deaths, only to have their beds filled by more dying children.

After her release, Judy spent a few months in Oslo with her father and brother before returning to America.

The following year, Judy decided to pursue a degree in education at the University of Minnesota. There, she met Brad Johnson, a business major, the man she came to love and marry—the man who eventually abandoned her, bringing even more pain to her already traumatic life.

CHAPTER
35

Wednesday, January 15. 1986

Judy and her father arrived at Bellevue in the afternoon. Mitchell stood on the front porch, wearing a winter jacket. He noticed the VW Bus pulling into the driveway.

"Mom's here," Mitchell called out to the others. He ran off the porch. "Mom. Mom."

By the time Judy parked and stepped out, Mitchell's arms were around her. Mark, close behind, gave her a hug and a kiss. Steve and Debbie came out of the house and stood back with careful smiles, letting Judy and the boys enjoy that long-awaited moment. Debbie held the hand of their eighteen-month-old son, Johnny, walking him toward his grandfather. Pastor Knutson picked up little Johnny and kissed his forehead.

That scene is one that every family knows, the safe arrival of beloved visitors—the warm welcome in the front yard. For Judy, it was as gleeful as she'd imagined it would be.

For the first few days, with Pastor Knutson at her side, Judy stayed grounded, calm, falling back into her motherly routine. She prepared the boys for school, sent them off and waited for their return. During the evenings they were a family again—homework, board games—a soothing pace that Judy kept up with.

But after a week, Pastor Knutson had to leave, and he worried that Judy had unreasonable expectations. Those few days of happiness, just a visit, hadn't changed anything. Judy could not go back to being Mark and Mitchell's caretaker.

On the morning of Tuesday, January 21, Steve drove his father to the airport. As they stood curbside saying goodbye, Pastor Knutson handed Steve a card, expressing his gratitude for the help that he and Debbie had given Judy and the boys.

"Power to you from the Holy Spirit," the pastor wrote. "We certainly admire what you both are doing so nobly. Will send more $ next month."

Pastor Knutson knew Steve and Debbie had been struggling financially, a young couple with a newborn. Stepping in to become the boys' legal guardians was a selfless act, and it made the pastor smile to know that his lifetime of homilies had found a home in Steve's heart.

When Steve returned home, he found Judy in a dark mood. She shouldn't have been there, not with Steve out of the house, and certainly not spending the night. They all knew it. Judy had already crossed the line, which Steve had put up with while Pastor Knutson had been in town. But it couldn't continue.

The tension built for about thirty minutes, an unspoken discomfort, before Steve broke the silence.

"So, where are you staying?" Steve asked.

Judy's blank stare revealed that she had no plan, but she flipped the script, playing the victim, casting her passive-aggressive guilt. "I can just stay at a motel," she said, grabbing her bag and packing her things.

Steve followed her around the house from a distance. "Do you have money?" he asked.

"I have enough for a few days. Don't worry about me," Judy said, hugging Mark and Mitchell. "I'll be back tomorrow after school," she said, then turned to Steve and Debbie. "Is that okay? Do I have permission?"

"That's fine, Judy," Steve said, dropping his eyes. "We'll see you tomorrow."

Judy shook her head slowly, holding back tears. She walked out and slammed the door behind her.

That episode, the first in a devolving cycle of interaction between Judy and the Knutsons, set the tone for the coming weeks. Each day, when the boys returned from school, Judy would be waiting, sometimes unannounced. Often times, Steve arrived home from work to find Judy in a conversation with Mitchell, which she'd been instructed not to do. Judy continued to bend the rules, forcing Steve and Debbie's hand. If she persisted, coming and going as she pleased, they had no way to predict what she might do next.

Judy, they knew, hadn't recovered psychologically. She'd been instructed by the courts to get treatment while in Bellevue, but Steve and Debbie weren't sure if she'd been going. Judy never discussed it.

On her January 1986 calendar, Judy penciled "Appt. 6:00, Trudi" on the 22nd, the day after her father left Bellevue. Trudi Campbell, a Seattle-based mental health specialist, had been asked to work with Judy on her "curing" and the "well-being of [the] kids."

From Judy's random notes, it showed that Trudi had been told to evaluate if "foster placement" with "visits arranged through a social worker" were an appropriate course, and it emphasized that if Judy violated the court order, she should be "taken into custody." A separate notation stated:

Trudi—Get Judy an interview with mental health team—3 with Trudi, with nothing to drink.

Over the last week of January, Judy got back into her habit of jotting down her daily schedule and observations on her calendar. She noted "Super Bowl" and "Flu" on Sunday, January 26, and "Motel" on January 27 and 28, as well as "Shuttle Exploded," referring to the tenth mission of the Space Shuttle Challenger, which broke apart before the nation's eyes. On January 29 she wrote, "Minister Comes Over," once again clinging to her faith.

Staying in the motel had drained Judy's funds. She should have headed back to Manhattan Beach, but she had nothing there, just the emptiness of a childless home.

"Can I *please* just stay a few nights?" Judy begged of Steve at his doorstep. "Brad owes me money…I swear…he's late with his check…he owes *you* money too, right? The child support checks…has he sent them?"

"No," Steve said, shaking his head. "I haven't—"

"You see," Judy said, her eyes widening. "He's late. He's always late."

Steve couldn't look at her. He just opened the door and stepped aside, letting her in.

Debbie stood in the threshold to their bedroom holding little Johnny. Her face told Steve how much she disapproved.

The days that followed brought immense strain upon the Knutson home. According to Debbie, Judy became difficult, wanting "to be in charge." Steve and Debbie tried to set ground rules for the boys, as parents do, giving them regimen and structure—homework, dinner, tub, and bed—but Judy, as Debbie put it, began to "openly interfere," refusing to accept their authority.

"It wasn't good for the boys," Debbie recalled. "She kept telling them on the sly that we weren't right, to not follow our instructions. But we were responsible for them, and they had to study and go to school."

It came to a head the afternoon Judy showed up at Mitchell's school and removed him from campus. Steve and Debbie got a call from the school's administrator.

"Mr. Knutson," the woman said. "I just wanted you to know that Mitchell's mother came and picked him up. She's visited him before, but this is the first time she's taken him with her."

Steve thanked her and hung up, furious. He knew, by law, he should have called the police and had Judy arrested for violating the court order. But could he really bring himself to do that?

Twenty minutes later, Judy pulled up in her VW Bus. She and Mitchell walked toward the house. Steve came out and told Mitchell to go inside. Steve got into Judy's face.

"What are you thinking?" Steve asked, keeping his voice down.

"What?" Judy replied, acting oblivious.

"Are you serious? Are you *actually* serious, Judy? You think you can drive to his school and take him out? Are you *that unaware* of what's going on here?"

"My god, Steve," Judy said, "you act like I kidnapped my own son. We just went to the park for fifteen minutes. It's no big deal."

"Judy, if the court catches wind of what you did, we're *all* in serious trouble." Steve looked at her sternly, but she gave no response. "The boys will go to foster care. Is that what you want?"

Still, Judy said nothing.

"Is it?"

Judy began to well up.

"Judy, listen to me," Steve said, placing his hands on her cheeks. "You have to stop this. This can't go on any longer."

Judy shook her head slowly, not wanting to hear what he was about to say.

"Judy, you need to leave. You can't stay here anymore. You gotta go."

Judy pushed him away, her sadness turning to rage. She turned and pointed at Debbie.

"This is *her* saying this, not you," Judy cried. "She just wants to get rid of me. She never wanted me here...never."

"That's not true, Judy," Steve said. "You know it's not true."

Debbie walked back into the house, then came out holding Judy's bag—her things were already packed. Debbie handed the bag to Steve and went back inside.

Steve gave Judy a hug, speaking softly through their embrace. "You can see the boys, Judy. You can see them whenever you want, but you have to follow the rules. You just have to do as the court says."

Judy lifted her head, nodding as if she understood. She grabbed her bag from Steve's grip, stepped into her van and pulled away. She drove to a nearby park, the same location she'd just taken Mitchell. Judy lay down on the floor of the VW Bus and settled in for the night.

* * * * *

By mid-February 1986, Judy had gotten used to living out of her van. The parks of Bellevue became her home during the day, while in the early evenings, when the boys came home from school, Judy hovered around the Knutsons' house.

When alone, Judy wrote in notebooks and on her calendars. On February 15, she scribed that she'd received the "last check from Brad," a helpful stipend but not nearly enough. On February 27 she wrote, "Bruises Bleeding," an indication that her health had worsened—the gastric ulcer tearing away at her stomach's lining. Her diet had become sparse and erratic. On February 25 she went to a "Recreation Center," but they'd offered "No Snack." As she spent each day mustering up free meals, the hunger pains worsened, and she had no way to neutralize the acids—no medicine or even natural foods to lessen her irritation. So, every few days, she threw up a spot of blood.

Compounding her physical ailments, Judy's relationship with Steve and Debbie had become less cordial. Judy had not stopped meddling in Mitchell's daily activity. One day she went by the school after he'd gone home, asking questions about him; another day she showed up in the morning to speak with one of his teachers. For Steve and Debbie, it seemed, kicking Judy out had made it more difficult to monitor her actions.

Despite their frustration, however, the Knutsons did their best to incorporate Judy into their home life, letting her take part in the most precious moments—such as a small get-together they had for the boys on Valentine's Day.

In a letter to Pastor Knutson, Judy told her story, the portrait of a woman destitute, left penniless by an ex-husband who'd refused to honor his word, a woman pitifully holding out her hand, asking her father what he could spare.

"Thank you for your Valentines," Judy wrote to Pastor Knutson. "It was very sweet. We had a little celebration at their [Steve and Debbie's] house." Judy mentioned that she'd "called Glenn Stevens to prosecute action against Brad," as he was "over $1,500 in back payments for child support." Judy said she was certain things would "work out," and she promised to "re-pay" her father.

> *The weather has been unbelievable; super storms, winds, ice, lightning and hail—Wow!*
>
> *Mark has been biking but got sick a couple of days ago. Mitchell has had a terrible cough. He is in school from 8:30am to 6:00-6:30pm every day.*
>
> *What a price to pay when it could have all been free.*

Judy said that she planned to see them all at church on Sunday, and she hoped they would get together later that evening "for *60 Minutes* and popcorn."

Apparently, as her letter illustrated, Judy wasn't up to speed with the McMartin case. She didn't know that Glenn Stevens had been identified as the "Judas" of the prosecution team, and that he was no longer with the DA's office. Judy had grown close to Glenn Stevens, her primary contact whenever she had a problem or an interesting story to convey. Judy had trusted him, confided in him, but that relationship, too, had come to an end.

As Judy spent her days in the park, beneath the dreary sky of the Pacific Northwest, with the damp air and the soft, muddy ground, her life resembled that of a homeless person. She scrubbed her body in the dingy public bathrooms, and she ate whatever she could get her hands on.

March became a busy month for Judy the Archivist, as she packed her words into the calendar box of each day, writing smaller to squeeze the words in. She wrote only in pencil, but very neatly, with no trace of eraser smudging. Her March 3 entry notes: "Mitchell crying; kids say he was going to be hurt" and "Mitchell Sick, Gas & Diarrhea," showed that Judy remained obsessed with Mitchell's daily doings, lurking in public view, pushing the legal limits.

By the second week of March, Steve had reached his wit's end. No longer willing to put up with Judy's behavior, Steve wrote her a letter to "recap the Court Order" and "the compliance requests" of the DSS. Steve informed Judy of the rules that she was mandated to abide by—she would "not have custody of kids unless under supervision"; if she picked Mitchell up from school again she would be arrested; an injunction could be placed upon her to keep her from even visiting their home.

"You can see that this makes me a policeman with my own sister," Steve wrote, "and I don't want that."

Steve warned Judy that the only way to avoid such conflict was for her to return to LA. He said that he "loved her very much" but he would have no choice. If she did not "comply with the court order," he would have her arrested.

But Steve's letter didn't faze Judy. The state had already taken her children away, and she was living out of her VW Bus in a park. Going to jail would have been a pleasant reprieve—a warm shower and a steady stream of meals.

Instead of backing off, Judy settled in, making a home of Spiritridge Park, an open lawn of 4.5 acres equipped with tennis courts, picnic areas, and hiking trails. The bathrooms were well-kept, sanitized daily—an upgrade of sorts—and most of all, a short drive to Steve and Debbie's house.

Nevertheless, the harsh elements of the Seattle winter took their toll on Judy. On her March calendar, she noted "Rain," "Storm," or "Cold" on fourteen occasions. She wrote "Sick" into several date boxes, that she was "Still Bleeding" and "Bleed Super," vomiting more and more blood by the day.

Then there was the isolation, the idea that she'd been spurned by those closest to her. On March 14, Judy went by Steve and Debbie's to see the boys, but they shut her out, not even letting her in.

"I just want to say 'hi' to my son," Judy said, raising her voice to Debbie, who stood in the doorway, blocking the path.

"Judy, you know you can't drop by like this," Debbie said, stepping out and closing the door behind her. "Your visits have to be scheduled. You know this."

"Whatever," Judy yelled, storming away.

The next day, Judy drafted a scathing note to Steve, a critical diatribe against Debbie, suggesting that Debbie was "oblivious" and "confused," challenging Steve's authority over his wife by asking, "Who's in charge here?"

That note also served as Judy's "written notification" of her next visit. She wanted to "come by" to see the boys "after counseling." She expected Steve to coordinate a visitation with the boys at Spiritridge Park; that he provide "a note" giving the boys permission to be with Judy, unsupervised, in the park.

Judy still hadn't received her monthly check from Brad—"No Ck," she wrote—so even if she'd wanted to, Judy had no way of traveling back to Manhattan Beach, no money for gas, no money for food, and no contingency plan in case the VW Bus broke down along the way.

With no realistic options, Judy hunkered down in her van, moving from park to park in a nomadic effort to survive.

PART VII
Blood of the Lamb

CHAPTER
36

April 1986

"Hoag here," the detective answered. "How can I help you?" The call had just come in. The woman—the mother of a teenage girl—wanted to file a complaint of child sexual abuse.

"Hello," the woman said, rather unnerved, "this is Nina Barron. I'm not sure exactly what to do, but my daughter, Heather, she's fourteen. She was molested."

"She told you this?"

"Yes, about an hour ago," Nina replied. "I got a call from the school counselor. She said that Heather was sitting in her office, crying. She wouldn't tell me why. She said that it wasn't something she felt comfortable speaking about over the phone. So I left work and rushed down there, and when I went into her office, Heather was sitting by herself… very upset…and she looked up at me and said, 'I'm sorry, Mom. I'm so sorry.' "

Nina told Hoag that, for five years, Heather had been keeping a secret, an indecent chapter from her past that she'd tried to forget, but the guilt had stayed with her. Heather had been sexually molested, several times, and the images of it had haunted her ever since.

"Did Heather say who did this to her?" Hoag asked.

"Yes. She said it was a janitor."

"A janitor? Like the janitor at her school?"

"No. Not at her school…a janitor up at American Martyrs."

Within hours, Detective Hoag received two more calls, the parents of the "other girls" who were molested along with Heather. The other two told a similar story, the eight to ten separate incidents between 1981 and 1982 when the girls had gone into the janitor's "private workshop."

The first encounter was on a Saturday in the summer of 1981, when the three girls—all eight years old at the time—came to the playground at American Martyrs. None of them were students at Martyrs Parochial, nor members of the church.

The janitor "invited them" into his workshop, promising to "give them chocolate." He talked to them "about sex," and he eventually undid his pants and "showed them his penis." They said that he "picked them up and hugged them," and proceeded to "fondle" them.

The secret liaison, as perverted as it was, intrigued the girls, and they continued to go back over the course of the summer. By fall, with the new semester, the girls stopped going, and the abuse ended, at least physically.

Five years passed, and the images of what had occurred in the workshop fell from the girls' immediate memory, but the scars were still visible. Heather Barron started acting up, going through a phase of anxiety and aggressive outbursts. Her parents recommended that she speak with a counselor at school, to express her feelings and to purge the anger she harbored. They had no idea what had been tormenting her. She'd always been such a well-balanced child.

After a few sessions, the counselor suspected that Heather had been repressing her memory, not willing to talk about her elementary years.

"Did something happen to you, Heather?" the counselor had asked.

Heather looked away, shaking her head.

"Heather, what happened? You can tell me."

Heather stood and walked to the corner, keeping her back to the counselor. When she turned around, her face flushed with shame. She couldn't bring herself to speak, to actually admit she'd been sexually abused.

After a few minutes, Heather began to tell her story, every detail of what had happened on those Saturday afternoons. Heather gave the counselor the names of the other two girls, and their parents were contacted as well.

Once confronted, those girls confirmed Heather's version. All three girls apologized for what "they had done," as if, in some way, they were at fault for their actions.

It didn't take Detective Hoag long to determine the identity of the suspect: "Clement Edmund Renaud," a fifty-seven-year-old native Texan who'd been married for twenty-five years, the father of two grown adults.

Known around American Martyrs as "Clem," he'd left his job in June 1983.

In her conversation with one of the three complaining mothers, Hoag was informed that "another girl," an "American Martyrs student"—the daughter of a friend of a friend—had also been molested by the janitor "sometime in 1982." The woman said that it occurred on the school grounds, in the workshop, just as it had with her daughter.

"My friend told me that many people knew what he'd done," the woman said. "And the Church *definitely* knew about it. But they didn't do anything. They dealt with it *in-house*. Not long after, the guy up and left."

If that were true, Hoag knew, then a crime and a cover-up had been committed. If Church officials had been aware that a child had been sexually abused, particularly by one of their employees, they had a legal responsibility to report it to the police. It would have been incumbent upon the police, after consulting with the parents and the child, to take the case to the district attorney, who would then decide if the case should be pursued. But it was certainly not up to the Church.

Hoag envisioned the firestorm this new allegation could create. If, as she'd just been told, the former American Martyrs janitor had molested multiple children on the campus—children who were the same age as the complaining witnesses in the ongoing McMartin case—then it was possible that the alleged McMartin victims had also been abused by the janitor, or—even more compelling—the janitor may have been part of the McMartin conspiracy.

Hoag placed a call to the Los Angeles District Attorney's Office and spoke with Assistant DA Steve Morgan.

"You need to find as many victims as possible," Morgan instructed her. "You can find them through the school records. Don't leave any stone unturned."

DA Morgan said that since the "potential victims" would be older, they could better articulate the details of their abuse.

"You need to speak with *every* family at American Martyrs about this guy," Morgan told her. "The more victims you can locate, the better."

* * * * *

Life had grown tiresome for Steve and Debbie Knutson. Judy's antics were more trouble than they were willing to put up with.

As a result, Steve informed the court he would be sending Mitchell back to Manhattan Beach to live with his father. Steve bought three plane tickets to travel on March 29. He phoned Brad and told him to be ready.

"I'll be there on Saturday," Steve told Brad. "I'll bring the boys for a visit, but when Mark and I leave on Sunday, Mitchell's not going with us. He's staying with you."

Steve loved Mitchell dearly, and he didn't want to create more instability in the boy's life. But this could not go on, something had to give, and the only way to lure Judy out of the Bellevue public parks would be to send Mitchell home. Hopefully, she would follow.

Being Easter week, Judy had plans for the boys. On Tuesday, March 25, she left a note for Steve on a sheet from a Christmas notepad. It had a cute illustration by American humorist and children's author, Sandra Boynton, where her "fat cat" struggled to hold up a giant candy cane. The greeting read, "Merry Christmas to You."

Yet it was far from Christmas, from the joyous celebration of Christ's birth. It was, instead, the harrowing days of his suffering and death. To Judy, it was the holiest season, a time to be spent with her children, and she expected her brother to honor that tradition.

> *I understand the boys leave Sat. or Sun. for LAX. As its Holy Week, I would like to see Mitchell Thurs. & Fri. afternoon for communion and Good Friday services, and local Easter events.*
> *Please call and clear with the school. There will be no problem.*

Two days later, on Good Friday, Judy again pressed Steve to let her spend some time with Mitchell before he left for California, but Steve didn't respond.

"Have attempted to reach you at office," Judy wrote in another note, and she asked if he wanted to "do lunch." She mentioned the "beautiful weather" and said that she hoped he had enjoyed his camping trip. She signed "Sis" and drew a heart around it.

But Steve didn't give in. As sincere as she may have been when she expressed her love, Judy was woefully misguided. If she expected him to let her spend unsupervised time with Mitchell, to take him out of school during Holy Week, then she was as unbound from reality as she'd been a year before, that last Good Friday when he found himself looking down the barrel of a shotgun.

With Mitchell back in Manhattan Beach, Judy became less

manipulative. Yet her skillful maneuvering gave way to a variety of altered emotions—fear, self-pity, anger, and spite. More than ever, Judy began to "check out," both physically and psychologically, as her spirit seemed to transmute into bi-polar moods and multiple personalities.

"It was amazing," Steve recalled about those months, "how lucid she could be one moment, and the next she'd be almost catatonic." Judy would arrive at the Knutsons' home with a bubbly persona, but soon after she would go to the couch and stare into space, completely unresponsive.

In conjunction with her mental decline, Judy's health continued to deteriorate. She noted being "Sick" on April 5, 6, 7, and 8, and wrote "Blood" on the 10th, sketching her caricature of the skull & crossbones on each of those days.

Another week passed, and Judy worsened. On April 15, she "Threw up" and got "Super sick," and four days later, she wrote, "Blood of the Lamb," as if to suggest that the blood she shed offered some hope of redemption.

Then, on the morning of Saturday, April 26, well before dawn, Judy woke in a cold sweat, breathing heavily, terrified. Unsure why, Judy only knew that her nightmare had been ominous, images of darkness that pulled her from her suspended consciousness.

Sometime thereafter, in her April 26 date-box, Judy wrote, "Lungs," "Russians," and "Warning Dream."

That day, while Judy and her fellow Americans slept soundly, a catastrophic nuclear accident occurred at the Chernobyl Nuclear Power Plant in the Ukrainian Soviet Socialist Republic, releasing massive quantities of radioactive particles into the atmosphere, the worst accident of its kind in world history.

Judy's claim of having a "Warning Dream" had likely been noted in retrospect. Judy made a habit of going back over her calendars and logging information with blue ink in a distinct quasi-cursive style, precisely what she'd done on that date. After hearing the news of the Chernobyl disaster, it seems, Judy recalled the visions of her dream, the premonition of mass destruction and widespread suffrage. To Judy, it meant that she'd been warned, as if she were a conduit of divine prophecies.

With the end of spring, Judy spent her days wandering aimlessly from public parks to food banks, and at night, she camped alone. She stayed occupied in her thoughts, in her constant scribing, cramming a whirlwind of words and expressions into the daily boxes on her calendar, leaving the impression she didn't have a minute to spare—but nothing was further from the truth. Most of the information had no rhyme or reason, a string of trivial observations: the diaries of an unstable woman.

Apart from her calendar, Judy kept a collection of random notes and letters. One of them, dated May 20, came from Deputy DA Lael Rubin, who, despite Ira Reiner's shake up of the case, remained the lead prosecutor.

Rubin wrote to Judy, saying that she was just "checking in," wondering when Judy would "return to Los Angeles," and instructing Judy to contact Rubin the moment she did.

* * * * *

In the aftermath of Glenn Stevens' resignation from the district attorney's office, Lael Rubin had to deal with Judy directly, to tie up whatever loose ends remained. Rubin knew that Stevens had spent a great deal of time with Judy. Rubin remembered the conversation she and Stevens had about Judy's "mental state," where they both agreed that Judy was "unstable"—back when they didn't give it much thought.

But recently, and far more concerning for Rubin, was the information that had recently surfaced. While going through Glenn Stevens' files, in the months after his departure, Rubin came upon two documents: a "hand-written" letter from Judy Johnson dated February 16, 1984—a bizarre account of a satanic ritual where, amongst other things, a baby had been sacrificed—and a transcription six days later, on February 22, by DA Investigator Tim Tyson, his follow-up interview with Judy Johnson in respect to her February 16 letter.

Rubin, "to the best of her knowledge," couldn't remember ever seeing the documents, and because of that, she believed they hadn't been handed over to the defense as part of discovery. If Glenn Stevens had been aware of the letter and the follow-up interview, he may have taken copies with him—a virtual ticking time bomb for the Los Angeles DA's Office.

On Friday, June 13, 1986, in an attempt to diffuse a potential ethical violation, Lael Rubin turned the documents over to the defense. Drafted weeks before the McMartin Seven indictments, the documents were considered the "smoking guns."

As Lael Rubin dealt with that controversy, Glenn Stevens had started another. Stevens, hard at work on his movie project with screenwriters Abby and Myra Mann, sat down with the couple for a thirty-hour, audiotaped account that told his story, the facts that he hadn't leaked to the press, such as the "bizarre letter" written by Judy Johnson.

Stevens implied that the letter had been intentionally lost in the shuffle by the DA's Office. Regardless, it was an authentic piece of evidence that suggested Judy Johnson may have been unstable when she filed the original complaint.

Stevens critiqued every aspect of the case, including how the DA's office had deliberately kept innocent people in jail, and he outlined the central theme of the screenplay. The basis of that tale, of course, would be the peculiar world of Judy Johnson. Stevens spoke of Judy as if she were a character in a novel, the misguided protagonist of a great social tragedy, the unstable mother whose false allegation spawned mass hysteria in a small community.

"Judy was a loner," Stevens told the Manns, and the McMartin case, he suggested, had given her "a cause" and a purpose in life, as it had for so many other parents.

He said, "She started hanging out with all these people who were acting like junior detectives, going through Manhattan Beach and looking for child molesters behind every billboard, looking through garbage pails and going through the trash of this house and that house."

As the parent who had initiated the case, Stevens said, Judy started to "really feel important." But with so much negativity happening around her, she grew increasingly paranoid. One night, Judy called Stevens and said that her "house had been broken into." Nothing had been stolen, but "the window screen had been slightly moved."

Stevens said Judy started to "see ghosts," and he recounted a day in late 1984 while Judy traveled through the Seattle area. She'd called Stevens collect.

"She was in a hospital," Stevens said. "She had no idea how she got there. All she knew was that she was with her kids in her Volkswagen Bus." Judy, extremely frightened, said that an "AWOL Marine from Twentynine Palms" had been stalking her. She'd met the man while visiting her folks in Yucca Valley. Judy couldn't give Stevens a description of the man, nor could she explain why she'd been admitted to a hospital or how she'd been released.

"So," Stevens told Abby and Myra Mann, "I'm beginning to think, you know, this woman's bananas."

What concerned Stevens most was that Judy started pointing the finger at numerous people: her husband, employees at the local Nautilus, and even the former head of the Los Angeles School Board, Roberta Weintruab.

When that happened, Stevens said, he discussed it with Lael Rubin, but, he admitted, neither of them took it seriously.

"We had a good laugh about Judy," Stevens told the Manns, "but we never discussed what it meant to the whole case."

Only in retrospect, after resigning from the DA's office, Stevens said, did he realize its significance.

"Well," Abby Mann suggested, "it's kind of extraordinary, because here's a woman who made the first charges, started the whole thing going. If something's wrong with her, chances are there's something wrong with the whole damned thing."

"I guess," Stevens replied. "Everything hadn't been put in place yet, Abby. That's the best I can explain it. I never really looked at it that way—when she started making these accusations—because I wasn't looking at the case skeptically yet."

But, Stevens said, once he did, he concluded that "Judy may be sort of a crucial piece," that "if you take Judy out of it, then you would've never gotten to CII" where Stevens believed that every child after Mitchell Johnson had been falsely programmed to say they were abused.

"Two hundred letters wouldn't have gone out," Myra Mann added, "and you wouldn't have had this mass hysteria."

Stevens knew she was correct, that if the police had done a better job of breaking down Judy's single accusation against Ray Buckey, they would have determined it baseless—the erroneous suspicion of a paranoid woman.

"Well," Stevens said, "I'm not going to sleep tonight, I can tell already."

CHAPTER 37

On Saturday, June 14, 1986, under an overcast dawn in Bellevue, Judy lay asleep on the floor of her van. With Mitchell back in Manhattan Beach, her thoughts were on Mark. Judy's latest camping spot at Robinswood Park, the parking lot next to the bathrooms, was ideal but not inconspicuous, not for someone in a Volkswagen Bus.

That morning, after first light, the banging on her driver's side window startled her awake.

"You need to leave, ma'am," a police officer said loudly. "I've told you before, you can't sleep here."

Judy nodded and rustled a bit before buckling herself in. She turned the ignition and pulled away. The officer watched and waited as she drove out of sight.

Judy headed southeast toward Lake Sammamish State Park. It was larger than Robinswood, and she could meld in without being bothered by the rangers.

Over the past two weeks, on a few occasions, Judy had stayed at Lake Sammamish, and she preferred its amenities, but it was five miles down the I-90 freeway, and the fuel cost ate into her already meager budget. Staying at Robinswood, a short drive to Steve and Debbie's, had allowed her to shoot by and see Mark, maybe get a meal, and get back to her reserved spot by dark.

No more.

On the move once again, Judy stayed in survival mode—"Food Banks," "Salvation Army," "Emergency Food," eating "Chicken & Rice" and "Soup," lots of soup, as well as "Bread" and a combination of "Egg-Onion Mush," all foods that gave her enough nutrition to get through the days while further activating her gastric ulcers.

The weather grew unpleasant, with heavy rains followed by severe heat. It wore Judy down. She wrote "Sick" and "Bleed" on seventeen days that month.

By late June she began to spend more nights at Iron Horse Trail State Park near North Bend, an additional sixteen miles southeast of the Knutsons. Judy camped along the Iron Horse Trail. She'd become even more secluded, living off the land, away from the parks from which she'd been banished.

During that stretch, Judy wrote to her father and Helen, stating that she'd "been out of funds" and had just been "making ends meet." Judy expressed how much she appreciated their help, leery about asking for more, but she would take whatever they could spare.

> *Seems a shame Brad is so disruptive. He and Gloria certainly make enough to live on, and then some.*
> *Perhaps, they need a good dose of Christian love!*

For the first time, her letter revealed, Judy had lost faith, giving up on her expectation that Brad would pay her what he owed her, or that she would ever be reunited with her children.

> *Everything has really gotten worse. I know how super you have been through all this, and I can't stop thanking you enough. I believe you can use me as a tax write off. I have no reportable income. My only funds have been from you, and that should be a sizable amount if I remember right.*

Judy worried about competing in a job market "overwhelmed with summer teenagers," and how she needed "re-training." She would have to "join a union" to make a livable wage.

> *I can survive on 300 dollars a month, but it requires a lot of budgeting. If you can help for the next three months, hopefully I will be nearly independent.*

Judy stressed that her "major concern" was getting her VW Bus repaired, and that she'd just managed "to stay afloat" since Brad cut off her funds.

I think I need some sunshine to cheer things up.

* * * * *

For weeks, Mark had grown feeble, a combination of nausea and difficulty with speech. Steve and Debbie decided to send him back to Manhattan Beach to be closer to his doctors. "Brad didn't want him," Steve said. Since their falling out at the custody hearing, they hadn't talked, so Steve arranged for Mark to live with Gayle and Jeep Schaeffer.

Debbie wanted Mark to stay. "Mark had been very happy in Bellevue," she said. "Steve had become his father figure, and he really needed that, especially with what he was going through. But he needed specialized treatment and attention that we couldn't provide. He deserved better…much better."

On top of his own well-being, Mark couldn't stop thinking of Mitchell, the fact that his little brother had been left alone with their father. Mark suspected that Brad didn't have Mitchell's best interest at heart.

"If he really cared about us," he said, "he wouldn't have let us go to Bellevue in the first place."

So as much as Mark wanted to look out for his mother, trying to keep her from fading into the shadows, Mitchell needed him more.

On the morning Mark prepared to leave—Monday, July 7—Judy came by the house to help him pack. She did her best to make a good impression, noting on her calendar, "Washed Hair" and "Washed Clothes," and that she'd "Slept a lot," catching up on some much needed rest.

"I'll miss you," Judy said, hugging him as she hid her crying face over his shoulder. "I'll be with you every minute, I swear."

"I know you will," he said. "Just get home safely, okay? Just get in the van and drive home, okay?"

"I will. I will. I promise."

Then Steve and Mark drove away.

Once again, Judy, alone, with no plan to get home, continued to lurk about the parks and campsites of the greater Seattle area.

Evidently, Mark's sudden departure left an impact on her psyche. Over the next two nights, July 8 and 9, as she lay beneath the clear night sky along the Iron Horse Trail, Judy wrote of "Nightmares." The first night she dreamed of her experience at UC Irvine, the mental health facility where she'd been incarcerated and diagnosed paranoid schizophrenic. The next evening her nightmare led her to write the phrase, "We Are Coming."

Over the next four days, Judy noted that she began "Bleeding" again.

Judy Johnson's calendar entries from July 1986, as she traveled through the Pacific Northwest, living in her VW Van, moving from public parks to camp sites.

* * * * *

Back in Manhattan Beach, Mark's health grew dire.

"Mark became very sick, sicker than I'd ever seen him," Gayle remembered. "As soon as we had him in our house, we could tell he wasn't doing well. Judy was still driving around Washington State, up there some place, but Mark spoke with her regularly. So we at least knew she was okay."

The Schaeffers, to their credit, had always thought of Mark as a son. He'd been a fixture in their lives since he was a child and had become friends with their son, Jason. Woefully, they witnessed the mornings he became dizzy and frail prior to discovering his brain tumor. They stood by him through the ordeal, and they saw the overwhelming fear in his eyes when told his life would not last much longer. They held him and hugged him and loved him like the precious gift that he was. And over the years, they noticed how his fear developed into bravery—when a boy becomes a man prepared to die.

"We got papers to adopt him as a foster child," Gayle said. "If that's what it took to take care of him and give him a quality life, then we would do it."

Yet they knew that even though he'd been rejected by his father, Mark, deep down, wanted to be with Brad and Mitchell, to be a family once again. The Schaeffers had always considered the arrangement to be temporary.

"We never filed the papers," Gayle confirmed. "We wanted to get him back with Brad."

Brad and his girlfriend, Gloria, lived nearby in a small home off Highland Avenue, a short walk. Mark would ride his bike there to see Mitchell each day, and sometimes he brought his little brother back to the Schaeffers' house.

Every so often, Gayle would run into Brad and Gloria on the block or at the corner market. "They couldn't avoid us," she said. At one point, the Schaeffers went to Brad's home to talk to him about Mark, to tell him he should be taking care of his dying son.

"Brad said he didn't want Mark," Gayle said, "that he wasn't going to take care of him, no matter what."

That moment, Gayle said, ended their relationship with Brad. "My husband, Jeep, really told him off," she said. "But Brad didn't care. He just walked back into his house."

Not long after, Mark took a turn for the worse.

"Mark was having trouble walking. His spine had sunken into his back," Gayle recalled. "I told him he *had* to go to the hospital…that he needed to see a doctor. He really didn't want to go. I don't think he wanted to know."

Gayle spoke to Gloria, a nurse at Kaiser, and she scheduled an appointment. Gloria told Gayle that it was the Schaeffers' responsibility to take him, not Brad's.

On Tuesday, July 22, the night before Mark's appointment at Kaiser, they had a small get together to celebrate Jason Schaeffer's birthday, a somewhat subdued gathering.

"Mark always liked fireworks," Gayle said. "He asked if we could take them down to the beach, so we all got into the van and drove across the sand and set them off. It was illegal, but we didn't care at that point."

When they came back from the beach, Brad stood in front of their house, waiting. "He didn't speak to anyone," Gayle said. "But he handed me a hundred-dollar check with his authorized release, giving us permission to make decisions. Brad didn't say a word to Mark. He just left."

The next morning, the Schaeffers took Mark to Kaiser.

"They administered a series of tests, many X-rays, but the doctors weren't ready to say anything definitive," Gayle said, "only that they would have results in a couple of days."

The next evening, while the Schaeffers were having dinner, they received a call from Gloria. She wanted to speak with Mark. She asked if he could come over.

When Mark and Gayle arrived at Brad's home, Gloria asked them to take a seat on the couch. Brad, seated in a chair, didn't speak but he looked distraught. Gloria, through her contacts at the hospital, had received an advanced report of Mark's examination. She'd seen the X-rays.

"Mark's bones are full of holes. The cancer is eating away at him. It's already spread. It's everywhere," Gloria said, tearing up as she saw the hopelessness in Mark's eyes.

"Mark just sat there and listened to Gloria for about an hour," Gayle said. "He never cried. He never said anything. He just listened and nodded."

It led to one conclusion: Mark could no longer be treated. His eight-year battle with cancer had ended. He would receive medication for his pain and nausea, and he would wait.

"Gloria eventually said that she and Brad would look for a bigger place," Gayle said, "so that Mark could live the rest of his life with them."

When they left, Gayle and Mark stepped slowly, taking in the surroundings of Vista Drive, the narrow block that held so many of their memories. They were in no rush. They had nowhere to go, nowhere to be. After being told that Mark would die, they were just glad to be together, thankful for that time to reflect.

Halfway down the block, Mark stopped. He turned to Gayle and grabbed her by the hand. "Well," he said with a tearful smile, "I've had a good life."

CHAPTER 38

August 1986

For months, Detective Jane Hoag had studied Clement Renaud, the former janitor, a man who fit the profile of every child molester she'd ever helped to convict. Renaud, a pedophile, a predator, had used his position at American Martyrs to prey upon girls between eight and eleven years old—an insidious scheme by a sick and unapologetic man.

When Hoag first took the complaint from the parents of the non-Martyrs children, she did everything by the book. She interviewed each of the children and their parents, fully aware that, since the incidents had occurred several years prior, as far back as September 1981, the children's memories may be clouded.

With all three girls telling the same story, Hoag had no doubt of Renaud's guilt. Still, with children not being the most reliable witnesses, she preferred a confession.

Hoag approached one of the fathers of the alleged victims and asked if he would take part in a three-way phone call, a sting operation to elicit an omission from Clement Renaud. The father agreed, and he placed the call. Hoag listened in, taping the conversation.

During the call, Renaud admitted that he'd answered the child's questions about sex, and that he'd "hugged" her, but he wouldn't admit to molesting her. He said there were so many children in the school that he had to constantly chase them away. Renaud said that he "liked the children," which was why he had kept a ready supply of chocolate in his workshop.

When the call ended, Hoag felt she had enough evidence to proceed with an arrest warrant. She filed the request to have Renaud served and extradited.

Within a week, suspecting Renaud may have molested other children within his workshop, Hoag arranged a second call between the father and the janitor. To her surprise, when the father got Renaud on the phone, Renaud said to direct all inquiries to his attorney—his California-based attorney.

Hoag had no idea why Renaud had retained a local attorney. She wondered if he'd been tipped off.

She soon found out that he had.

As Hoag had been preparing her next move, someone in the Manhattan Beach Police Department had mailed a copy of the arrest warrant to Renaud's home in Texas. Upon receiving the document, Renaud retained a California lawyer, and all conversations with the police halted.

Knowing that someone in her department had undermined her, Hoag went to her direct boss, Sergeant Jim Noble, for answers. What he told her made her cringe.

According to Noble, several months earlier, Manhattan Beach Police Chief Ted Mertens had told him that he "did not want the Renaud case pursued any further than the original victims." Following that conversation, Noble said that Mertens frequently made statements that he "didn't want the Renaud case getting ensnarled in an investigation the size of McMartin."

Sergeant Noble, feeling obligated to follow up on the family's complaint, had allowed Hoag to set up the telephone sting, but he never intended for Hoag to expand the investigation to include the entire student body of American Martyrs.

Despite her chief's instructions, Hoag had pushed forward. Her best tip had been related to the "Martyrs student—a young girl," who also had been molested by Renaud back in 1982, when the Church had allegedly covered it up.

Hoag went to the rectory at American Martyrs to speak with Church officials, and she confirmed the story. But it all fell back on the late Monsignor Robert Deegan who'd dealt with the controversy at that time. Deegan, after consulting with the victim's parents, decided that "counseling" would be the best remedy. None of the parties—the girl, her parents, the Church—had been interested in getting the police involved.

Unfortunately, Hoag was told, Monsignor Deegan died in the midst of the ordeal. Monsignor John Barry, who had been assigned to the American Martyrs parish in July 1983, a few months after Deegan's passing, had never met Clement Renaud, as the janitor had been relieved of his duties in June 1983, just weeks prior to Monsignor Barry's arrival.

For Hoag, it proved to be another dead end, one born, she believed, from deception more than veracity. She suspected Renaud had more victims, likely Martyrs students, but the Church, once again, wanted the story to go away.

But it hadn't, not entirely. Like most scars, it healed over time, leaving a faded mark—the dim memory of the parish community, those tumultuous days in April 1983, when the salacious rumor of "the janitor's workshop" had impressed the minds of certain parents.

Thus, in the months leading up to Judy Johnson's accusation against Ray Buckey and the McMartin Preschool, the idea that multiple children may have been molested on school property had become a disturbing reality.

* * * * *

On Thursday, August 21, 1986, Detective Jane Hoag entered the Torrance Municipal Courts Building with documents in hand, her felony complaint against Clement Renaud: eight counts of "lewd and lascivious acts with a child under the age of 14."

The court set Renaud's bail at $25,000 and scheduled his plea hearing for mid-December.

For Hoag, a case that had seemed like a massive discovery with potential links to McMartin had ended up as a reduced filing—two of the "non-Martyrs" children abused in 1981.

Hoag, content that justice had been served for those two victims, couldn't get over the fact that she'd been double-crossed by her superiors, treated like a pariah for merely doing her job.

And it wasn't just Chief Mertens who'd worked against her, but the Los Angeles District Attorney's Office as well. Knowing that Renaud may have abused American Martyrs students in the early 1980s—children who were complaining witnesses in the McMartin trial—the DA had no interest in looking deeper. It would only muddy the water.

Hoag, following her orders, filed the paperwork and let it be.

Months later, at his hearing, Clement Renaud pleaded "no contest"—a negotiated deal that sentenced him to five years' probation, with 124 days of time served.

Clement Renaud left the Torrance Courts Building and returned to Texas, free to walk the streets.[14]

---

[14] Eleven years later, in December 1997, Clement Renaud was charged for "indecency with a child," a third-degree felony. He pleaded guilty.

CHAPTER
39

Despite the grueling conditions of her life in Bellevue, Judy remained there for another seven weeks.

By Sunday, August 24, her time had run out. School would start in a matter of days—Mitchell's first day of kindergarten—and she wanted to be there to see him off.

In his latest note, Steve had urged Judy to head home. "You must return to LA," he wrote, "or you will lose the kids."

Judy knew it to be true, yet she wondered if she'd already lost them. Sitting in her van on a blustery afternoon, Judy wrote of herself:

> *I'm an actor for causes. The McMartin case took so much out of me.*
>
> *Being so close to the boys might be unhealthy for them, bringing back memories of us all living together.*

Before she set out on that Sunday, Judy stopped by Steve and Debbie's to say farewell. She wrote, "Shower—Clean" on her calendar, as if she'd used their bathroom to freshen up before her trip. She also wrote, "Leave before the storm."

The air had been uncomfortably warm and muggy, the calm before a late-summer lightning storm. Judy stood on the porch looking up. The clouds grew darker, a low cumulous shelf ready to break.

Debbie could see Judy's anger, the resentment in her eyes.

"I'm bringing these clouds upon you for all that you've done to me," Judy said.

Debbie didn't know how to respond.

"I am *Christ the Redeemer*!" Judy said to her, as if, despite her apparent psychosis, she'd achieved some level of salvation.

Minutes later, Judy stepped into her VW Bus, turned the ignition, and drove into the wall of rain and rolling thunder.

Judy Johnson's calendar entries from August 1986, where she continued to chart her chronic bleeding and her struggle to survive. On August 24, she "leaves before the storm," returning to Manhattan Beach to be with her children.

* * * * *

The smell of the Labor Day barbecue filled the air. Music ruled the day. Parents and children walked to and from the beach, enjoying the three-day holiday. At the home of Gayle and Jeep Schaeffer, their annual street party had begun, as friends and neighbors dropped by to see what was cooking.

For days, Gayle had been on edge. Mark's latest diagnosis, coupled with not knowing Judy's whereabouts, made it difficult for her to enjoy the festivities. Gayle had expected Judy to return by then, but she hadn't. Steve said she left Bellevue on August 24, and he hadn't heard from her since. Both boys had been asking about their mother.

The high-pitched sound of a young boy, one of the neighborhood kids, caught Gayle's attention.

"Judy! Judy!" the boy yelled. He stopped in front of the Schaeffers' door. "Look," he said to Gayle, "it's Judy."

Judy stood next to her VW Bus, smiling at Gayle, a thankful expression for all she'd done. Judy stepped across the narrow street and gave her a hug.

As happy as Gayle was to see her, she noticed Judy had let herself go. "She'd put on weight and she was dirty—her clothes, her skin, and her hair. She looked plagued, something about her aura."

Gayle decided not to tell Judy about Mark's diagnosis. The timing wasn't right. Judy needed to know, she deserved to know, but not then.

Word spread through the neighborhood of Judy's homecoming. Mark and Mitchell came running through the door and into her arms. They talked for a while, and then they all headed down to the beach, just like old times.

Two days later, Gayle sat down with Judy, taking her by the hand. "Judy, Mark's real bad," Gayle said, trying to keep it together. "We just took him to Kaiser, and they did X-rays. The cancer's spreading. It's all over his bones. There's nothing they can do."

Judy remained silent, not clearly acknowledging what she'd been told. She stood, gave Gayle a thankful nod, and walked out.

* * * * *

For Judy, those early days of September were endearing—her reunion with her boys—but she couldn't escape the pressure of the Los Angeles District Attorney's Office.

On September 2, the day after she returned, she heard a knock on her door. She crept slowly across the living room and peered through the blinds. She saw a man but didn't recognize him.

"Who is it?" Judy asked loudly.

"It's Bill Brunetti," he replied. "You remember me, right?"

She certainly did. Brunetti, an investigator with the DA's office, had met with her before. Judy slid back the deadbolt and cracked opened the door, the security chain still attached.

"What do ya need, Bill?"

"Can you let me in, Judy?" he asked. "I came to talk to ya."

Judy looked over her shoulder, then back to Brunetti.

"My house is a mess, Bill. What do you want?"

"Lael wanted me to check in on ya. She said you haven't returned her calls."

"I just got back."

"And that's fine. But she asked you to call her when you got back to town, and you didn't."

Judy looked away, rolling her eyes a bit.

"She's just worried about ya, that's all," Brunetti said. "So give her a call back, okay?"

Judy closed the door, sliding the bolt, then rushing to the window. She watched Brunetti pull away.

* * * * *

Considering the way that former prosecutor Glenn Stevens had leaked his misgivings to the press, the Los Angeles District Attorney's office suspected that it wouldn't be long before Judy's mental health became a public topic.

And the DA was right.

Over the summer, when Stevens and the Manns recorded those 30 hours of conversations—audiotapes transcribed into more than 2,000 pages of dialogue—they manufactured a body of evidence. The former prosecutor's claims of corruption against the DA's office had been classified as "discovery" that would have to be handed over to the McMartin defense.

According to the Manns, upon evaluating the transcripts, they became concerned that "vital information" had been withheld from the defense, the information that Stevens had referenced. The Manns took the audiotapes to their lawyer, a former state judge, and he recommended they give the tapes to the state attorney general's office as well as the McMartin defense. If they didn't, they could be charged with obstruction of justice.

"We agonized over what to do," Abby Mann had said, concerned that they risked compromising their future project by releasing some of their most exclusive information prematurely. But as Abby Mann put it, "Two people's lives were at stake [Ray and Peggy Buckey's]. And we realized we had no choice."

Glenn Stevens, after conferring with his own attorney, agreed with that decision, saying, "I couldn't argue. The information was too critical to be ignored."

But that scenario, as altruistic as it sounded, contained other statements that put their motivations into context. Stevens and Mann also discussed how the success of their project would be dependent upon an acquittal for both Ray and Peggy Buckey. They went so far as to "toast" to that hopeful outcome.

"I'll tell you something," Stevens had said. "You get an acquittal, and then this project comes out, and we're all just absolutely sitting on top of the world."

"Absolutely," Abby Mann replied.

The Manns followed the advice of their counsel and turned over the information to both the attorney general and the McMartin defense team.

Upon receiving the information, Danny Davis, Ray Buckey's attorney, hired the Manns as "defense investigators," gaining access to all of their information, including anything they had discussed with Glenn Stevens. Davis sought information regarding "prosecutorial misconduct," looking to have the charges dropped before the trial began.

Notably, the information that most interested Danny Davis was related to Judy Johnson.

* * * * *

Halloween night 1986 brought little activity to the narrow block of Vista Drive, as most of the neighborhood children flocked to the Tree section. Judy sat at home, alone as always, in the low-lit solitude she'd grown accustomed to.

Since her return to Manhattan Beach, Judy had stopped noting her daily events on her calendar, choosing instead to simply jot down important items, such as "Sick—Orange," suggesting that she'd been throwing up bile, and that she was "Bleeding Still," that her eighteen-month struggle with stomach ulcers had not subsided. In fact, she'd been bleeding more than ever.

Making matters worse, Judy continued to drink, a habitual pace that sullied the world around her, leading her to obsess. The exorcism she had conducted months before eased her mind, but her deep-rooted fear of the devil had not fully diminished. Her move to the Seattle area had been her way of staying near her children, but getting away from Vista Drive—the dark energy that thrived within it—had been further incentive.

Upon her return to Manhattan Beach, that demonic entity—real or imagined—consumed her. In a separate notepad, Judy wrote incessantly, drafting what is best described as a "personal manifesto"—a twenty-three-page document that illustrated her mindset, her confrontation with the evil that threatened her.

Judy, apparently fixated with cleansing her soul, wrote of the reincarnation of humans into animals—the retribution of sinners:

> *The system of rebirth as an animal was typical punishment for an erring human—foxes became beautiful men and women; seduced opposite sex and slowly consumed them to prolong their lives.*

Judy wrote of the ancient celebration of the "Eve of Samhain"—which eventually became Halloween—where cattle were returned from summer pastures to be slaughtered, a "bonfire ritual" that offered "protection and cleansing."

Judy jotted down random thoughts and phrases:

> *Know that evil abundantly exists*
> *Man listens for whispering voices that guide him*
> *Bleed to Death*
> *Conversation with Devil Illusion*
> *Drugged, Raped, Tortured*

Then there was the lucid side of Judy, where she tried to reconnect with the ongoing events around her, mainly her role in the McMartin case. Knowing that he was no longer with the DA's office, Judy continued to communicate with Glenn Stevens.

On the back of her October calendar, Judy wrote, "Glenn Stevens—H—859-9129; Office 625-8373." Evidently, Stevens had contacted Judy, hoping she would collaborate on his film project with Abby Mann, giving her a chance to tell her story.

Judy may have shown an interest. On Thursday, October 30, she noted, "Called Glenn," and the next night she wrote, "Glenn Here" and "Abby Mann—6:00—7:00."

Next to it, in the blank box following October 31, Judy wrote, "Note from Glenn 10/29/86" and "Mike Wallace in So. America."

On the upcoming Sunday night, *60 Minutes* would be airing a Mike Wallace segment on the "McMartin Preschool Case."

CHAPTER

40

Sunday, November 2, 1986

Just before 7:00 p.m., Judy sat in her bedroom, her television tuned to CBS. Like many Americans on Sunday nights, she waited for another episode of *60 Minutes*, this one a special report by Mike Wallace.

Wallace, an icon of American journalism, opened his segment with a slow-panning close-up of the five McMartin teachers whose charges had been dropped—Virginia McMartin, Peggy Ann Buckey, Babette Spitler, Betty Raidor, and Maryanne Jackson.

Wallace's voice-over asked, "Do these women look like child molesters?"

After nearly three years of intense media coverage, Wallace's segment was the first major network investigative report that offered the point of view of the accused. Every major anchor had covered the most salacious aspects of the story—Peter Jennings, Tom Brokaw, Dan Rather, and Diane Sawyer—each of whom told their national audiences of the horrific tale of the "preschool in Southern California." *20/20* had aired two separate segments, one on McMartin, one on Satanism—but after the majority of charges were dropped, there was no incentive to remind their viewers that they had egg on their faces.

60 Minutes, with no apparent skin in the game, did the right thing.

The segment opened with each of the former defendants making statements of their experience, and how their lives had been ruined.

"The United States has the rottenest judicial system in the world," proclaimed Virginia McMartin. "Don't let anybody tell me about Russia or South Africa or anything. We have it right here. You are *guilty*,"

Virginia said, "and God help you if you try to prove you are innocent. That's the way we've been treated since the first day."

The camera moved to Betty Raidor. "My character, my, my reputation, has been destroyed," she said.

Maryanne Jackson explained rather calmly, "We lost almost everything we'd accumulated in thirty-eight years of our married life."

Babette Spitler told the story of how, while in jail, her children had been taken into protective custody, that her young son was told that "*he* was under arrest."

"Under arrest for what?" Wallace asked.

"He doesn't know for what," Babette replied, her voice cracking. "I don't know for what. I don't know why they took him into custody. I was behind bars. If I was such a threat to him…" At that point, Babette began to weep.

Peggy Ann Buckey gave a stoic response, but her anger and disgust came through loud and clear. "I, along with everyone else, lost every material possession that I had. I saw my family lose their home, their school, their bank account, everything. Everything went to attorneys, every last penny. I lost my career. I went six years to college to teach special education, and the state has revoked my teaching credentials."

As Wallace gave a general narrative of the case, he asked rhetorically, "How did this case get started?" He went on to talk about "the mother" who had not only accused Ray Buckey, but had implicated others as well, saying her son had been "attacked by wild animals." The mother, Wallace said, was "later diagnosed to have mental problems."

Judy, stewing in anger, couldn't watch anymore. She jumped from her bed and turned off the television—but the rest of the nation continued to watch.

Wallace gave both sides an opportunity to speak. Current DA Ira Reiner defended his decision to drop charges against the five women, while moving forward with the case against Ray and Peggy Buckey.

"This was a case that involved the molestation of *some* children," Reiner argued. "It was blown massively out of proportion to become the *case of the century*. It is nothing of the sort. It is simply a case of some children, a few children, over a period of years, being molested."

Reiner directed most of the blame toward his predecessor, former DA Robert Philibosian, who Reiner claimed had conducted "no investigation whatsoever," that he'd simply submitted the case to a grand jury which "started the ball rolling."

The camera cut to Robert Philibosian, who said that it was "sad that [Reiner] is expending his time and energy attacking me" when he should instead be "supporting the children."

When asked by Wallace, "So, you feel no sympathy or deep concern for these five defendants?"

"These five defendants are not the subject of sympathy or deep concern," Philibosian replied. "The subject of sympathy and deep concern are the children who were molested." Philibosian, after losing his special election to Ira Reiner in June 1984, went into private practice, eventually joining the international law firm of Sheppard, Mullin, Richter & Hampton.

The most poignant moment of the segment was Wallace's interview with Ray Buckey, Ray's first public statement since his formal plea of "Not guilty, Your Honor."

After denying he had ever abused a child, and speaking candidly about "the reality of prison," where he was unlikely to survive, Ray put his condition into perspective.

"They've ruined my life," Buckey said. "I've watched them ruin my mother and grandmother's lives. I've watched them ruin my sister's career. I was just starting at that school," Ray explained. "I hadn't made up my mind what I wanted to do in life. But they've burned a scarlet letter on me that I can never get rid of. I'll never know what kind of life I could've had. I can't trust people anymore, because I've seen too much of the politics, the corruption, the evil, the anger, and the ignorance."

Peggy Ann Buckey gave the final statement for the group: "I think people in the world need to know this was a witch-hunt; that nothing happened at this school. And this could happen to *anyone*. And because of this case, it has happened everywhere, and people need to realize that nursery schools are not places where children are being molested, raped, and sodomized."

* * * * *

On the morning of Wednesday, November 12, within the Los Angeles Criminal Courts Building, the McMartin defense dug in.

"The facts," said defense attorney Andrew Willing, "paint an ugly picture of a prosecution team which has completely lost sight of its obligation to seek justice and which has lied and deceived the court."

Willing, a member of the team defending Peggy Buckey, had filed a motion to have the charges dropped due to the prosecution's "deceit" of the "entire judicial system." The motion, a 118-page document filed jointly by Willing, Dean Gits, and Danny Davis, was based primarily on information they had obtained from former prosecutor Glenn Stevens.

In the motion, Stevens alleged that Chief Prosecutor Lael Rubin and others within the district attorney's office had committed "conspiracy" and other "civil rights violations," a clear case, the defense argued, of "prosecutorial misconduct."

Danny Davis pressed to have Lael Rubin removed from the case, even if the judge chose to reject the defense's request for a full dismissal. Davis argued that she should be disqualified on the grounds that she was "having an affair" with a Superior Court judge whose child had once attended McMartin. Davis suggested that Rubin had an "intense personal and emotional" drive as "opposed to merely professional involvement."

Amongst the complaints was the controversy surrounding Judy Johnson, the unnamed "mother of the child who had initiated the McMartin investigation." There was "evidence," the motion alleged, written and transcribed testimonies of this mother—a woman with "a history of mental illness"—that may have exonerated his client years ago.

A hearing was set for a later date.

Back in his cell, suspecting that corrupt members of the district attorney's office were working around the clock to cover up the truth, Ray Buckey once again sat down and recorded his thoughts, a harsh assessment of a prosecutorial machine pandering to the emotion of a distraught and misguided community of parents:

> *Giving an investigation over to emotionally involved and untrained parents by law enforcement's own standards is a suicidal melting pot of alleged facts with blind fear.*
>
> *Where does any belief come from but an assumption of fact or facts?*
>
> *In come the words of children. Belief in this case comes from the words of children...children obviously tainted by adults, yet still coming from their mouths.*

Is any child's words their own, or the product of adults who control their world?

"A child cannot lie," they say...and yet a child lives in a world of make-believe and fantasy.

Somehow this case has evolved into an acceptance of a core one can find in the onion of a child's story coupled with so-called physical evidence. Logically the physical evidence must match the extent of the accusations. Which I believe and know does not and never could.

My knowledge, one may say, is based on my own awareness of my innocence, yet the physical realities and logic my mind walks upon can sidestep the truth and still see impossibility.

One must show the total lack of physical evidence to support the accusations if the first wedge of understanding is to pry open the closed door of ignorance.

One must be able to see the chain of events these children went through that molded their beliefs. An overview of the pool of adults will show their attitude and actions that molded their children...

Jane Hoag and the parents must be shown in the light for their part as plotters. CII was a force in fueling the fear and belief, but to me the fuel they supplied was to a fire that on its own had already begun and would have probably grown in size without CII...

Jane Hoag gave them the fear and belief initially, and from there the parents communally grew their own monster...

* * * * *

Inside the dark walls of 3112 Vista Drive, Judy Johnson had fallen by the wayside. The world around her had closed in, as everyone knew she was the "unnamed mother" who had been the subject of America's #1 television news journal.

Judy, in that moment of self-loathing, may have begun to believe that the criticisms about her were true—that she was a disturbed woman driven by her fear of evil.

At the top of her calendar, Judy wrote, *Reader's Digest: Into the Unknown—Witches*, the magazine's comprehensive guide to the occult, and she referenced two other books on witchcraft: *What Witches Do*, the 1971 publication by Stewart Farrar—written as an eyewitness account of the Alexandrian coven—and *Witchcraft from the Inside: A Llewellyn Occult Manual* by Raymond Buckland.

On a blank piece of white paper, using a black calligraphy pen, Judy scribed various phrases, drawings, and symbols—such as "Judy the Devil," and next to it the sketch of a small human-like creature with horns. "Compliments of the Staff," Judy wrote, along with "Judgment" and "Hexagram." Another sketch showed the devilish creature holding a lamb waist high, with the staff running through its body—a caricature of the Paschal Flag she had once hung on her porch.

Distinctly, Judy drew a symbol—two variations of an "X." Next to them, she identified them as "Hebrew letter—Aleph—initial of Aradia." The symbol appeared as: א.

"Aleph," originally influenced by Egyptian hieroglyphs, depicted the triangular head of an ox (𓃾) with its two horns extended. Her reference to "Aradia" indicated her fascination with witchcraft.

Aradia, also known as the *Gospel of the Witches*, was an 1899 publication by American folklorist Charles Godfrey Leland, a religious text he claimed had once belonged to a coven of witches from Tuscany. Aradia, the principal figure of Leland's *Gospel*, was the daughter of Lucifer and Diana. The witches of Tuscany were said to have exalted Diana as the "Queen of the Witches," and Aradia, her child, the Messiah, had been sent to Earth to unleash witchcraft against the Roman Catholic Church by empowering the peasantry with black magic. Diana, according to the *Gospel*, instructed Aradia to "go to earth below" and to be "a teacher." Upon Aradia's descent, she became the first of all witches.

* * * * *

On November 19, Judy wrote, "BIRTHDAY," the day she turned forty-two years old. According to Gayle, in the early afternoon, she took Judy a birthday card. "I left it under the door," Gayle said, "but I never got a response."

Later that evening, Steve and Pastor Knutson stopped by to wish Judy a happy birthday.

"We wanted to give her a gift," Steve said. "We asked her if she wanted to go out to dinner, to celebrate. But she said 'no.' "

"She wouldn't even let us in the house," Pastor Knutson recalled. "I don't think she wanted us to see her."

They spent several minutes speaking to her through the closed door. Judy sounded nervous, as if she were being held hostage—but she was alone.

CHAPTER
41

Wednesday, December 17, 1986

In the early evening, sixteen-year-old Jeff Beck drove through the brightly decorated neighborhood, delivering a bag of items to Judy Johnson. Her name and address had been added to the Rolodex at Super Sam's Liquor & Deli. Beck had made four deliveries to Judy's home in the first three weeks of that Christmas season.

Beck meandered along Marine Avenue and continued up the rise that led to Vista Drive. The neighborhood had a picturesque quality. Flashing colored lights had been strung across rooftops. Ceramic Nativity scenes were set reverently on display, each home cared for, aglow with Christmas trappings—with, of course, the exception of Judy's.

Beck noticed it the moment he turned onto 31st Street. It stood out, a lone patch of darkness. The flower pots were cracked and crumbling; a mound of newspapers yellowed on the doorstep. Only the porch light and the fluttering images from a television set indicated someone was home.

Beck knocked and waited. The deadbolt disengaged. The door cracked open, chain still hooked, and eyes looked upon him. The door closed and re-opened. Judy motioned him inside and stepped back. She walked to the table next to the kitchen. She dug through her purse.

To Beck, Judy looked worse than she had the time before. She appeared uneasy, frightened; her nightgown hung loosely with nothing underneath, so that her breasts and abdomen were partially revealed. The inside of her home was as disheveled as the landscaping. Trash lay scattered about the kitchen floor, dishes piled in the sink, with dirty laundry strewn along the hallway and into the bedrooms.

Beck pitied her demise, but what he remembered most about his prior deliveries was: "She never tipped."

Judy turned from the table and handed him the exact amount. Beck walked out, and the door shut firmly behind him.

* * * * *

Two days later, Friday, December 19, at approximately 1:00 p.m., Mark Johnson rode his bike to his mother's home. He hadn't spoken to her since Monday. He arrived, jumped off his bike, and knocked on the door. No answer. He rang the bell and called out to her repeatedly. Not a sound. He walked to the side of the house and peered through the bathroom window. He knew she was inside. She had to be. Her VW Bus sat parked in the alley against the fence, covered in dust. It hadn't been driven in weeks. He yelled again, pounding on the window.

From across the narrow street, Gayle watched Mark circling the house, knocking on the window pane, crying out for Judy.

"Mom. Open up," he yelled. "It's me, Mark. Open up. Please."

Mark stepped back, dejected, and crossed the street into Gayle's backyard. Gayle grabbed the phone and dialed the district attorney's office in an effort to reach investigators Bill Brunetti and Tim Tyson. She was told, however, that the two investigators were tied up in court, and that someone else would be sent to check on Judy.

Gayle, having not seen or heard from Judy in over a week, had a bad feeling. Four days earlier, Gayle had written Judy a letter, saying that she had "come over many times in the last week," calling out her name and knocking repeatedly. "I know you are in there," Gayle wrote, "and I'm very sorry that you won't answer me. Please don't shut us all out again. What if Mark gets sicker and we can't reach you? Would you want to do that to him?" But Judy never responded.

As Gayle hung up the phone, Mark walked in. The look on his face froze her heart and confirmed her deepest worries. Trying not to frighten him, Gayle asked Mark to go back to his father's apartment and get the spare key.

Without questioning, Mark left.

At the same moment, heading west on the Pomona Freeway, Pastor Knutson and Helen drove toward Manhattan Beach. Pastor Knutson had called Judy dozens of times over the past few days but reached only an unrelenting busy tone.

Just before 2:00 p.m., Manhattan Beach Police Chief Ray Burgess knocked on Gayle's door. Being closest to the site, Burgess had been contacted by Detective Brunetti and told to get to Judy's home immediately. As Gayle and Burgess discussed the situation, Mark arrived with the key.

Burgess asked Mark to hand over the key and to wait with Jeep while he and Gayle went to check on Judy. Mark wanted to go with them, but Burgess refused. Mark obeyed the officer and sat stiffly on the couch, silent in his thoughts.

Gayle and Burgess hurried across the street. Gayle knew about the deadbolt securing the front door, so she took Burgess to the back. She unlocked the door, stuck her head inside, and called softly, "Hello...Judy, it's Gayle." She waited a few seconds, but got no answer.

Burgess stepped past her and went inside—but he stopped abruptly, halted by the putrid stench.

"Stay outside," Burgess instructed Gayle, walking toward her and closing the door.

Burgess covered his nose and mouth, careful not to inhale. He stepped through the kitchen and into the hallway that led to the bedrooms. He turned the corner and came to the entrance of the boys' room, and there she lay, naked, face down in a pool of blood.

Judy's lifeless body told her story. Her arm stretched out, clutching the phone receiver. Her head tilted left; one blue eye stared vacantly. A greenish-brown substance dribbled from the corner of her mouth. The sheets on the bunks were stained with blood, a trail of gore that led to the spot where she'd fallen.

In the adjoining master bedroom, a black-and-white television had been propped on the bed, also covered in blood, flickered a shadow across the dim walls. A wastebasket filled with rancid, vomit-tinged blood sat on the floor, next to a scattered mix of papers. Near the headboard, a copy of C.S. Lewis' *Mere Christianity* lay next to an opened *Home Medical Guide*.

In the kitchen, Burgess found three unopened cans of Pepsi, and a 1.75-liter bottle of Bacardi lay empty atop the trashcan. Every room in the small, two-bedroom house had been stained with some portion of Judy's blood—the type of splatter more commonly found in a multiple homicide.

As far as Burgess could tell, Judy had hemorrhaged internally and vomited to her death. In the midst of the attack, she apparently fled to each room, frenzied, spewing blood, stumbling around in a half-conscious effort to save herself, gripping the telephone receiver to call for help as she slumped to the floor and died.

It appeared as if she'd been conscious up to the end, evidence that her final moments were immensely frightening and extremely painful.

Chief Burgess regained his composure and went outside to tell Gayle. The moment he said, "I'm sorry," Gayle turned away and began to cry, a silent weeping that grew into uncontrollable sobs.

Burgess put his arm around Gayle, guiding her across the street. Gayle tried to pull herself together, to be strong for the boys, but as she entered the living room, searching for the right words, she looked at Mark's face, his lost expression, and she told him the truth.

"She's dead, Mark. I'm so sorry…I'm so sorry."

Mark shook his head, refusing to accept it. He pleaded with Burgess to let him see his mother. The chief gently refused. He told Mark he could not go inside until the police completed their work. Burgess pulled Gayle and Jeep aside.

"You *cannot* let him go in there," Burgess said. "He *cannot* see that. Do you understand?"

Mark started to leave, stepping out the door, but Jeep grabbed him and held him firmly.

"I want to see her," Mark cried. "Why can't I see her?"

"Just stay with me," Jeep said, hugging him, rocking him. "Stay here with me."

"Somebody killed her," Mark screamed, trying to pull away. "You know it, Jeep. Somebody killed her."

Jeep pulled Mark in even closer. "Don't say that. Don't say that, Mark. Be strong. Be strong for her."

Jeep, knowing that an onslaught of media would soon arrive, walked Mark down to the beach, where they sat in the sand near the shore.

News of Judy's death spread quickly. A team of investigators arrived at the scene, soon outnumbered by a group of reporters and photographers.

Pastor Knutson arrived just after 3:00 p.m. He got as far as the front door before a young officer stopped him.

"Who are you?" the policeman asked.

"I'm Judy's father," he replied, "What's going on here?"

The officer shifted his eyes away from Pastor Knutson and said, "I don't think you want to go in there."

The tone of the officer's voice told Pastor Knutson all he needed to hear. His daughter was dead. An investigator came out of the house and told him they were about to seal off the area to take fingerprints.

"Sorry," he told the pastor, "but we can't let you in."

As they spoke, TV cameramen and news photographers squeezed against the windows and jockeyed for position to get a shot of the body through the tightly drawn shades.

"I don't think they should be able to do that," Pastor Knutson said.

The officers agreed and ordered the reporters to step back to the middle of the street.

Pastor Knutson turned and walked back to Helen, who had waited by the car. She needed no explanation. The Knutsons crossed the street to the Schaeffers' home, where they were met by the inconsolable grief of their oldest grandchild.

Mark clutched his grandfather, but after a long hug, he sat back on the couch and stared aimlessly at the crowd of people gathering on the street. Residents from all sides joined the commotion as the narrow alleyway filled to capacity. Traffic through the neighborhood had been blocked by police cars at both ends. An ambulance sat parked at the side of the house, and two paramedics stood outside their vehicle, waiting for the coroner.

Standing in the middle of the street, Bob Currie spoke with Kevin Cody, the editor of the *Easy Reader*. Currie had rushed to the site as soon as he'd heard the news. In a crowd of more than fifty onlookers, only Bob Currie stepped forward to say that he understood the troubled woman.

"She made the McMartin case," Currie said. He described himself as a "close friend" of Judy's, saying their relationship had strengthened through their private investigative work.

"We are indebted to this mother for helping us to protect future children," Currie proclaimed, "not only in this country, but throughout the world. There's now awareness about sexual abuse that wasn't in existence prior to the McMartin case."

"Very few of us even knew her," Currie told *Los Angeles Herald* staff writer Shawn Hubler. "And when it got around that she was something other than, well, normal, a lot of people—you know, the pseudo-intellectual types—refused to have anything to do with her. They didn't want to be involved with her problem."

* * * * *

At the Criminal Courts building in downtown Los Angeles, while forensic investigators stood over Judy's body, Ray Buckey came before Judge William Pounders for his bail reduction hearing. In an attempt to keep the bail at three million dollars, Lael Rubin repeated the list of allegations that had kept Buckey behind bars for so long, pleading with the court to keep him off the streets.

Ray Buckey stood and spoke in a somber tone on his own behalf. He told Judge Pounders how his family had lost everything, everything but each other. Through the most difficult times, he said, the love of his family had kept him believing he would survive. His plea for a reduced bail would allow him to be home with the people he loved while he awaited his fate.

"Your Honor," Buckey stated, "though I know I'm not guilty of these crimes, I still believe this is a case that must go to trial. Only through a complete trial will we reach the truth. Sir, the truth of my innocence is all I have left. And the truth, to put it simply, will set me free."

Judge Pounders denied Ray Buckey's request.

Minutes later, the court clerk approached the bench and spoke privately to the judge. Judge Pounders called the court to attention.

"I need to inform you that Judy Johnson has died," he said. "She was just found dead in her home."

The courtroom broke into disarray. Those in attendance shuffled in their seats, and within moments their quiet murmuring grew into loud, open conversations. Some of the people—parents, lawyers, and media personnel—had only known Judy indirectly. But everyone had been aware of her importance to the ongoing proceedings, that her testimony could determine the future of the case. In fact, the subpoena ordering her to testify lay among the mail that had piled up on her doorstep.

* * * * *

Back at Vista Drive, Bill Sheffield, the investigator for the Los Angeles Coroner's Office, arrived at the crime scene, sent to determine the cause of death in a situation deemed "suspicious."

Entering the living room, Sheffield found that the sheriff's department had already dispatched its own investigator, Homicide Detective Frank Salerno.

Detective Salerno, who a year earlier had tracked Richard Ramirez, the Night Stalker, headed to Manhattan Beach the moment word that Judy's death hit the station. Taking no chances, the department sent its finest homicide detective, a man who had played an integral role in solving some of Los Angeles's most notorious murders. His professionalism and objectivity could never be called into question.

In his notes from the scene, Detective Salerno said it appeared that Judy had been dead for three to four days. He made several general observations: that "no Christmas tree or decorations" were visible throughout the house; the "yellow pages by her right foot" had been opened to "Sam's Liquor Store," and in the margin, she'd scribbled "1.75." He noted that the living room was relatively tidy, but the master bedroom was in total disarray, with trash all over the floor. The television had been placed on the bed, still on. The kitchen phone had been disconnected, but the phone in the boys' room was still working. "A pool of blood was found near the body," he wrote.

Detective Salerno concluded that Judy Johnson had died from "Natural Causes."[15]

* * * * *

In the following weeks, a pre-trial hearing commenced to determine if, because of the departure of Judy Johnson, the McMartin case would continue. Amid accusations of a "cover-up," the district attorney's office had been put on the defense.

The hearing focused on the two letters from February 1984—identified as the "smoking guns"—where Judy had made statements about satanic rituals and sacrifice. Those documents, the defense argued, indicated that Judy had deep psychological problems prior to the case being filed. Instead of treating those letters as "discovery," handing them over to the defense as they were required, the district attorney's office withheld them—grounds for a dismissal.

In the days immediately after Judy's death, over the Christmas recess, co-prosecutor Roger Gunson had discovered a "copy of one of the letters" within a file that had been assembled for him when he was assigned to the case, following the departure of deputy DAs Glenn Stevens and Christine

---

[15] Eva Heuser, MD, the Deputy Medical Examiner for Los Angeles County, concluded that Judy had bled out after acute hemorrhaging as a result of extreme alcohol poisoning. In effect, her liver had stopped working. The clinical diagnosis was "Fatty Metamorphous (or Sclerosis) of the Liver," which is common to alcoholics. Judy had developed "Acute Esophagitis, Acute Gastritis and Chronic Pancreatitis."

Johnston. Inscribed on the letter, in "Jane Hoag's handwriting," were the instructions: "Do Not Copy."

Amongst those notes, which had been given to DA Investigator Bill Brunetti, contained a statement written by Detective Hoag dated June 24—June 28, 1984, where Hoag had written, "If it wasn't for the McMartin case" she would have taken Judy Johnson's children into protective custody since Judy had allowed her son to be alone with his father after both the boy and Judy had accused the father of molesting him.

The firestorm of "lost discovery" continued, including a summary of Judy's "smoking gun" letter where Hoag had attached a typed note: "Confidential Information—not to be turned over to the defense—per D.A. Rubin."

With all of this exposed, the defense called their witnesses—Chief Prosecutor Lael Rubin and DA investigators Bill Brunetti and Tim Tyson—but each testified that they "didn't recall" having knowledge of the two letters, and were "unsure" if the letters had been turned over as discovery.

Lael Rubin, contradicting the sworn testimony of both her former colleagues, Glenn Stevens and Christine Johnston, said that she didn't learn of Judy Johnson's "mental infirmity" until November 1985, seven months after Judy had been incarcerated and diagnosed as a "paranoid schizophrenic."

Before she left the stand, Rubin admitted that she'd been "negligent," and said that she never considered any of the information surrounding Judy's mental state to be "exculpatory."

Harry Sondheim, the head of the district attorney's appellate division, presented the prosecution's defense. Sondheim, considered one of the top appellate lawyers in the state, conceded that Judy Johnson was the "cornerstone" of the case, and he agreed with the defense that her psychosis may have fueled a "social contagion."

Nonetheless, Sondheim argued, Judy Johnson, as real or imagined as her claims may have been was merely "a key," a key that "opened the McMartin Preschool," giving the public a "chance to see what was inside." The defense, he posited, wanted to use that same key to "close the doors" of the other complaining families, while leaving Judy Johnson's door wide open, the only home where no one was available to testify.

Thus, Sondheim further argued, Judy Johnson's mental state, although germane to her own experience, had no relevance to the independent and collective testimonies of the other alleged victims and their parents. Those citizens, by law, had an absolute right to be heard in court, irrespective of the mental capacity of a single witness who had since died.

Sondheim's brief was well-received.

Judge William Pounders ruled Judy Johnson to be "irrelevant" to the McMartin case.

Judge Pounders set the trial for the summer of 1987.

The defense team disagreed with that ruling, and they took their argument to the press.

Danny Davis, Ray Buckey's attorney, suggested that "one woman's paranoia" had caused an entire community to erupt into a state of hysteria. He believed that Judy Johnson was mentally unstable from the moment she initiated the investigation.

"Her complaint was the seminal, misleading event that led to the contagion that was McMartin," Davis told reporters from the steps of the courthouse. "With her death," he said, "the truth may never be known."

PART VIII

The Proverbial Snowball

I CAN COMPANY

Consultants • Fundraising

Myrus L. Knutson, Ph.D., President   April 26, 1989

Dear Friend,

The heat wave we had with our present cold snap has not blown my cork. What you are reading is a true rational act on my part.

So the next question is "what is the occasion that would twist my arm into scratching a few lines"?

The reason I'm writing is to introduce two fine young men writing a book about the Manhattan Beach attitude after the McMartin pre-school sexual abuse exposure. This of course involves Judy.

Attorney Glenn Stevens, formally a Deputy District Attorney, is now on the side of the McMartin's. He has stated that Judy was a loner all her life and was crazy for a very long time. A genuine liar. Mr. Matt LeRoy and Dave Haddad are attempting to write an accurate account of what happened. What they need is some evidence of what Judy was before the McMartin happening.

I have presummed on our long friendship to suggest you might be willing to give them your honest opinion of Judy's personality and character before the McMartin situation.

I would personally appreciate your receiving them by visit or telephone and giving them your honest opinion what ever that may be.

Helen and I leave for Minnesota about May 3rd and plan to return sometime in July. She would like to be back here for my 75th birthday. Amazing how old everybody else is getting.

Have a good summer. I pray God is blessing you with a growing faith and a positive attitude.

Love through Christ,

CHAPTER
42

In the aftermath of Judy Johnson's death, we began our three-year inquisition—a quantitative research of the people and the events behind the phenomena of Manhattan Beach.

Between 1987 and 1990, in parallel with the McMartin Preschool trial, we conducted hundreds of personal interviews—Peggy Buckey, Virginia McMartin, Michael Ruby, Bob Currie, Steve and Debbie Knutson, Gayle Schaffer, and many others—the subjects of the aforementioned story.

The high point of our investigation came on the morning of Thursday, April 27, 1989, when we arrived to the desert home of Pastor Myrus Knutson, Judy Johnson's father, who handed us a garbage bag filled with Judy's hand-written notes. He had drafted a letter to dozens of friends, asking that they speak with these "two fine young men" who were analyzing the "Manhattan Beach attitude" in the wake of the McMartin case. Pastor Knutson wanted to know more about the fervor that'd brought an end to his daughter's life.

We promised him that we would preserve the documents, that we would organize and archive them into a data-base, and above all, that we would use them judiciously.

As we pulled away, waving goodbye to the pastor standing on his dusty porch—a man who had endured such tremendous loss—we never expected that thirty years would pass before we made our findings known.

* * * * *

The contents of the garbage bag embodied Judy's experience. Each notation symbolized her mindset—a jumble of disbanded thoughts and emotions, confined to a single chamber, howling to escape, to be heard.

Many of the notes were dated—like her calendar entries—and some were not. Still, they came together into a sensible time-line: the paradigm of a schizophrenic in decline, where her misguided fear was the microcosm of the community around her.

Sifting through Judy's notes and missives, we had a single purpose: To relive the days that led her to the McMartin Preschool, and to better understand how she came to believe that Ray Buckey had abused her son.

In the spring of 1989, when we first opened the garbage bag, the McMartin trial was well underway, as the defense was presenting its case. Judy Johnson had been ruled "irrelevant," so nothing we possessed could've been admitted as evidence. With that being said, for the sake of history, for the invaluable reward of knowing the truth, we found ourselves in a race against the trial, our attempt to prove how relevant Judy was.

Our first order of business was to measure the credibility of Peggy Buckey and Virginia McMartin, our primary sources in respect to Judy's relationship with the preschool. We had conducted dozens of interviews with Peggy and Virginia, and they'd always maintained that on May 12, 1983, Judy Johnson secretly escorted her son through the entrance of the McMartin Preschool and walked away.

That story, a bizarre tale, hadn't been told until after Judy's death. Thus, some argued that Peggy and Virginia—*diabolic, child-molesting Satanists*—had fabricated the story after Judy died, once they knew that Judy had been diagnosed mentally ill.

If there was ever a single event in a major criminal case that could reconcile the truth, the alleged "drop-off" seemed to be it. The events of May 12, 1983, if true, said much about Judy Johnson—but a plausible story considering her strange behavior thereafter.

Yet in respect to the McMartin-Buckey family, their account of that fateful day, if credible, supported the notion that they were telling the truth. And if they were truthful about the events of May 12, they were likely being honest about everything else.

* * * * *

Within the garbage bag, several curious pieces of evidence surfaced, documents Judy intended to be found. About a year before the alleged drop-off, Judy placed a clump of blond hair in an envelope, writing on the front, "Brad pulls hair, 3-26-82."

Judy scribed several accounts of their volatile arguments—sometimes about his affairs, other times about money—but on more than one occasion, according to Judy, Brad became physically aggressive.

Coincidentally, those encounters seemed to have affected Mitchell, causing the two-year-old to grow anxious—a fact supported in a greeting card addressed to Judy.

The card, dated October 3, 1982, was from the owners of "The Children's Place," a home daycare in San Pedro. They'd reached out to Judy by mail, saying that they'd "repeatedly tried to contact [her] by telephone" with no success. They were "concerned about Mitchell," wondering why he'd been "so upset" the last time they'd seen him. They hoped that Judy had a "good trip to his doctor," and they recommended "a change in his diet."

That card was written seven months before the alleged drop-off, demonstrating that Mitchell Johnson had illnesses and anxieties that pre-dated his attendance at McMartin.

From there, according to her notes, Judy began searching for answers to what was ailing Mitchell. In doing so, she may've linked Mitchell's problems to his father's aggression and the volatile atmosphere within their home.

On Wednesday, March 2, Judy wrote, "Brad Yells at Boys." On March 3 and 4, she wrote, "Mitchell Home" and "Blood," respectively, but she didn't state where Mitchell had been prior to that or if the blood she'd seen was his.

Week after week, Judy researched incessantly, noting "Books Due" on ten occasions.

And then came the date of May 12, the most infamous day in her mysterious saga—a day she was said to have done something so reckless that many objective, fair-minded arbiters of fact have simply found it too hard to believe. They've asked, "What evidence do you have to support such a claim?"

Judy, it appears, preserved that evidence.

On her May 1983 calendar, Judy boldly boxed around the date of Wednesday, May 11. From there, she drew a long, snaking arrow to the

They Must Be Monsters

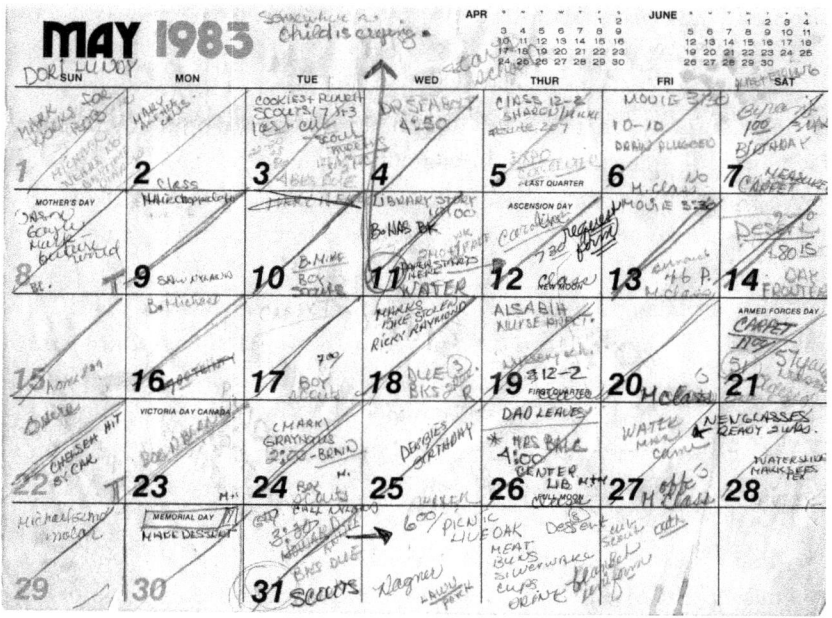

top of the page where she wrote two phrases—"Somewhere a Child is Crying" and "Mitchell Starts School."

From the May 11 date-box, Judy drew another arrow that hopped over to the next day, Thursday, May 12, the day of the alleged drop-off—the date also noted on her Christian calendar as "ASCENSION DAY."

Somewhere a Child Is Crying is a revolutionary book written by Vincent J. Fontana, M.D. Published in 1976, it'd been reprinted in April 1983. Dr. Fontana, the long-standing medical director and principal pediatrician of the New York Foundling Hospital, had been a national voice for abused and neglected children. His 1964 *The Maltreated Child: Maltreatment Syndrome in Children* had called upon medical professionals and social workers to lead the crusade against child abuse.

Dr. Fontana contended that massive programs on parenting and family care were needed to effectively support the welfare of children. "We should engage in an all-out effort to recognize and report and protect the maltreated child," Fontana wrote, "while at the same time offering help to the parents," many of whom were in need of "psychological treatment."

Dr. Fontana expressed sympathy for both the children and the parents, saying that it is "very difficult for the most remorseful and guilt ridden maltreating parents to seek help," and that it is "not only the children who cry for help."

Judy's interest in *Somewhere a Child is Crying* is undeniable—the way she isolated the title and associated it with Mitchell's introduction into the world of McMartin.

But most compelling is how her mindset on that fateful day centered on "maltreated children," those neglected and abused within their homes at the hands of their parents.

As tragic as it seems, Judy's decision to lead Mitchell through the entrance of the McMartin Preschool, stepping away without informing an administrator, ends up being a case study that validates Dr. Fontana's theory. Fontana told Judy precisely where Mitchell's problems were rooted—but Judy did not hear his message.

Furthermore, and most germane, was what this discovery meant to the McMartin case.

Prior to unveiling Judy's lost chronicles, the story of the drop-off could've been discounted as fiction—a convenient tale spun by sinister women accused of unthinkable crimes.

But by Judy's own hand—her reference to *Somewhere a Child is Crying*—she brings clarity to that critical moment, a concrete piece of evidence that illustrates her psyche on that day.

Peggy and Virginia had no way of knowing what Judy had written on her calendar, no clue as to what she would've scribed on those specific dates. Thus, if they conjured up that sensational story about Judy's actions on May 12, 1983, then its correlation with Judy's calendar entries is a profound coincidence, one too improbable to accept as chance.

* * * * *

Having established through her chronicles that Judy Johnson had likely dropped her son off at the McMartin Preschool—just as Virginia and Peggy had claimed—we set our focus on determining: *Why did she go after Ray Buckey?*

Three months passed—from May 12 to August 12, 1983—between the drop-off and Judy's initial complaint, of which less than eight weeks—June 21 to August 11—Judy and Mitchell were in direct contact with the McMartin Preschool.

According to the police report, Judy told Detective Hoag that Mitchell had redness on his bottom when she brought him home on his first official day at McMartin, June 21, 1983, and that the redness continued through July. Judy told Hoag that she had no idea what'd caused it; she even told the detective her account of a July 28, 1983 conversation she had with her brother and sister-in-law, where they discussed the issue, and again, Judy claimed to be mystified.

But Judy's private notes reveal several facts that contradict the version she gave to Detective Hoag.

Judy's July 1983 calendar, coupled with her hand-written notes, confirms that, four weeks before she filed the complaint, she was already zeroing in on Ray Buckey.

On an undated sheet of paper, Judy noted that she'd seen "blood" dripping from Mitchell's rectum on Thursday, July 14; and on her calendar, on that same Thursday, she wrote and underlined the words, "Here" and "Sodism"—as if *here*, on July 14, an act of sodomy had occurred.

Moreover, there's a particular entry in Detective Hoag's police report, an odd statement that made little sense—until it could be correlated with Judy's calendar.

On August 12, during her first meeting with Detective Hoag, while

Judy was describing Ray Buckey, she said that her "Cousin Kathy had attended a birthday party for Virginia McMartin on July 23rd," and that Kathy had "seen Ray there."

"Cousin Kathy" was Kathy Terret, a distant relative of Judy's, a woman Pastor Knutson described as "a bit out there" before disclosing that there was "quite a long line of schizophrenia running through the family." Kathy had come to Manhattan Beach in the summer of 1983, spending ten days with Judy and the boys, from July 15 to July 24.

Kathy arrived the day after Judy wrote "Sodism" (July 14), and according to Judy's calendar, Kathy accompanied Judy and Mitchell to Kaiser Hospital four days later, July 18, where Judy told the doctor she believed she'd given Mitchell her "vaginitis."

Then, five days later, July 23, Kathy went to Virginia McMartin's seventy-sixth birthday party—and immediately after the party, Kathy returned to Vista Drive and discussed it with Judy. They talked about the people Kathy had seen there, namely Ray Buckey.

Kathy's attendance at Virginia's party is a bit odd—neither Peggy nor Virginia could recall her name. Still, there could be a reasonable explanation as to why she'd attended—like maybe she'd accompanied one of the invited guests.

Far more suspicious, however, is that Kathy and Judy discussed Ray Buckey; the fact that Kathy had seen Ray at the party and felt the need to relay that information to Judy.

Ray was not Mitchell's teacher at the McMartin Preschool, and Judy had never had any personal contact with the twenty-five-year-old instructor.

It was five days after her conversation with Kathy about Ray that Judy discussed Mitchell's problems with Steve and Debbie, where Judy never mentioned the thought of "Sodism" or that Ray could be the potential culprit. Instead, Judy claimed to "have no idea."

All the while, every Tuesday and Thursday thereafter, Judy took Mitchell to the McMartin Preschool.

Two weeks later, on August 12, Judy filed the complaint, telling Detective Hoag that she'd come to suspect that it "must have been Ray" while giving her son a bath the night before, the evening of August 11.

In Judy's undated retrospective of the morning of August 12, where she sat with her preacher, she spoke of her "social obligation," and how it'd already been "burning a hole in [her] psyche." Judy thought of "the

They Must Be Monsters

angels at the school," and she proclaimed that "this madman must be stopped."

* * * * *

On a weekend in the late summer of 1989, we met with Dr. John Byrom (Haddad's "Uncle Jack"), a psychiatrist and an expert in paranoia and schizophrenia. We'd given him Judy's notes and a detailed summary beforehand, allowing him time to study and analyze the information.

"Wow," he said decisively as we entered his office. "This is a textbook case."

He had our attention.

"First of all," Dr. Byrom said, "she was a *paranoid personality*...which means she was *non-psychotic*...totally functional...but unstable all the same."

Dr. Byrom explained that a key dynamic of The Paranoid is the "transference of blame," where instead of accepting responsibility for their condition, they look for a scapegoat.

"She projected, impulsively," he said, "because she couldn't accept what she'd become. Subconsciously, she found herself to be unacceptable and intolerable...and through her natural progression, the gradual demise of a paranoid personality, she turned her attention externally, to an object, or, in this case, a person—a man, like her husband, who wasn't her husband—or, more specifically, the guy who worked at her son's preschool... Ray Buckey.

"Then, once she identified her target, the object of her paranoia, it crystallized...and he became precisely what she wanted him to be...a monster, or as she said, 'a madman.' "

Dr. Byrom presented the concept of the *paranoid pseudo-community*, how Judy sought attention, trying to be seen as meaningful and worthy to those around her. She did so by becoming an *injustice collector*.

"After her husband left, she may've had such an acute need to be significant and useful," Byrom said, "that she put herself at the center of a controversy...for it was better for her to be ostracized or persecuted than to be ignored."

Over the course of that four-hour meeting, we took Dr. Byrom through Judy's steps leading up to the drop-off, asking his opinion of her reference to *Somewhere a Child is Crying*.

"It makes perfect sense," Byrom said, "that any mother who thought her child was neglected or abused would look to such a book for answers—and it makes just as much sense that Judy, a *paranoid personality*, would misinterpret...or should I say, misdirect its meaning. She *knew*, at least subconsciously, that the source of the problem derived in her own home, and yet she made a conscious decision to find that *scapegoat* with whom she had no emotional connection."

When asked if he thought that the drop-off itself may've been part of a setup, that Judy had targeted Ray Buckey from the beginning, Dr. Byrom shrugged in disbelief, not wanting his clinical analysis to wander into the land of wild conspiracies.

"That," he said, "I can't say. That's a reach much farther than I am willing to stretch. At the same time, her actions are beyond suspicious... and if anyone would be capable of such a scheme, justifying their actions for the good of what they perceived to be a higher cause...it would be *the paranoid*."

CHAPTER
43

By the fall of 1989, having exhausted our investigation, we went our separate ways, moving on with our lives. The information we had obtained on Judy Johnson was, as only we knew, highly provocative—a virtual roadmap to the truth.

Yet in that same light, we could see that we were way ahead of our time; that the society of Believers who had propagated this case was still clutching to its ethos. The notion that heinous crimes had been committed was no longer an impassioned accusation, or even a steadfast ideology—it had, instead, produced a generation of victims and advocates whose sheer identities were vested in its certitude. It had become a religion.

Thus, with so many interested parties demanding an outcome, the Mc-Martin case continued, an unstoppable machine.

The day-in-and-day-out courtroom scene became tedious. The evidence—fantastical stories from the mouths of babes coupled with medical theories that proved to be erroneous—didn't live up to the hype. No third-party witness ever testified that they had seen, or even suspected, the workings of a secret conspiracy of pedophiles. The notion of a child pornography ring fell apart as no kiddie porn related to the preschool ever surfaced. No evidence of animal slaughter was presented, not a shred of proof to suggest that a satanic cult had thrived for decades within the neighborhoods of Manhattan Beach.

Still, the seemingly devastated parents sent their allegedly damaged children to the stand, one by one, giving their eyewitness accounts of the legend—a flawed story, a fairy tale of sorts, but a narrative that left society suspecting that "something must have happened."

* * * * *

One of our final interviews was conducted at the office building of Dr. Roland Summit, situated across the street from UCLA-Harbor General Hospital in Torrance. Dr. Summit, the leader of the advocate movement for sexually abused children, and a true believer in the genuine threat of satanic ritual abuse, was identified several times in Judy Johnson's notes—and on dates that contradicted Dr. Summit's sworn testimony.

Dr. Summit had long maintained that he "first met Judy" in a private consultation they had in early February 1984, just days before she drafted her "smoking gun" letter about the ritual of the "Goat Man." Dr. Summit testified that Judy was "quite sane and emotionally contained" during their meeting—but, as the evidence proved, Judy was anything but stable at that time.

Furthermore, Judy's 1983 calendar told a different version of her and Dr. Summit's history. Her notes suggest that they may have met, in some capacity, well before February 1984.

On Sunday, January 16, 1983, Judy wrote "American Martyrs," where she had gone to listen to a lecture by Dr. Summit regarding "teenage sexuality." According to Gayle Schaeffer, Judy had taken Mark, who had just turned thirteen. The next day, Monday, January 17, Judy wrote "Roland"; and she wrote it again on Wednesday, January 19—as if she'd scheduled appointments with Dr. Summit following his lecture. Notably, Judy referred to Dr. Summit by his first name.

Those notations, in and of themselves, proved nothing, other than that Judy had to gone to see Dr. Summit speak, and that, over the proceeding days, she'd written down a name that was the same as his—but still, it reveals that Judy had some type of interest in Dr. Summit prior to dropping off Mitchell at McMartin, the same period she was reading *Somewhere a Child is Crying*.

In addition, scribed in large cursive letters on the back of her August 1983 calendar, just days before her initial accusation against Ray Buckey, Judy wrote, "Roland Summit Harbor General." Also, three months later, on Thursday, November 22, in the wake of the McMartin hysteria, when the first families returned from CII with the devastating news that their children had been abused, Judy wrote, "Roland Summit Meeting 7:00."

Thus, it's fair to assume that in the context of such a meeting, the nation's foremost expert in child sexual abuse had come in contact with the "mother who uncovered it all," especially considering that the mother had shown an inclined interest in the doctor beforehand.

Based on those calendar entries, we suspected that Dr. Summit had either had a critical lapse in memory, or he'd been wittingly dishonest in his public statements and sworn testimony.

Whatever the case, in the years following her death, Dr. Summit maintained his public support for Judy, challenging those who said she was mentally unstable from the start—and he went so far as to suggest that her paranoia had "helped her" to unveil a crime that no one else was willing to consider.

Just two months before our interview with Dr. Summit, in April 1989, at a lecture before the Costa Mesa chapter for the Study of Multiple Personality Disorder and Dissociation, Dr. Summit told the audience, "Eccentric, alienated, un-socialized and paranoid personality types are needed to ferret out allegations of child sex abuse in the face of lack of evidence and conventional, well-socialized parents and professionals. It takes somebody paranoid to continue to express suspicion and to take the child from doctor to doctor until someone confirms that maybe there is abuse."

Our interview with Dr. Summit lasted more than two hours. He spent the first forty-five minutes explaining the background of the clinical movement that pre-dated McMartin, and how he and his colleagues had long suspected the existence of "multi-victim perversity," where conspiring perpetrators were dead set on the "deliberate destruction of children."

Around 1980 and 1981, Dr. Summit recalled, the professional community began to realize that sexual abuse went beyond traditional incest—a man and his young daughter—and that "females were also perpetrators." In some cases, these female culprits took part in the sexual abuse.

By 1983, Dr. Summit said, on the precipice of the McMartin case, the awakening of "multiple perpetrators" had become an "evolutionary phenomenon."

Summit's mention of that time period—January 1983—was the perfect segue for us to present what we'd discovered in Judy's notes. January 1983 was the same month that Dr. Summit had published his "Child Sexual Abuse Accommodation Syndrome" which he'd promoted across the South Bay.

When presented with Judy's 1983 calendars—the January 16

"American Martyrs" reference; the January 17 and 19 meetings with "Roland"; the August 1983 "Roland Summit Harbor General" notation, as well as Judy's mention of the November 22 "Roland Summit Meeting"—Dr. Summit was taken aback.

Are you sure you didn't meet her earlier than February 1984?

Dr. Summit looked over the calendars, not sure what to make of them. There was a long silence between the three of us, an uncomfortable pause that changed the mood, and not in a good way.

We then showed him Judy's May 1983 calendar. We asked him to look at the date of May 12 from which the arrow pointed to the two handwritten phrases: "Somewhere a Child is Crying" and "Mitchell Starts School."

What do you think Judy meant when she wrote, "Somewhere a Child is Crying?"

Dr. Summit's blank expression said more than he intended to reveal. He awkwardly looked up and shook his head. "Judy was a very mysterious woman," Summit said, his dismissive way of sidetracking the discussion. He ended the interview.

Upon leaving Dr. Summit's office, we were convinced that Judy's notation, *Somewhere a Child is Crying*, had a resounding impact on Dr. Summit—the way he shifted nervously before shutting down the conversation. He had to have known that Judy was referring to the title of the heralded book, a body of work that he'd likely studied while drafting his own groundbreaking thesis. For Summit to suggest that the phrase was simply part of Judy's "mystery" seemed to demonstrate that he was being evasive, that he had something to hide; or, at the very least, he didn't want to admit the obvious truth.

Days later, we received a call from Bob Currie, who, up to that point, had granted us several interviews.

"I just got a call from Dr. Summit," Currie said in a confrontational tone. "He says you guys are asking some *provocative* questions."

We're just looking for the truth.

"I'm done talking to you guys. I've said enough."

* * * * *

Six months later

On the morning of Thursday, January 18, 1990, nearly six years after the McMartin Seven indictment, the jury rendered its verdict.

Unlike most mornings in that Superior courtroom, where only a handful of regulars attended, this day, like the indictments in March 1984, found the pews packed; an agitated mix of onlookers with no control over who sat beside them. Much different than a wedding, where the bride and groom segregate their families and guests, this situation placed *Believers* shoulder to shoulder with *Friends of McMartin*, the makings of a perfect storm.

Stan the bailiff, a rotund black man, entered and instructed all in attendance to rise in respect for the Honorable Judge William Pounders. The crowd sat and settled, and the jury entered. The jury foreman handed a sheet of paper to Stan, the panel's decision after a nine-week deliberation. Stan handed it to Judge Pounders, who read over it and handed it back to Stan with his nod to proceed.

Stan read through the counts of molestation and conspiracy. Of the 65 total, he read the first 52—all of the charges against Peggy and the majority against Ray—then he stopped and said, "The jury finds the defendants…not guilty."

A single scream shot through the courtroom, the cry of a mother who believed her child's abusers had escaped justice. Others wept soundlessly, covering their faces with their palms—the friends and family members of the McMartin Seven who had thought this day would never come, that the twelve people who had sworn to render a fair verdict had done just that. The jurors had come to the courtroom for three years, listening carefully, and then took nine weeks to reach a conclusion. Justice, at least as a process, had worked.

But it wasn't over.

On the remaining 13 counts, the jury could not reach a unanimous decision. Seven of the twelve jurors voted to acquit Ray on all counts.

Judge Pounders declared a mistrial on those 13 counts and ordered Ray back to court on a later date to determine if he would be retried.

Outside the courtroom, Prosecutor Lael Rubin spoke to the cameras in a humbled and defeated tone. "We ultimately must respect the jury's decision, even though I personally disagree with it." Rubin defended the DA's determination to bring the case to trial, even after admitting that the evidence was "incredibly weak."

Ray Buckey left the courtroom without making a comment, but his mother, Peggy, expressed her anger and resentment for the system and the process. "I've gone through hell," Peggy said, on the verge of tears, "and now we've lost everything. My concern was for my son and what they've done to him, because my son would never harm a child."

Peggy stood silently, panning the reporters and photographers as they snapped shot after shot. After so many years of incarceration, after the jury finally told the world that she'd been falsely accused, that her life had virtually been destroyed, the media was only interested in capturing her expression with no understanding of her pain.

Peggy shook her head and walked away.

The following weeks brought great pressure upon District Attorney Ira Reiner, mainly from the parent activists who held his department responsible for this debacle. Their children continued to claim they were sexually abused, so they demanded that Ray Buckey be retried on the unresolved counts.

DA Reiner agreed to a second trial on eight of the thirteen counts, a reduced filing limited to three girls.

Six months later, on Friday, July 27, 1990, a second jury again failed to reach a unanimous verdict, although a majority favored acquittal.

The defining issues, the flimsy evidence and implausible scenarios that the case had been built upon, were even more glaring the second time around. Kee MacFarlane's suggestive interviewing techniques—where she provided information to the children until they simply nodded, affirming that "yes," all of "those things" had happened—left jurors bewildered as to how the case could have come so far in light of what seemed so apparent from the video tapes. The physical evidence, the evaluations by CII's Dr. Astrid Heger—where 90% of the children she examined were determined to have "scarring that was consistent with a history of sexual abuse"—proved to be the result of fallacious theories and methods. Dr. Heger's techniques in 1984 were so flawed that by 1990, as she stated on the stand, "we don't use them anymore."

And still, despite the unfounded charges and the complete lack of evidence to support them, a few jurors chose to *believe the children*, as if their blind loyalty to a lost cause would in some way bring comfort to innocent young girls whose childhoods had already been stolen.

Following the second trial, lead prosecutor Joseph Martinez announced that the district attorney's office would not seek a third trial of Ray Buckey.

"These kids have lives to live," Martinez said. "They can't be McMartin kids forever. There's no sense in trying this case again. The evidence is not going to change. As far as we're concerned, the McMartin case is over."

After nearly seven years, at a cost of more than $15 million to the taxpayers of California, after enduring what was, at that moment, the "longest, most expensive criminal case in the history of the United States," Ray Buckey, like Michael Ruby four years earlier, was set free.

Ray stood outside the courtroom and made his statement to the press. He looked older and more refined than he was when he was indicted six years earlier. Now thirty-two years old, his glasses had been replaced with contacts, and he'd developed a deep tan while out on bail.

At the center of that portrait, standing at the top of the courthouse steps, Ray Buckey had the look of a distinguished and uniquely handsome man. "I know I'm innocent," Ray said proudly, chin high, panning the scrum of reporters. "I've proclaimed my innocence since day one. I'm pleased that I wasn't found guilty. Of course, I would've wanted a full acquittal."

Turning away from the press, Ray reached out and embraced his father, Charles. Ray struggled to hold back his tears.

"It's all over," he said to his father, rocking him in his arms. "It's all over."

* * * * *

During the years leading up to those verdicts, as he'd remained confined to his cell, Ray Buckey had nothing but time to think, to dwell upon the life he could have had, the life that had been taken from him, and he struggled to make sense of it all. It was maddening for him to accept that something so unjust could have happened in a modern society. It was as if his constitutional rights were not recognized simply because the charges against him were so heinous—charges based on evidence manufactured by adults who'd used innocent children as their weapon.

Time and again, to blow off steam, Ray sat atop his stationary bicycle, pedaling for miles, closing his eyes and taking himself to another place. He rode until his body dripped with sweat, until his legs became numb from exhaustion, a pleasurable pain for a man in his predicament.

Once he reached his daily goal, Ray would step down to relax, lying back on his cot. Often times, he picked up his yellow legal pad to scribe his thoughts. After so many years in isolation, Ray had gained composure, no longer letting the bitterness degrade his spirit. His anger, his fury for the injustice that imprisoned him, had morphed into a solemn rationale, where he stood at the peak of a mountain looking down upon the band of fools and their campaign of mindless persecution.

Ray filled page after page, making several poignant arguments in his defense—but at the heart of his journals, one rather eloquent paragraph stood out, a profound concept that put the entire phenomenon into perspective:

A beginning of hysteria—

> *The proverbial snowball carelessly dropped from the top of a mountain whose path was unforeseen.*
>
> *Could not it have been that the hands that shaped the snowball had no rock at its core of assumptions that come from a solid foundation of truth?*
>
> *It is so hard to believe that the core of the snowball that rolled down the mountain causing destruction and fear had no more substance than the snow of absurdity it picked up along the way.*

Epilogue

Following his trial, Ray Buckey didn't say much, although he agreed to an interview on CNN's *Larry King Live*. When Larry asked, "What do you want to do with your life?" Ray replied pointedly, "I just want to be left alone...to live my life in peace."

Other than a few magazine articles—where he invited the public to take a closer look at his rather uneventful life before becoming one of America's most infamous criminals—he essentially vanished.

Danny Davis, his attorney—the man who represented Ray for more than six years—later said that he had more respect for Ray Buckey than any other client he'd ever had, that Ray had handled the situation with a "quiet wisdom," the posture of a hero, not a martyr.

For the McMartin-Buckey family and their former staff—the infamous McMartin Seven—life went on. Yet there was no heartfelt apology from the society that had persecuted them.

In February 1990, Peggy, Virginia, and Peggy Ann filed a joint civil suit against Bob Currie, seeking damages for his incessant slander—his stories about Peggy lifting her dress and urinating in front of him, and his appearance on Geraldo Rivera's prime-time special, *Exploring Satan's Underground*, where Currie announced that "more than twelve hundred children had been molested," each forced to drink a "mixture of blood and urine."

While on the stand in that civil trial, Currie broke down crying. "They raped my children," he sobbed, his justification for spreading rumors he had no evidence to support.

A year later, on May 8, 1991, Superior Court Judge G. Keith Wisot ruled in favor of Peggy, Virginia, and Peggy Ann—but only awarded them $1 each, saying that they "had not proved that their reputations were damaged."

"I didn't care a snip about the money," Virginia said after the ruling. "I just wanted him [Currie] to shut up."

Eventually, however, the mainstream media gave the McMartin Seven their regretful acknowledgement. It came in the form of an HBO movie released on May 20, 1995. The film, *Indictment: The McMartin Trial*, produced by Oliver Stone, was the project that Glenn Stevens had taken to Abby and Myra Mann. The film won several Golden Globe and Primetime Emmy awards, telling the world that the McMartin case was a terrible mistake.

Seven months later, on December 12, 1995, following the 53rd Golden Globe nominations, Geraldo Rivera, who for so many years had promoted the "satanic ritual abuse" theory, issued a formal apology, admitting that the McMartin case and the Believe the Children movement was a hoax.

The next week, on Sunday, December 17, 1995, after suffering a series of strokes, Virginia McMartin died in a Torrance hospital at the age of eighty-eight.

Five years later, on Friday December 15, 2000, Peggy Buckey died in her home from what appeared to be natural causes. She was seventy-four.

On October 30, 2005, nearly five years after Peggy's passing, an article in the *Los Angeles Times*, headlined "I'm Sorry," told the story of Kyle Sapp, a thirty-year-old former McMartin preschooler. Kyle was eight years old in 1984 when he claimed to have been abused in unimaginable ways by the McMartin Seven.

Kyle made an emotional plea to the good people he had falsely accused. He gave a detailed account of how the case "took over the whole city and consumed our whole family."

Having become a father himself, Kyle remained haunted by the case. He knew he had lied and helped to ruin the lives of his former teachers. "I would love to look at the defendants," Kyle said, "and tell them 'I'm sorry.'"

* * * * *

As for Manhattan Beach, the quaint seaside town found a way to move on. The McMartin Preschool disappeared—literally and figuratively—demolished and reconstructed into a dry cleaners, leaving no visual evidence of what had taken place.

Over time, the community modernized, changing its complexion, all part of a city plan that was underway when the scandal broke in 1983. The concrete sidewalks and asphalt intersections were uprooted, replaced with an elaborate streetscape of soft blue and light-gray tiles that take patrons on a stroll to their favorite cuisines and posh franchises.

The mom-and-pop shops that had once made Manhattan Beach such a "special place to live" seemed to have died a natural death, now a faint memory to the old guard that remembers its golden age.

Yet at the center of town, at the intersection of Highland Avenue and Manhattan Beach Boulevard, a line of patrons remain in front of The Kettle, just as it had before.

Hungry people stand at the corner, waiting for their tables, enjoying the view of the pier and how the sunlight reflects off the crashing tide. They're so innocent in their milieu, so unencumbered by the past. They don't realize that directly above them, hanging ominously is that dark cauldron, the boiling crucible that watches over their small town. They don't consider what it symbolizes, or the profound irony it represents. They have, one might say, simply forgotten about those who suffered.

Author's Postscript

"Those who cannot remember the past are condemned to repeat it."
—George Santayana

In the corner of my garage sit two gray file cabinets. The cabinets have not left my sight since Deric and I finished our investigation in 1990, the day we moved out of my parents' house. They are filled with legal documents, newspaper articles, magazines, cassette tapes, and personal notations that represent our three-year inquiry. They reflect our accomplishment, a journalistic feat that went beyond our wildest dreams; yet, those file cabinets were a constant reminder of the promise we'd failed to keep. Over the years, as I looked at them each day, I was left with an unshakeable feeling of guilt.

That promise, I told my daughters one afternoon, was to all the individuals who'd entrusted us with their stories, that we would chronicle the facts—their impassioned testimonies—to "set the record straight." It was the promise we made to Virginia McMartin, who reminded me of my grandmother, or anyone's grandmother for that matter, as she sat us down and spoke from the heart, retelling of the destruction her family endured. She knew, like we knew, that what happened in Manhattan Beach could happen to anyone at any time. The story needed to be told, and only in those files could the truth be found.

The truth can be haunting, especially to those keeping it secret. In our case, the truth was a simple debt, a personal guarantee, to make sure that society had some understanding of what caused the hysteria to infect an entire community, to spread across the entire nation, without pause.

In the bottom drawer of the last cabinet sat three journals, my personal thoughts of our investigation in real-time. Each night, when Deric and I returned to our "War Room," I filled the pages with our daily activities, charting our every step. When I wrote them, back in the late 1980s, I'd considered them my private missives, something for myself, a way to one day reflect upon that period of my life.

Now, almost 30 years later, I've discovered that my journals, which lived and breathed within those file cabinets for decades, were an essential part of the story we'd uncovered. In fact, my journals were "the story." The files merely contained the data that supported our thesis. Together, in parallel, they inspired us to finish what we started.

—Matthew LeRoy

Acknowledgements

Like any collaborative non-fiction project, it would not have been possible without the unwavering support of those who got us started—Jill (Haddad) Martin and Lloyd Martin for giving us our "inside track," and of course, Carl and Deneen LeRoy for providing the "comforts of home" that kept us going.

We are forever beholden to Virginia McMartin and Peggy Buckey, who were determined to "get to the truth"; and to Ray Buckey, Peggy Ann Buckey, and Charles Buckey, for allowing us (two strangers) to spend countless hours with their family's matriarchs.

There will always be a warm place in our hearts for Pastor Myrus Knutson, who trusted us with a volume of never-before-seen archives—the documents that shed light on his daughter's death. Today, as we too have daughters of our own, we can only imagine the pain he endured, and we pray that he's watching over us with a gracious smile.

Our thundering applause to Steve and Debbie Knutson, Gayle Schaeffer, and Noreen Noel—your painful memories had more value than any of you could've ever imagined.

We give our profound thanks to Michael Ruby and his parents, Glenn and Evelyn Ruby, who welcomed us into their home and convinced us that "God was on our side."

To Jackie Starmer, a.k.a., *The Walking Library of the McMartin Case*—your nickname needs no commentary—but of course, it doesn't say what a great friend you were to so many.

A very special appreciation to Claudia Krikorian who opened doors that would've otherwise remained closed. You, madam, are a true educator.

To Chuck Elliott, despite your damage, your infectious laugh inspired us forward.

To Dr. Jerry Todd, a truly wise and selfless man, who took us under his wing and helped us to get *something* on paper (oh, the memories of those floppy discs).

To Dr. John Byrom, who provided a view of *paranoid schizophrenia* that we would've never fathomed.

To the dedicated journalists: Bob Williams, Mary Fischer, Chris Woodyard, Faye Fiore, Shawn Hubler, Lisa Endig, and Martin Burns, each of whom provided information and insight that led us to a treasure of discovery.

To all the players on both sides of this case who, irrespective of their beliefs or dispositions, gave us their time and candid recollections: Kay Larson, John Banta, Tommy Allen, Mary Mae Cioffi, Bob Currie, Dave Allen, Father John Calhoun, Father Jack Eales, Monsignor John Barry, Glenn Stevens, Dr. Roland Summit, and all others who made themselves available.

To our broad range of beta readers—Mary Olson, Danielle Mathison, Jeff McLaren, Summer Grace, Anna Amundson Esq, Lynn Gahman, Valerie Kinder-Davis, Joe Duffel, Tony Small, Veronica Rodriguez, Rosemary Rodriguez, Whitney Johnson, Angelo Haddad, Maureen Wylie, Marie Haddad, Christopher Jacobs, Brian Bloodgood, Michael Weber, Sean ("El Chano") Todd, Veronica Vonk, and Heather Haddad.

To the unsung heroes, for their tireless work behind the scenes: Arthur Gallegos—the chronicler, Adam Poe—website design, Timothy Brittain—book designer extraordinaire, Margret McBride—literary agent (with us from the start), and a special thanks to our editor and mentor, Larry Edwards.

Our resounding *shout-out* to San Diego State University, and a vociferous "thank you" to undergraduate advisor Dr. David Johns, who helped forge our path.

To Delta Upsilon, who brought us together and provided endless encouragement and cold beers during those early days. Nordstrom and Larry Shelton, head basketball coach at Downey High School, for giving us jobs so we could continue our investigation. Lastly, to Pops and Jewel for providing us food, hoops and unending entertainment.

And, most heartfelt, we express our gratitude to our wives and children. To Brenda and Heather, who've found a way to love us unconditionally, and to our beautiful children (in order of age): Gabriella, Jacqueline, Wylie, Abraham, and Scarlett. This book is as much yours as it is ours.

Timeline

May 11, 1983—Judy Johnson drops her two-and-a-half-year-old son at the McMartin Preschool in Manhattan Beach, California.

August 12, 1983—Judy Johnson contacts Detective Jane Hoag of the Manhattan Beach Police Department and accuses Ray Buckey of child molestation.

September 7, 1983—Ray Buckey arrested by the Manhattan Beach Police Department and released hours later for insufficient evidence.

September 8, 1983—The Manhattan Beach Police Department mails 200 letters to current and former McMartin families.

November 1, 1983—Kee McFarlane conducts her first videotaped interview with a McMartin student at Children's Institute International (CII).

January 13, 1984—Virginia McMartin voluntarily closes the McMartin Preschool.

January 23, 1984—Judy Johnson alleges that Ray Buckey took her son to the Manhattan Ranch Preschool where the boy was abused by strangers.

February 2, 1984—KABC-TV's *Eyewitness News* reporter Wayne Satz makes initial broadcast on the McMartin Preschool case.

February 16 and 22, 1984—Judy Johnson writes two bizarre letters describing satanic and ritualistic abuse. These two documents would later be referred to as "smoking guns."

March 6, 1984—The Manhattan Beach Police Department raids eleven schools in three counties. No arrests are made.

March 22, 1984—Grand jury indicts the *McMartin Seven*: Ray Buckey (25), Peggy McMartin Buckey (57), Virginia McMartin (76), Peggy Ann Buckey (28), Babette Spitler (36), Betty Raidor (64), and Mary Ann Jackson (56) on one hundred fifteen counts of child molestation.

April 1, 1984—Los Angeles District Attorney Robert Philibosian announces that the seven defendants are linked to a wide scale conspiracy, the largest in United States history.

June 4, 1984—The McMartin preliminary hearing begins.

June 5, 1984—Judy Johnson accuses her husband of sexually abusing their son.

July 17, 1984—Police raid nine locations across the South Bay believed to be connected to the McMartin conspiracy.

They Must Be Monsters

July 24, 1984—Michael Ruby, the seventeen year old teacher's aide at the Manhattan Ranch preschool, is arrested for child sexual abuse.

October 31, 1984—the twenty member Sheriff's Child Sexual Abuse Task Force is formed and located in a vacated lifeguard station next to the Manhattan Beach Pier.

April 6, 1985—Judy Johnson is hospitalized and undergoes psychiatric evaluation at the University of California Irvine's Medical Center. Fourteen days later she's released, diagnosed as a "paranoid schizophrenic."

October 8, 1985—The Sheriff's Task Force shuts down its yearlong investigation having spent over one million dollars without making a single arrest.

November 22, 1985—Michael Ruby's trial ends in a mistrial. All charges are dismissed.

January 9, 1986—the eighteen-month McMartin preliminary hearing ends, the longest in California history.

January 17, 1986—Los Angeles District Attorney Ira Reiner dismisses counts against five of the seven McMartin defendants; only Ray and Peggy Buckey remain charged.

January 23, 1986—Peggy McMartin Buckey is released on bail after spending nearly 2 years in jail.

August 22, 1986—Clement Edmund Renaud is charged with eight counts of child molestation at American Martyrs Parochial School from 1981 to 1983. He pleads "no contest" and is released based on his time served.

December 19, 1986—Judy Johnson is found dead in her home.

April 20, 1987—the McMartin Preschool trial commences.

February 15, 1989—Ray Buckey is released on bail after spending nearly five years in prison.

April 27, 1989—the McMartin trial hits the two-year, four-day mark, becoming the longest criminal proceeding in United States history, surpassing the trial of the Hillside Strangler.

January 18, 1990—Ray and Peggy Buckey are acquitted on 52 counts, as the jury remains deadlocked on 13 counts against Ray Buckey. Judge William Pounders declares a mistrial.

January 31, 1990—District Attorney Ira Reiner announces Ray Buckey will be retried on eight counts of felony child molestation.

May 7, 1990—Ray Buckey's second trial begins.

July 27, 1990—the second McMartin trial ends in a hung jury. A mistrial is declared. All charges against Ray Buckey are dropped.

Δικαια Υποθηκη
Justice, Our Foundation

About the Authors

MATTHEW LEROY, thirty years ago while attending San Diego State University, left college to investigate the McMartin Preschool. This decision would profoundly change his life and mark the beginning of an incredible journey that continues to this day.

LeRoy is owner of Five Star NDT, an export management company (www.soldinmexico.com) that specializes in selling U.S. made products in Mexico.

Haddad & LeRoy, c. 1988

LeRoy, an entrepreneur, holds several patents and currently manufactures a line of proprietary products sold and used worldwide in the Aerospace Industry (www.fivestarndt.com).

The author resides in San Diego, California with his wife, Brenda, and their two daughters, Gabriella and Jackie.

* * *

DERIC HADDAD became interested in the McMartin Preschool case through his mother and stepfather, who were experts in child abuse and hired as McMartin defense consultants.

Following the authors' investigation, Haddad relocated to Los Angeles to pursue a career in screenwriting and film production. In 1996, he co-wrote the independent feature film *Cannes Man*, shot on location at the Cannes Film Festival. He currently works as the Vice President of National Accounts for Cleanetics, a consulting and engineering firm for the life sciences.

Haddad resides in southwestern Pennsylvania with his wife, Heather, and their three children, Wylie, Abraham, and Scarlett.

Haddad & LeRoy, c. 2018

CPSIA information can be obtained
at www.ICGtesting.com
Printed in the USA
FSHW022220211121
86370FS